IMAGES
of America

The Japanese on the Monterey Peninsula

I0807102

On the Cover: This 1912 photograph shows the congregation of the Monterey Peninsula Presbyterian Mission standing in front of its new church building on Washington Street in Monterey. Washington Street was the center of Monterey's Japantown. The Monterey Japanese community referred to this area as "the village." (Matsuyama family collection.)

IMAGES
of America

The Japanese on the Monterey Peninsula

Tim Thomas and the
Monterey Japanese American Citizens League

ARCADIA
PUBLISHING

ISBN 978-0-7385-7497-4

Published by Arcadia Publishing
Charleston, South Carolina

Printed in the United States of America

Library of Congress Control Number: 2010941974

For all general information, please contact Arcadia Publishing:
Telephone 843-853-2070
Fax 843-853-0044
E-mail sales@arcadiapublishing.com
For customer service and orders:
Toll-Free 1-888-313-2665

Visit us on the Internet at www.arcadiapublishing.com

This book is dedicated to Otosaburo Noda and all those early Monterey Japanese pioneers who took a chance and ventured across the Pacific so long ago, and to Roy Hattori, whose journey inspires me.

Contents

ACKNOWLEDGMENTS

I give special thanks to the Monterey Chapter of the Japanese American Citizens League (JACL) and the Heritage Committee—especially to Larry Oda. Thank you, to all the families both here and in Japan for use of their family photographs. Thanks go to my good friend Dennis Copeland in the California History Room, Monterey Library. Thank you, David Yamada, for your wonderful book *The Japanese the Monterey Peninsula* and Sandy Lydon, for all the amazing work you have done over the years on this incredible story. And special thank-yous go to John Castagna and to Linda, who makes me look good!

Introduction

After the United States imposed the Chinese Exclusion Act in 1882, the number of Japanese immigrants to the West Coast increased in large numbers. One of those immigrants was a man named Otosaburo Noda, who settled in Watsonville (about 25 miles north of Monterey) in 1895. One day, while working in Monterey as a lumberjack for the Pacific Improvement Company (precursor of the Pebble Beach Company), Noda noticed the incredible variety of fish and red abalone in Monterey Bay. Nobody was utilizing this vast resource. He quickly gave up his lumberjack days, moved to Monterey, and started a small fishing colony made up of fishermen from the Wakayama Prefecture of Japan. Noda was so taken with the Monterey area that he even wrote to the Japanese Agriculture and Commerce Department about this marine abundance. Almost immediately, abalone divers from the Chiba Prefecture arrived, and for the next 20 years, the Japanese dominated the fishing industry in Monterey Bay. By the turn of the 20th century, a small group of farmers from the Hiroshima Prefecture came and developed farms just south of Carmel. By the mid-1930s, 80 percent of the businesses on the Monterey Wharf, from fish markets to abalone processors, were Japanese-owned.

The Japanese fished for abalone, salmon, and sardine. Running small business all around the Monterey Peninsula, they also farmed strawberries, potatoes, corn, and artichokes. But fishing ruled, and salmon was king. In August 1909, at the end of salmon season, the *Monterey Daily Cypress* reported that there were 185 salmon boats fishing the bay, and 145 of these boats were Japanese-owned. Monterey is most famous for sardines. Everyone knows that it was Sicilian fishermen who fished for sardines. This is only part of the story. Around the turn of the last century, the salmon fisheries along the Sacramento River were not doing very well. But due to some changes in fishing gear, coupled with the arrival of the pioneering Japanese fishermen to the Monterey Bay, large salmon landings began in Monterey. Salmon processors on the Sacramento River heard of those large landings and sent Frank E. Booth to investigate. Booth was so impressed that he opened a small cannery at the foot of the Monterey Wharf. Unfortunately for Booth, the Japanese fishermen already had good contracts with the fish markets in San Francisco. Booth stuck around, though, and he eventually got a deal to buy salmon from the Japanese fishermen. By 1900, there was a great deal of anti-Japanese sentiment in the United States, coming mainly from Caucasian workers who were afraid the Japanese would take their jobs. In 1905, Booth said that he would not hire Japanese fishermen anymore, an easy call for him considering that salmon was fished only in the spring, and he was interested in developing a sardine fishery in Monterey for the fall and winter months. Yet every spring, he continued to buy his salmon from Japanese fishermen.

There were also many Japanese families who lived in Monterey year round, which created a need for other businesses like fishing supplies, general merchandise, food markets, hotels, restaurants, barbershops, shoe repairmen, dry cleaners, and every kind of enterprise that can be found in any town in the United States. The difference was that these businesses were owned and operated by issei (first-generation immigrants) and nisei (second-generation immigrants). All these small businesses—be they fishing, farming, or radio repairing—made up a community. Monterey had its own *nibon-machi*, or Japantown, which was bounded by Alvarado, Adams, and Pearl Streets. The Monterey Japanese referred to this community as a colony.

On January 25, 1932, eighteen charter members organized the Monterey Peninsula Chapter of the Japanese American Citizens League (JACL), two years after the national organization was formed. The chapter was originally formed for the same purposes as the parent organization: fighting against discriminatory legislation and racial prejudice, and to help issei with navigating through the American bureaucracy, such as legal matters in alien registration and property contracts.

Throughout the 1930s, the chapter involved itself in the larger community. In 1937, to take part in the Independence Day parade, the chapter made a giant American flag to carry. The rationale was that only a few people could ride on a float, but it would take 60 people to carry the flag. Another way for the community to assimilate was to participate in organized sports. The JACL sponsored Monterey Minato, and it established a formidable reputation with high records in several sports because of its gifted athletes. From 1934 to the outbreak of World War II, the Monterey Minatos virtually dominated all other teams within the Central California Coast Counties Athletic Association (4CAA). In 1938, just three Minato trackmen won nine of the 11 events at the YMCA Olympics at Kezar Stadium in San Francisco and took the whole meet.

The chapter, today, continues to fight for tolerance and diversity, looks after its members to preserve their cultural heritage, and assists new immigrants to assimilate into American society.

Monterey has always been a special place. After World War II, the Monterey Peninsula heralded the return of its Japanese citizens. Locals, including John Steinbeck and Ed Ricketts, even placed a full-page advertisement in the *Monterey Peninsula Herald* to welcome them all home.

Today, the Monterey Japanese community is as strong as ever and very active in the community. These citizens are a vital part of what makes the Monterey Peninsula what it is today.

One

The Pioneers

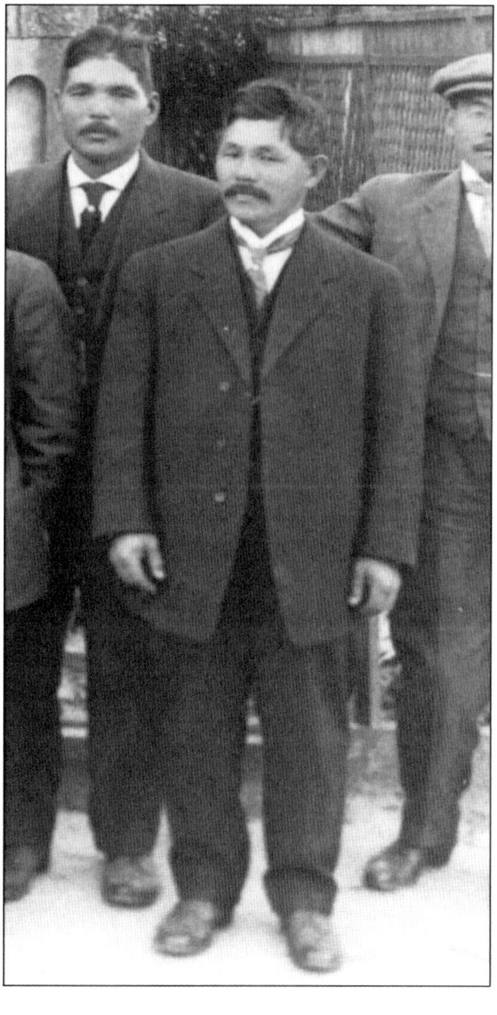

Otosaburo Noda. Noda was a leader in the early Japanese community. He was the first to recognize the potential use of Monterey Bay for commercial fishing and of the fertile land for agriculture. Coming from the Saga Prefecture of Japan, Noda immigrated to California at the age of 19 and farmed throughout central California, eventually settling in Watsonville. In 1895, he was hired to cut wood by the Pacific Improvement Company, which then owned several thousand acres of the Monterey Peninsula. It was while working as a lumberjack that Noda first noticed the incredible abundance and unlimited possibilities of the Monterey Peninsula. (Kodama family collection.)

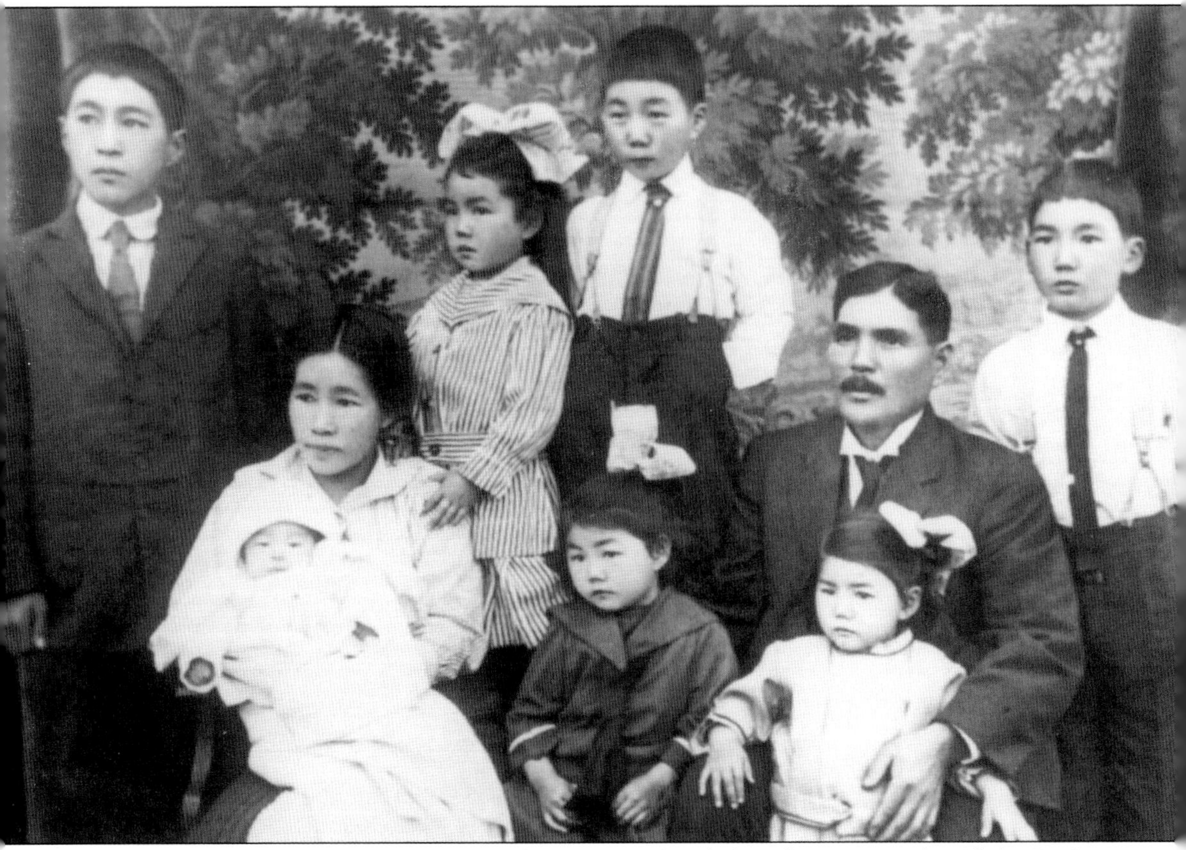

GENNOSUKE KODANI AND FAMILY. Kodani was in the abalone business in the Chiba Prefecture of Japan. He first came to the Monterey Peninsula in early 1897, at the request of the Japanese Agriculture and Commerce Department, which was acting on a letter it received from Otosaburo Noda, who had written that there was so much abalone in Monterey Bay that it was like "a carpet of abalone." In this photograph, from left to right, are (first row) Fuko, Yoshiko (baby), Kumiko, and Takeko; (second row) Hideo, Fusako, Seizo, Gennosuke, and George.. (Kodani family collection.)

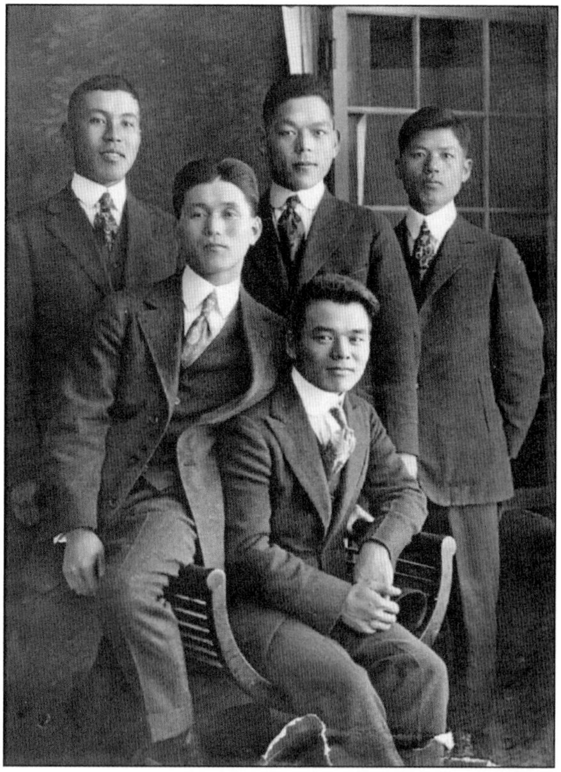

Pacific Mutual Fish. Unosuke Higashi was an early issei pioneer and a major influence in Monterey's Japanese community. From the Wakayama Prefecture, he first came to Monterey at age 16 in 1906 to get into the fishing business. He eventually opened a hotel, the first Japanese restaurant on the Monterey Peninsula, and a fish market. In this photograph are, from left to right, Azuma Toi, Zanchiro Oda, Jack Hamaguchi, Junchi Oda, and unidentified. (Higashi family collection.)

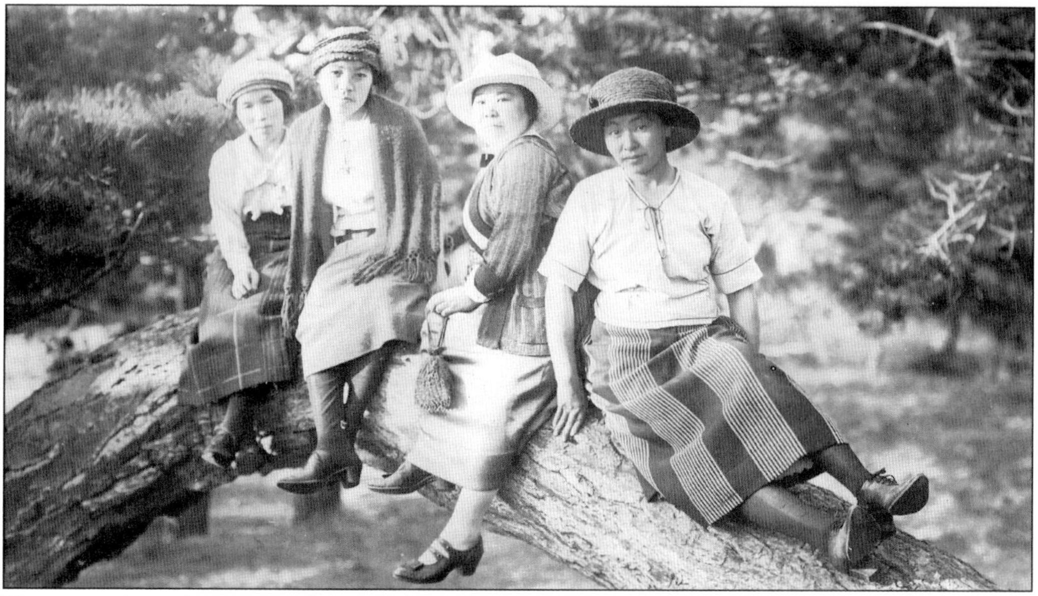

Katsuno Sobe Ichiuji. Kikujiro Ichiuji first came to the United States from the Shimane Prefecture in 1906, landing in San Francisco. His initial plans were to make as much money as possible and return to Japan. Instead, he met his future bride, Katsuno Sobe (right). The two married in Seattle, Washington, and moved to the Monterey Peninsula in 1916. Kikujiro went to work on the Monterey Wharf for Coast Abalone Co. Katsuno and unidentified friends are pictured here sitting on a limb. (Ichiuji family collection.)

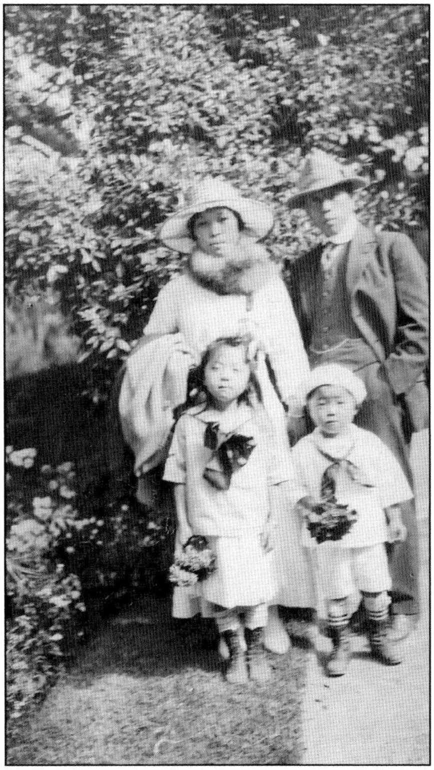

KODAMA FAMILY. Setsuji Kodama came from the Hiroshima Prefecture and settled in Sacramento. After marrying Fujiko Nagatani, they moved to Monterey in 1914, where Kodama entered into a partnership of a wholesale fish business on the Monterey Wharf. (Kodama family collection.)

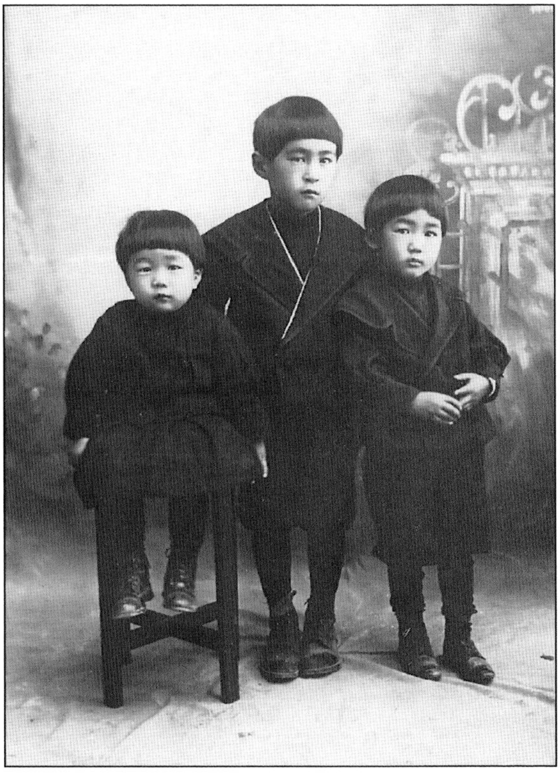

KODANI CHILDREN. From left to right are Sizo, Fusakao, and Kuniko Kodani. (Kodani family collection.)

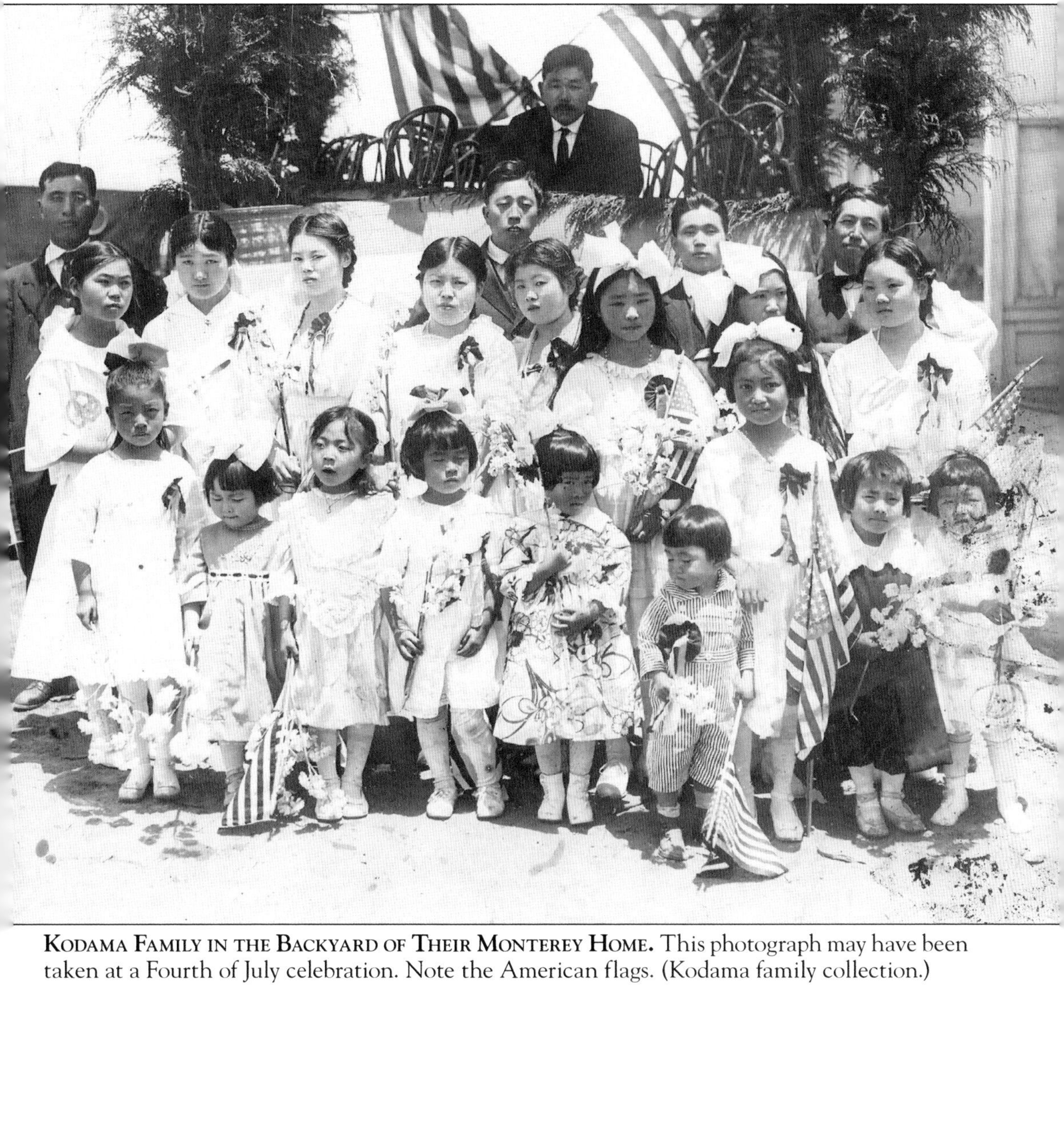

KODAMA FAMILY IN THE BACKYARD OF THEIR MONTEREY HOME. This photograph may have been taken at a Fourth of July celebration. Note the American flags. (Kodama family collection.)

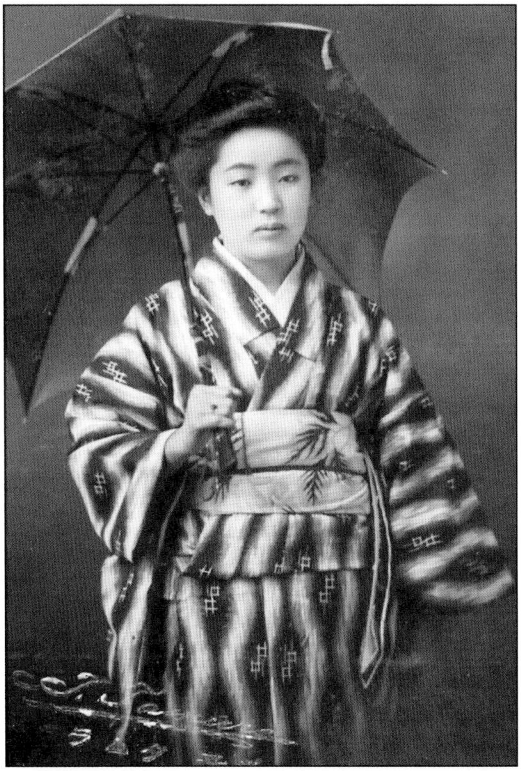

Kikujiro Ichiuji's Mother in Japan. Kihujiro Ichiuji originally came to the United States from the Shimane Prefecture in 1890. He first went to work in a nursery in San Francisco. His eldest son Mickey said of his father, "My father was an adventurous -type person who wanted to make his mark in this country, make quick money, and go back to Japan." (Ichiuji family collection.)

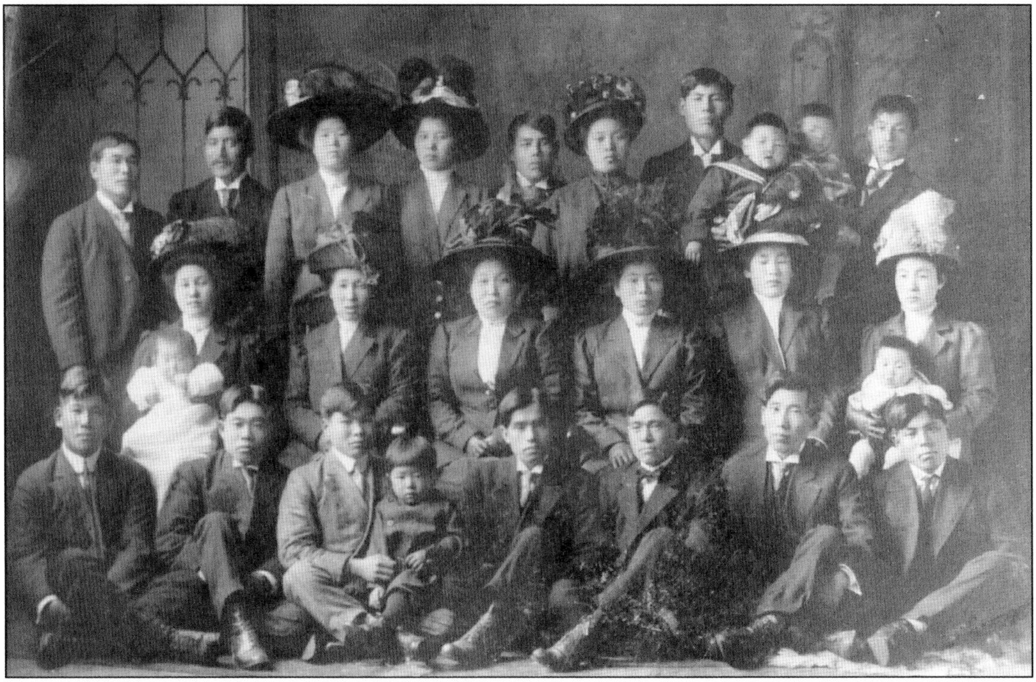

Matsuyama Family. The Matsuyama family members were early pioneers to the Monterey Peninsula and were actively involved with local chapter of the JACL and the Presbyterian Church. (Matsuyama family collection.)

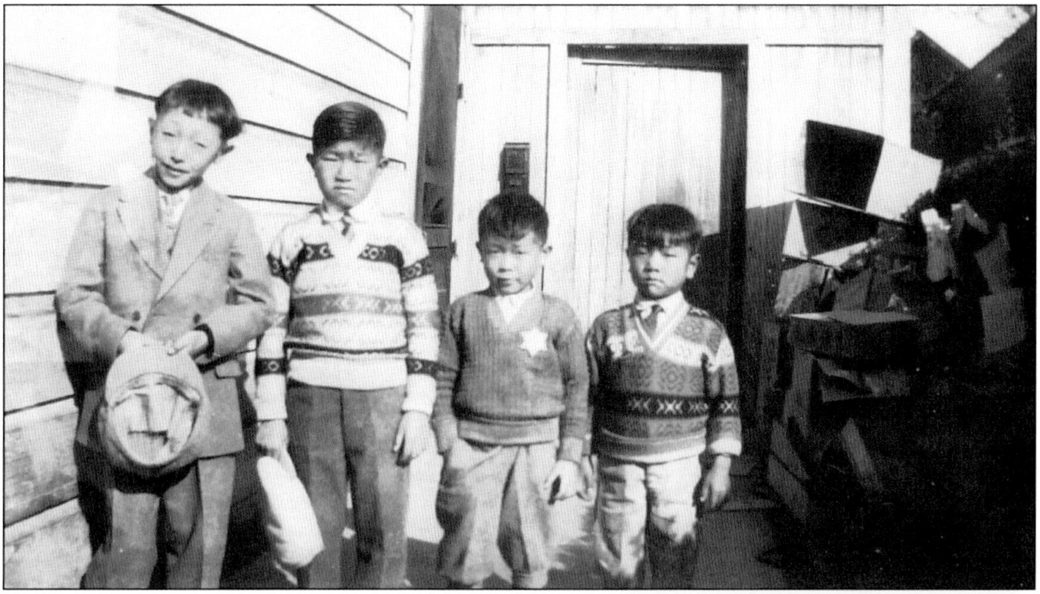

KODANI CHILDREN. The Kodani children—from left to right, Hideo, George, Seizo, and Kumiko—are pictured at Point Lobos around 1910. (Kodani family collection.)

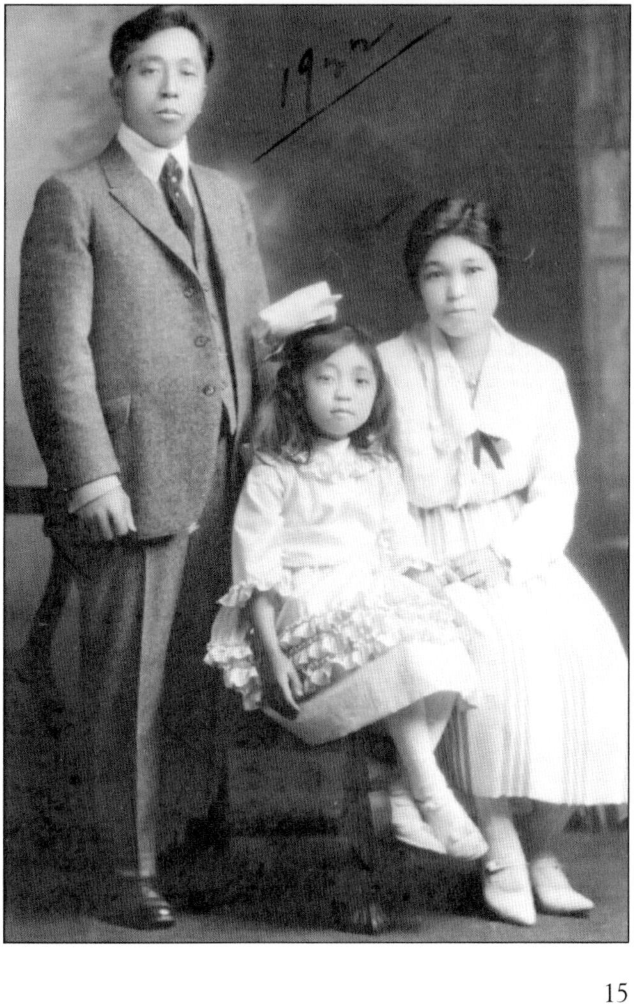

KODAMA FAMILY PORTRAIT. Setsuji and Fujiko Kodama are pictured with their daughter Rose. (George Kodama and Monterey Library Collection, California History Room.)

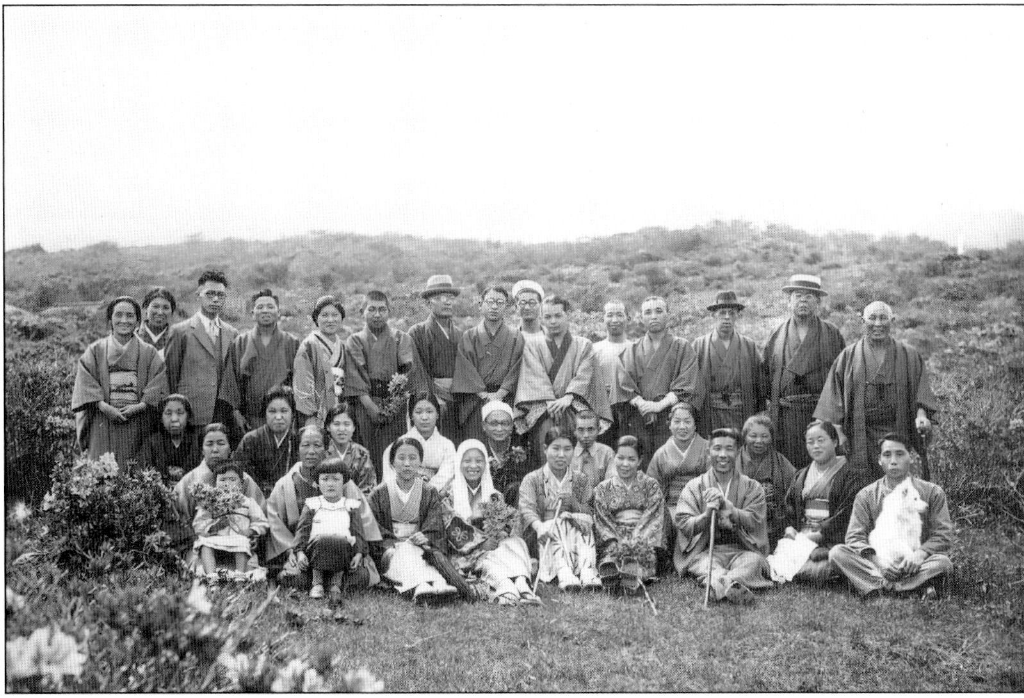

Kodama Family in Japan, c. 1900. This photograph shows an early Kodama family picnic in the Hiroshima Prefecture. (Kodama family collection.)

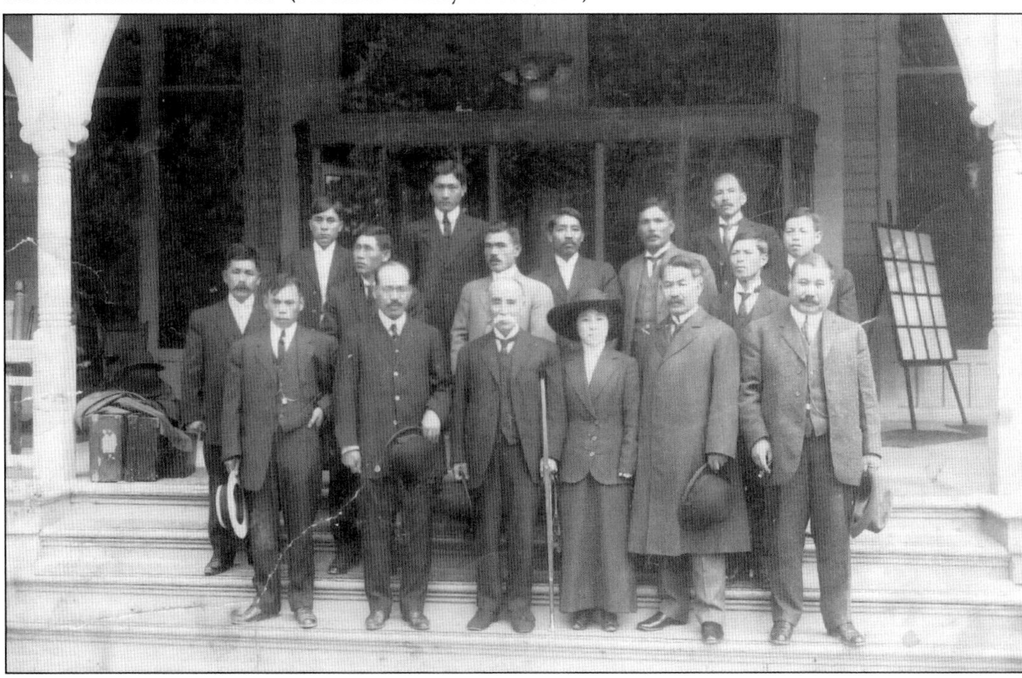

Hotel Del Monte, c. 1909. A group of Japanese visitors stands on the porch with Gennosuke Kodani (third row, third from left) and Otosaburo Noda (second row, left) at the Hotel Del Monte. As one of the leaders of the local Japanese community, Kodani met with visiting dignitaries. (Kodani family collection.)

Kikujiro Ichiuji and Family, c. 1910. It was important for early Japanese families to assimilate to Western ways as soon as possible. Reasons for assimilation were to avoid social and economic conflict so that Japanese immigrants and their children could be law-abiding, loyal American citizens. (Ichiuji family collection.)

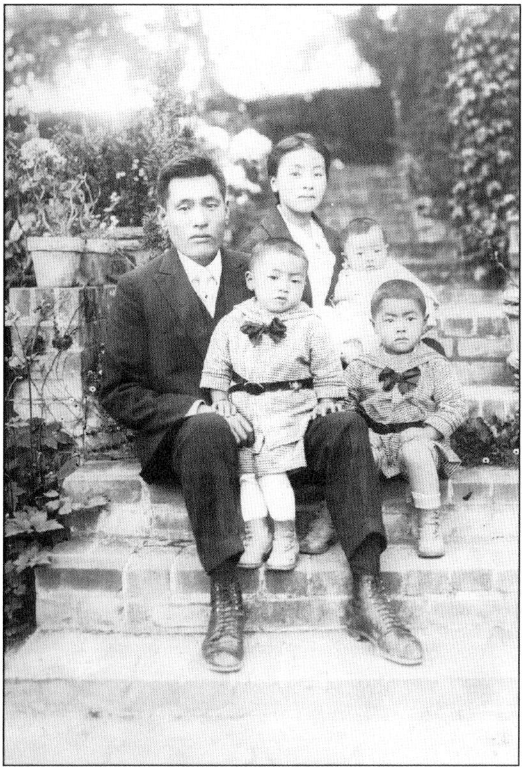

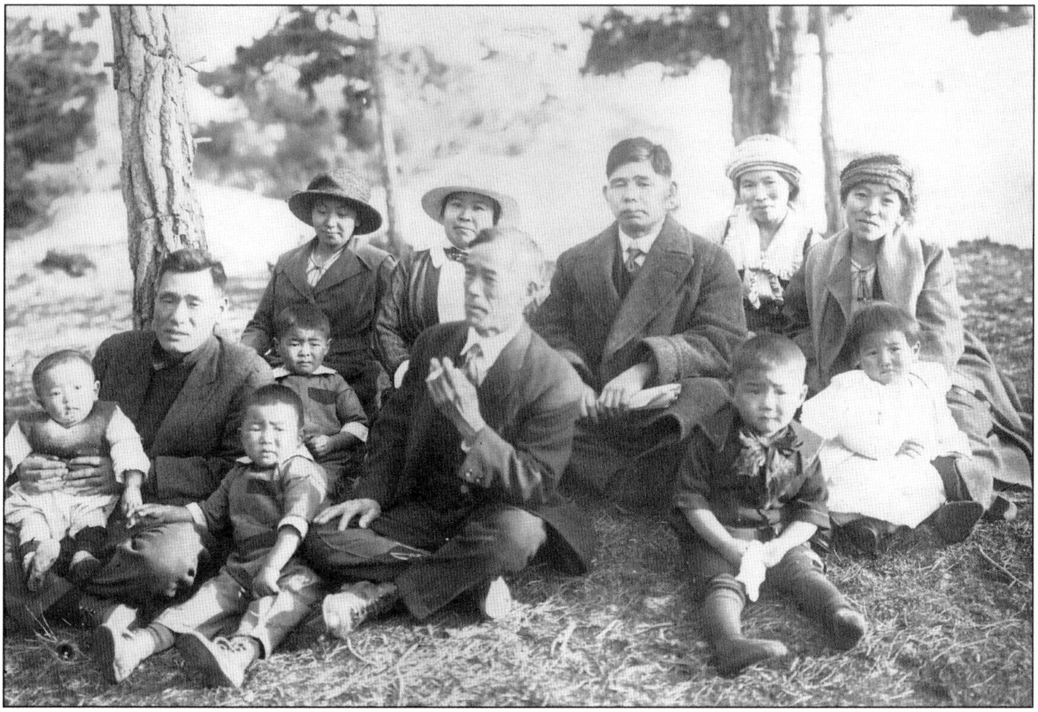

Ichiuji Family, c. 1915. Members of the Ichiuji family are pictured with friends at a picnic in Del Monte Forest. (Ichiuji family collection.)

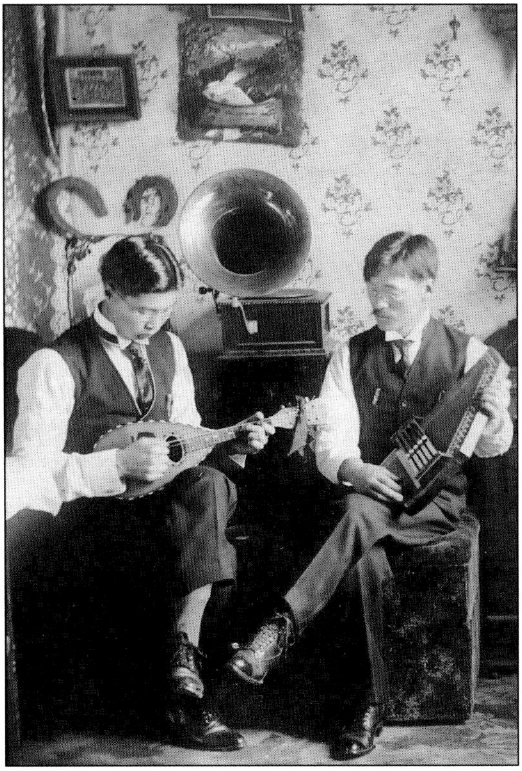

Ichiuji and Music, c. 1915. This beautiful photograph shows some of the Ichiuji men enjoying playing and listening to some music. The instrument on the right is an autoharp; on the left is a lute. (Ichiuji family collection.)

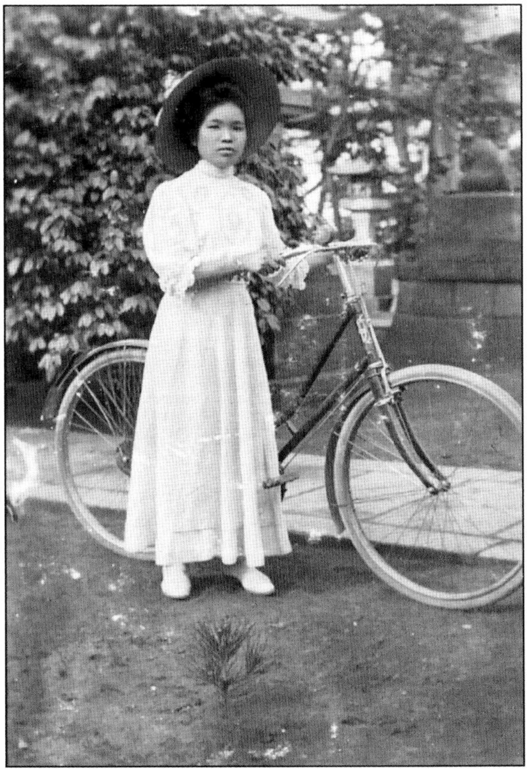

Bike Ride, c. 1910. Katsuno Ichiuji is pictured here getting ready to go bicycling. (Ichiuji family collection.)

Two

Abalone, Salmon, and Early Japanese Fishermen

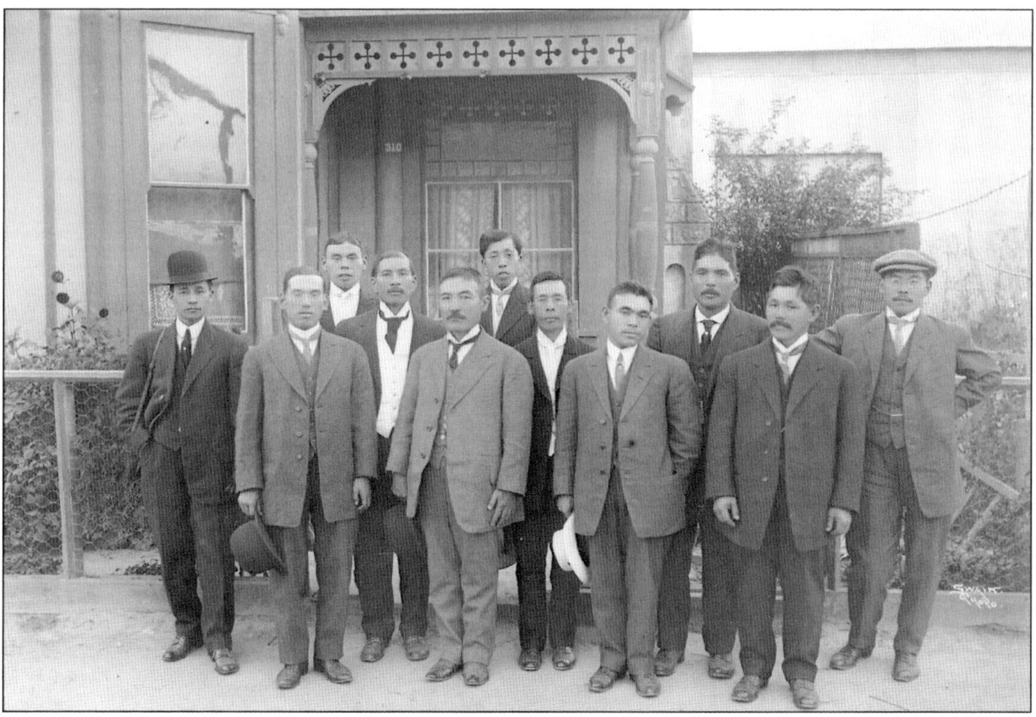

Group of Monterey Japanese Businessmen, 1909. Otosaburo Noda is standing at right in the first row. Gennosuke Kodani is behind Noda's right shoulder. (Kodama family collection.)

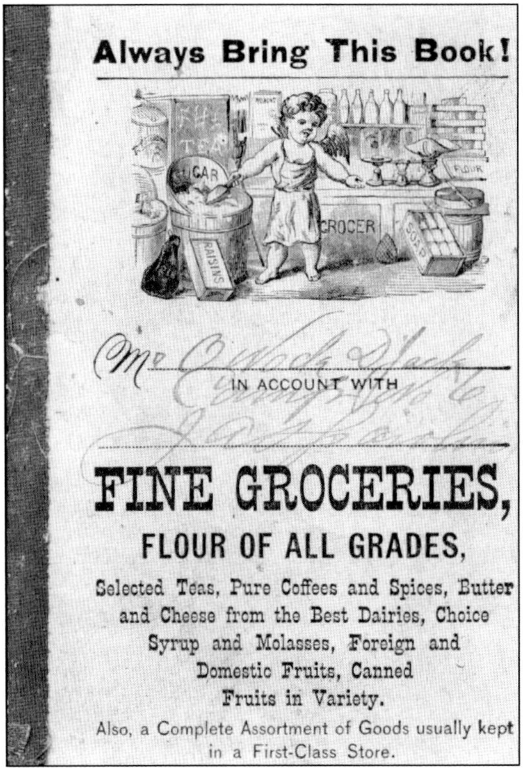

PAMPHLET, C. 1907. Besides being a woodcutter, Otosaburo Noda was also supplying other Japanese businesses and fishing camps with foods and materials. He kept separate books for each camp he supplied. (Larry Oda collection.)

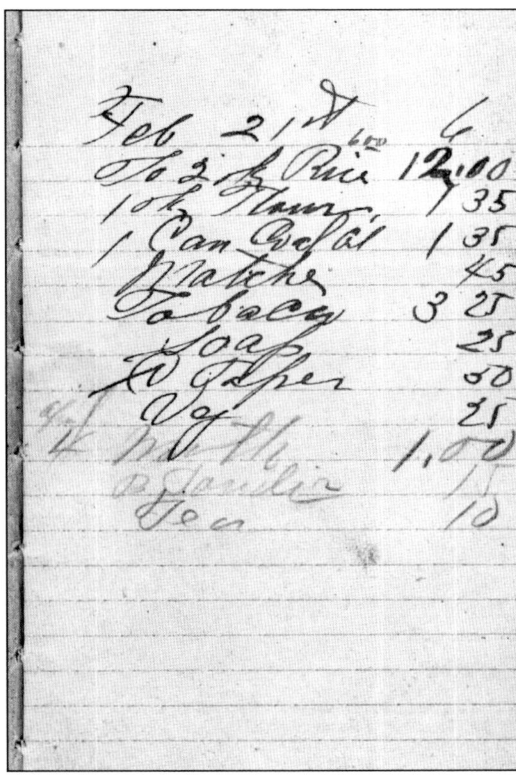

PAGE FROM NODA'S ACCOUNT BOOKS, C. 1907. Otosaburo Noda also set up his own camp, made up of 10 fishermen from the Wakayama Prefecture, along the present day Cannery Row. This camp was the first Japanese colony on the Monterey Peninsula. (Larry Oda collection.)

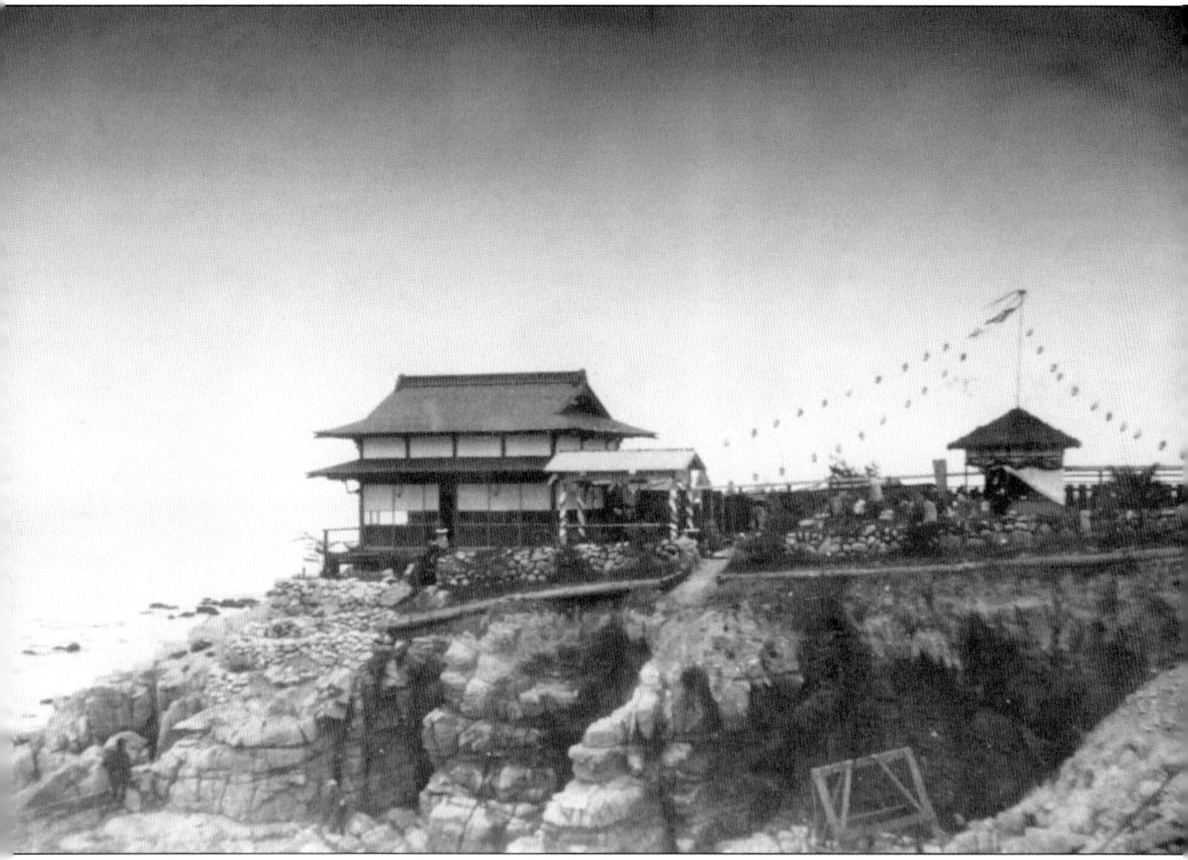

JAPANESE TEAHOUSE. In 1904, Otosaburo Noda brought in artisans and carpenters from Japan and built this traditional Japanese teahouse at Lover's Point in Pacific Grove. It was constructed, as it would have been in Japan, without nails. (Monterey Library Collection.)

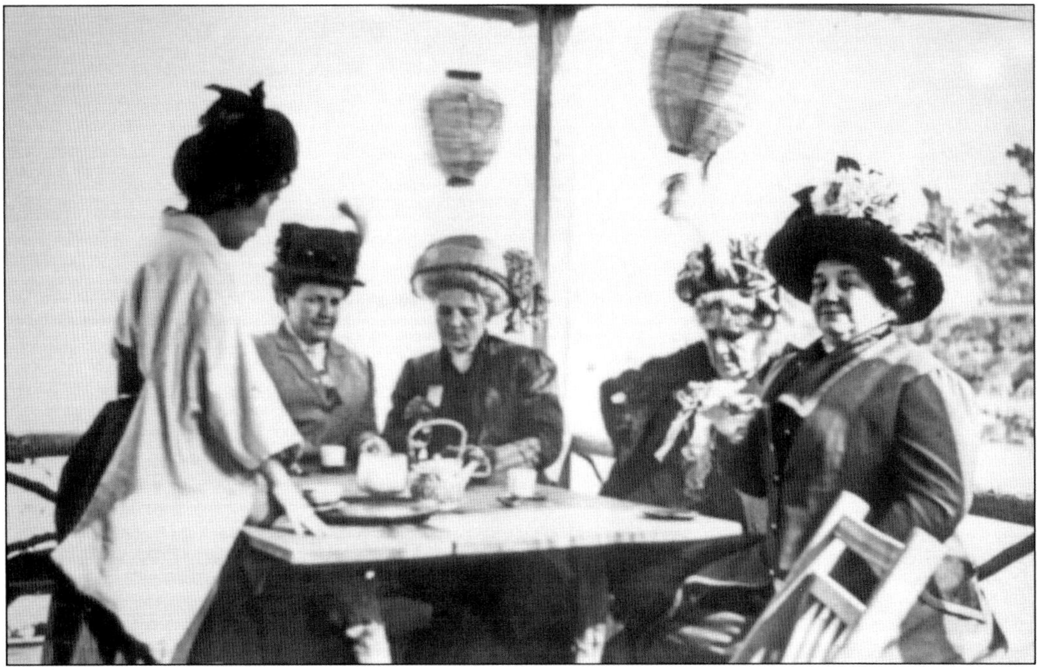

Tea Ceremonies. Otosaburo Noda also brought in women to serve tea and to perform tea ceremonies. Tea and rice cakes were sold for 10¢. It is also believed that Noda brought female divers, known as ama, to dive for abalone. (Tom Fordham collection.)

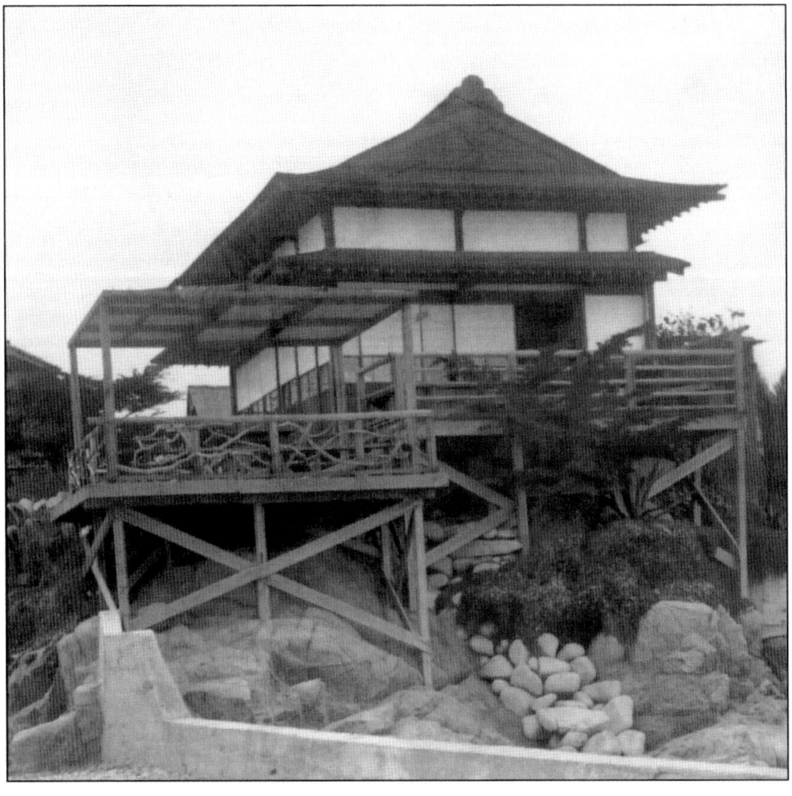

Noda's Teahouse. Although very popular with the tourists, Otosaburo Noda's teahouse was torn down in 1918. (Paulette Sugano Walker collection.)

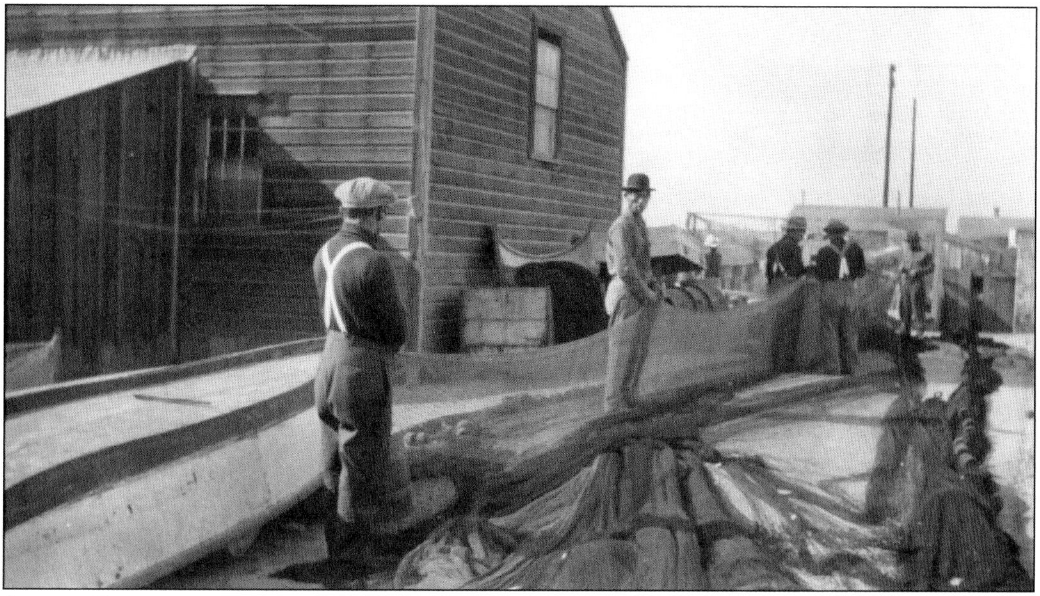

Salmon Fishermen, c. 1919. Besides abalone, Otosaburo Noda brought fishermen to the Monterey Peninsula to catch salmon. These men, working on a net, were mostly from the Wakayama Prefecture and were professional fishermen. Many were graduates from fisheries colleges in Japan. (Monterey History and Art Association [MHAA] Collection.)

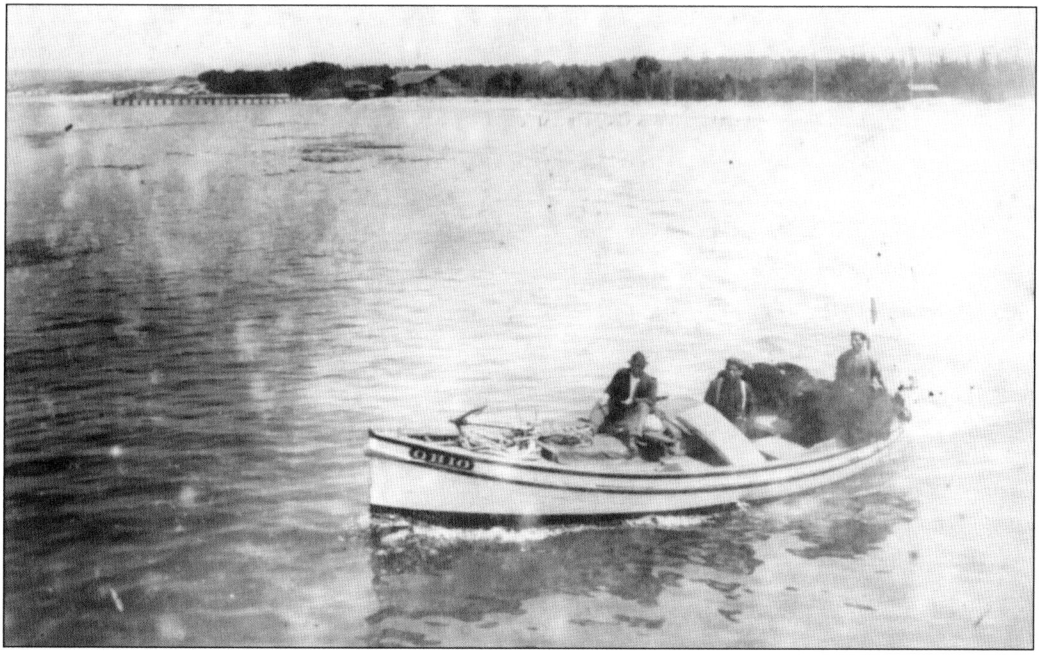

The *Ohio I*, c. 1909. From 1898 to 1915, the Japanese dominated the Monterey fishing industry, and salmon was king. Pictured here is an early Monterey salmon boat, named the *Ohio I*, on the bay. (Manaka family collection.)

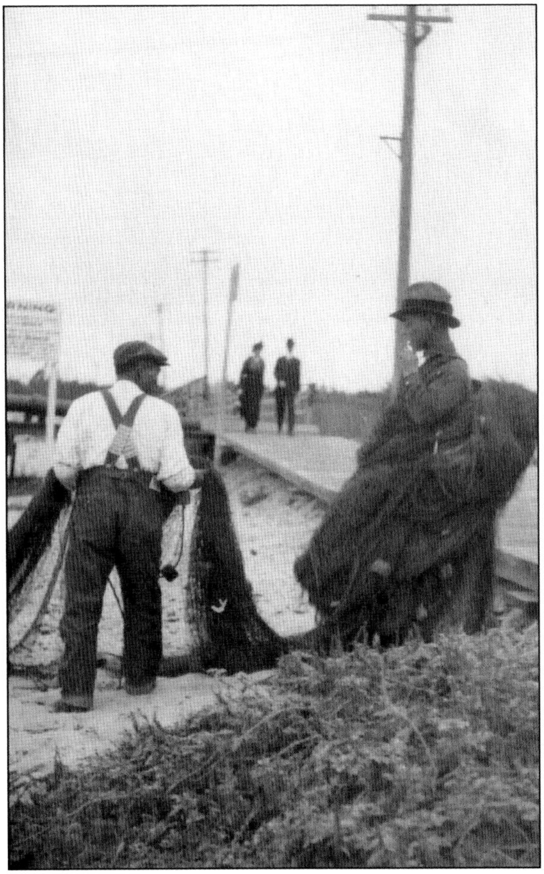

Noda's Fishermen Working near the Monterey Wharf. In 1902, Noda formed a partnership with American businessman Harry Malpas and opened the Monterey Fishing and Canning Company to can salmon and abalone. This was the first cannery on cannery row. (MHAA Collection.)

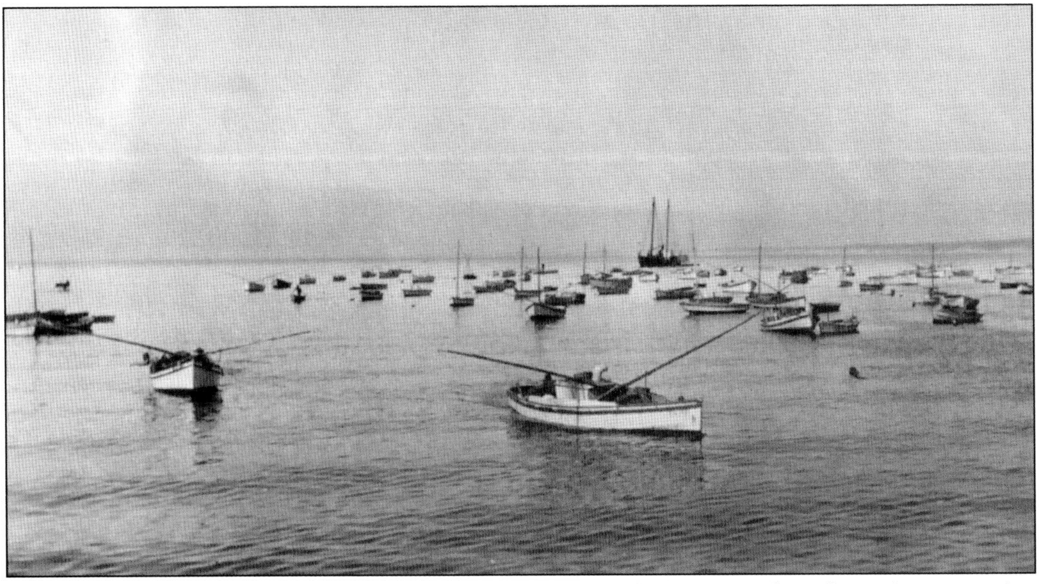

Japanese Salmon Boats in Monterey Harbor, 1909. Salmon season lasted just three months, from May 15 to August 15. Together, these small boats would catch an average of one million pounds of salmon every season. (MHAA Collection.)

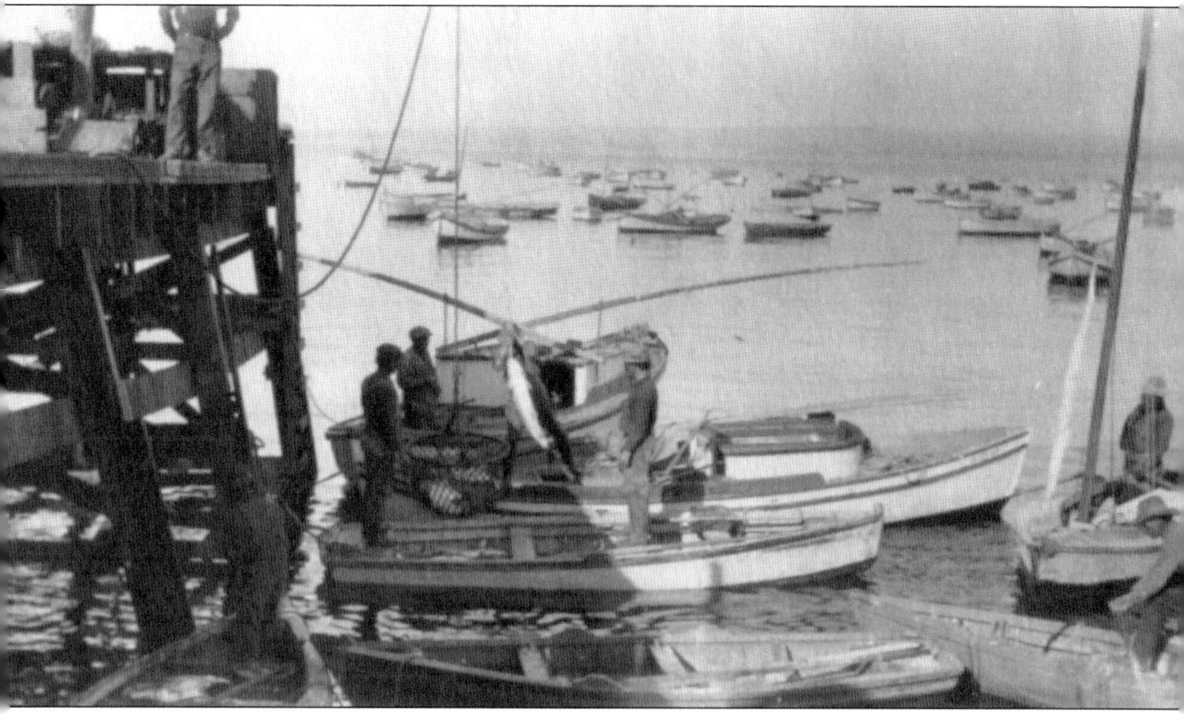

UNLOADING SALMON AT THE MONTEREY WHARF. At the end of the 1909 salmon season, the *Monterey Herald*, the local newspaper at the time, reported that there were 185 salmon boats working the bay; 145 were Japanese owned. (MHAA Collection.)

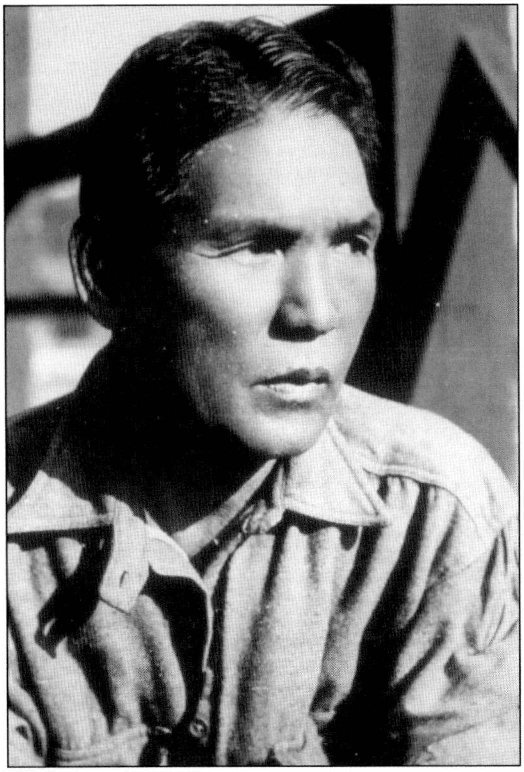

Gennosuke Kodani. Utilizing divers from the Chiba Prefecture of Japan, Gennosuke Kodani opened an abalone company and cannery at Point Lobos, south of Monterey, in 1898. (Kodani family collection.)

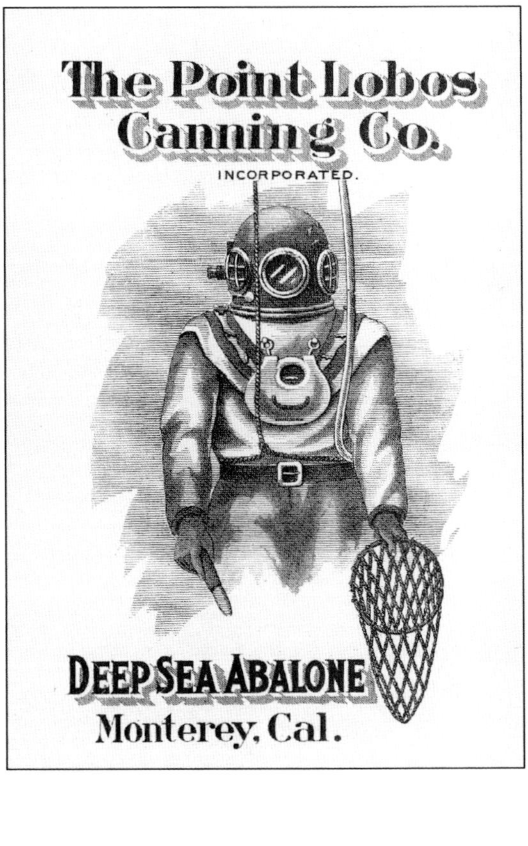

Label for Kodani's Point Lobos Canning Company. Because Kodani was an issei, a first-generation immigrant, he was prohibited from becoming a US citizen or owning property. (Kodani family collection.)

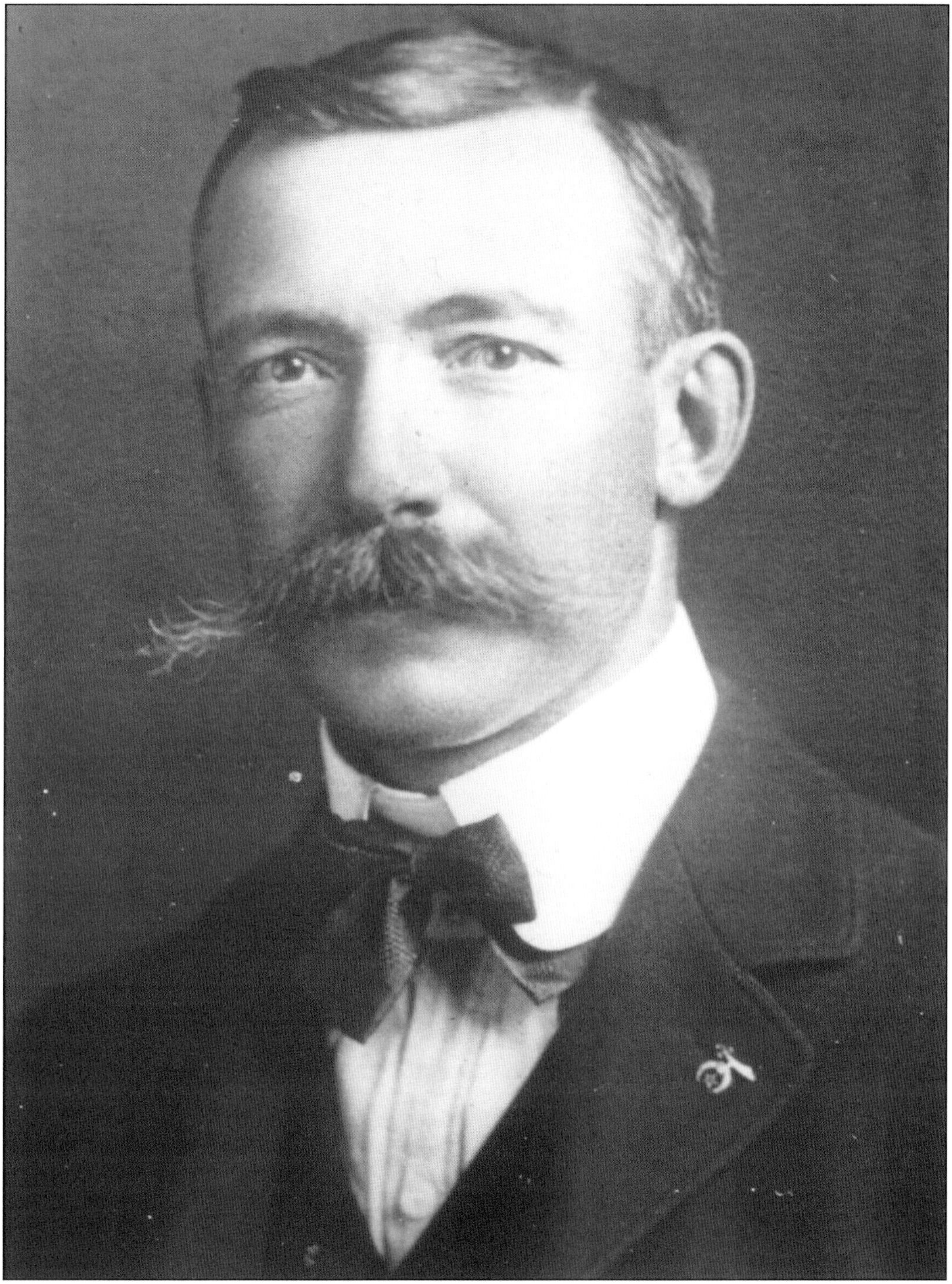

A.M. ALLAN. Allan purchased the Point Lobos property in 1898 and went into partnership with Kodani. Allan was a progressive thinker, who saw a great opportunity in working with the Japanese fishermen. He championed the Japanese cause and abalone fishing at every turn. Allan and Kodani became great friends. That friendship continues to this day with both the Allan and Kodani families. (Kodani family collection.)

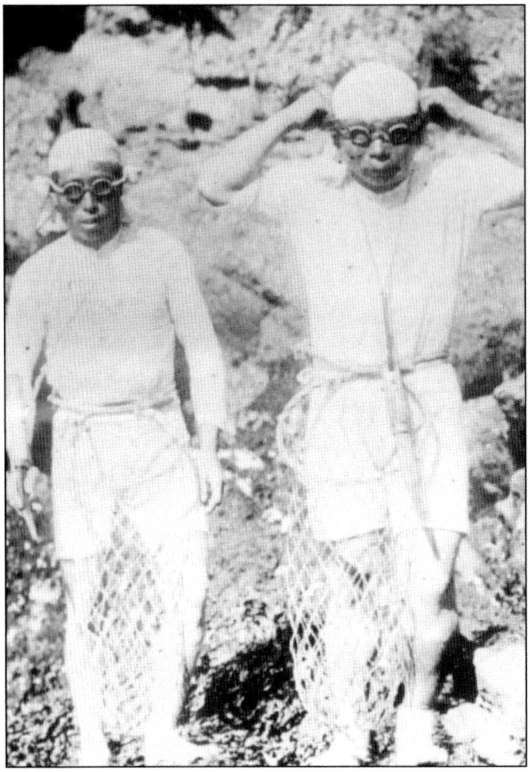

Ama, the First Abalone Divers, c. 1900. In Japanese, *ama* means "sea people." These early divers all came from the Minamiboso Peninsula in the Chiba Prefecture of Japan. Professional divers initially dove in Monterey dressed in their traditional cotton diving gear, because in their home country the water temperature was about 15 degrees warmer. They wore goggles so they could see and protect their eyes. The goggles were fitted with pig's bladders, with one on each side, that the diver would squeeze to help release pressure. (Kodani family collection.)

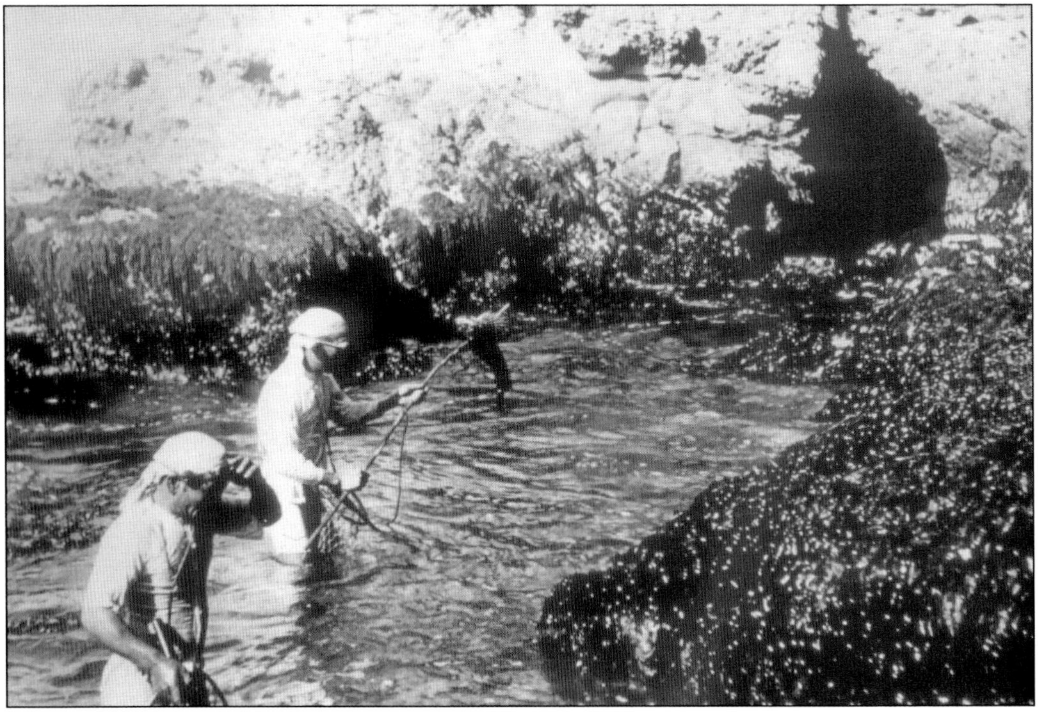

Two Ama in the Water at Point Lobos. The large rockfish on the end of the spear of the diver on the right is perhaps his lunch. (Kodani family collection.)

DIVER CHOMATSU KAWAKAMI. Kawakami first came to Monterey in 1907. In Japan, he was a rice farmer and not a diver. Within a day of arriving in Monterey, he was diving for abalone, and he stayed in Monterey for 20 years. (Kawakami family collection.)

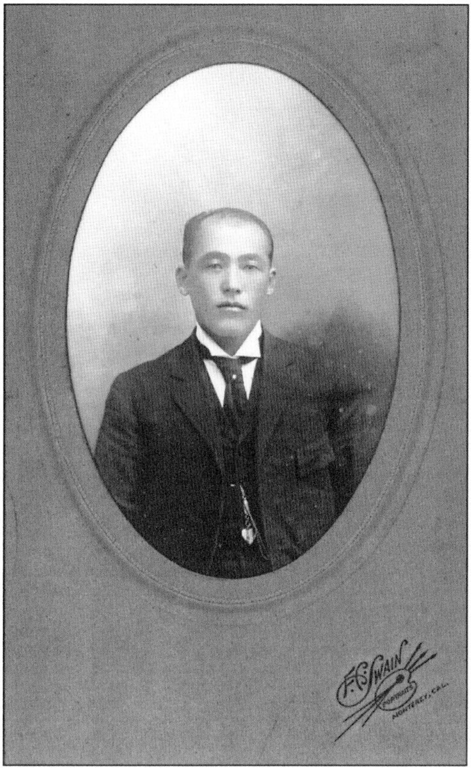

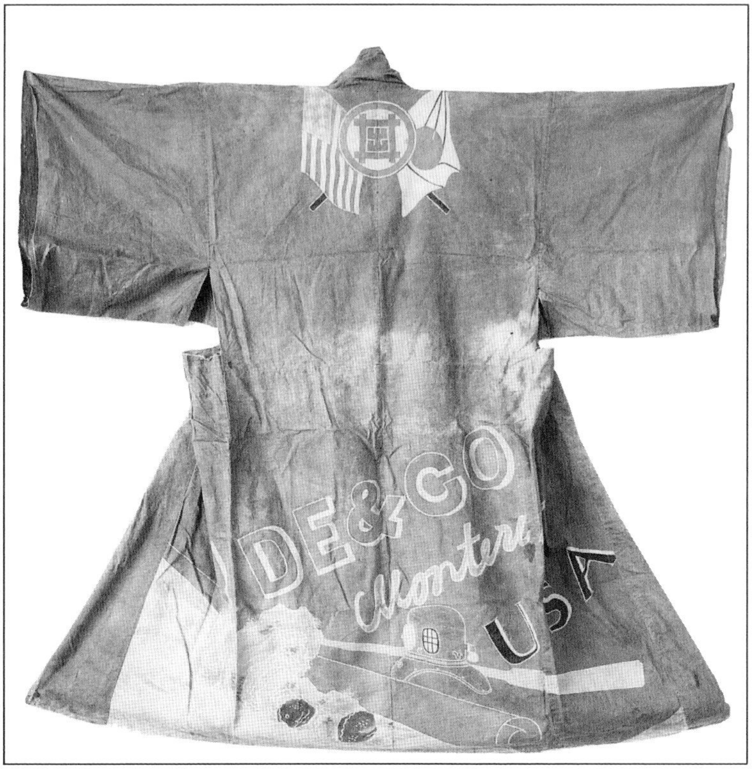

JAPANESE MAWAI, C. 1905. This is a celebratory coat given to Japanese fishermen at the end of a very good season. Written on the jacket is "Ide & Company, Monterey, USA," which was a Monterey abalone company. Haykutaro Ide was an early partner of Otosaburo Noda. The jacket is one of only two known to exist. Chomatsu Kawakami was given one of these. When he returned home to Japan, he had it made into a bedspread so he could sleep underneath it and dream of Monterey. (Photograph by Yoshie Mitsuhashi.)

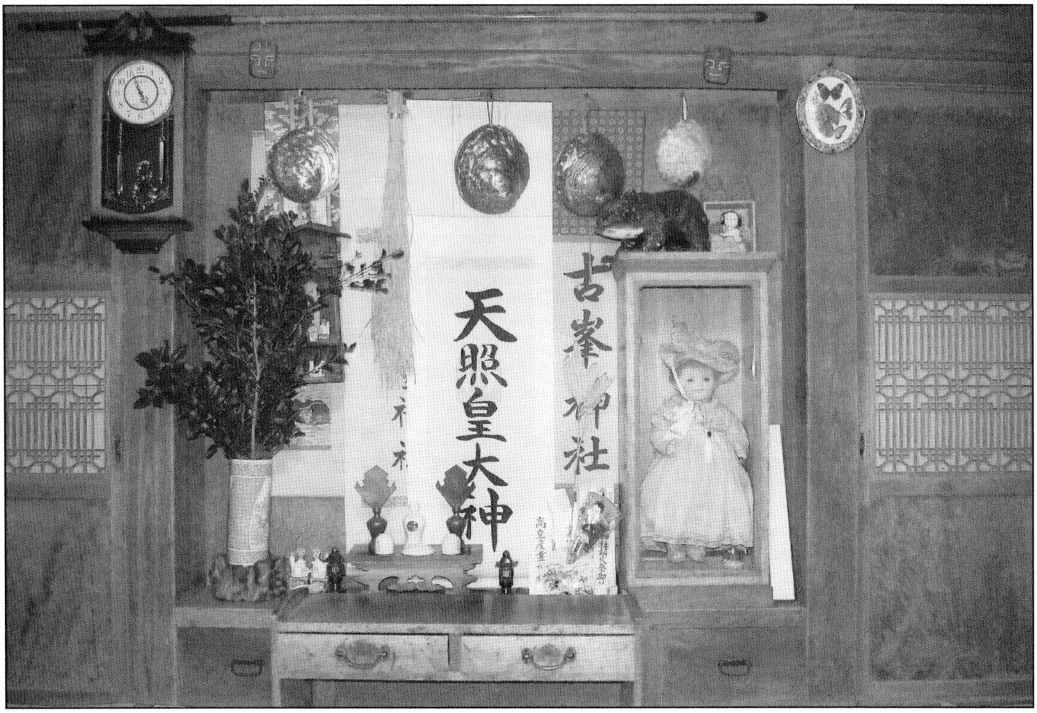

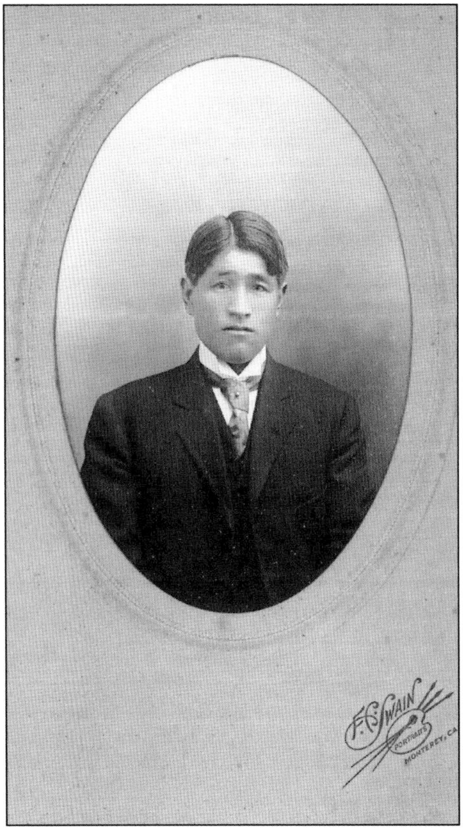

SHRINE TO MONTEREY, c. 2006. This is the home of Chomatsu Kawkami in the village of Chikura, which is on the Boso Peninsula in Japan. Many of the Monterey divers came from this small village, and their families, to this day, still have these shrines to Monterey that honor their loved ones who risked their lives and limbs to travel across the Pacific to dive for abalone. The large abalone shells came out of the Monterey Bay over 100 years ago. The doll on the lower right was purchased at Holman's Department Store in Pacific Grove in 1927, and it is now a family heirloom. (Photograph by Tim Thomas.)

DIVER TOYOMATSU YAMAGUCHI. Yamaguchi came to Monterey in 1908. In the late 19th century and early 20th century, divers off the Boso Peninsula were having a difficult time finding abalone because of a disease that was killing all the brown kelp, which was what the abalone fed on. Divers had to go elsewhere to work so they could care for and feed their families, and many came to Monterey. Kodani's brother Nakajiro Kodani, a trained marine biologist with a degree from the Imperial Fisheries Institute in Tokyo, stayed in Japan and was responsible for recruiting divers for the Point Lobos abalone fishery. (Yamaguchi family, Japan.)

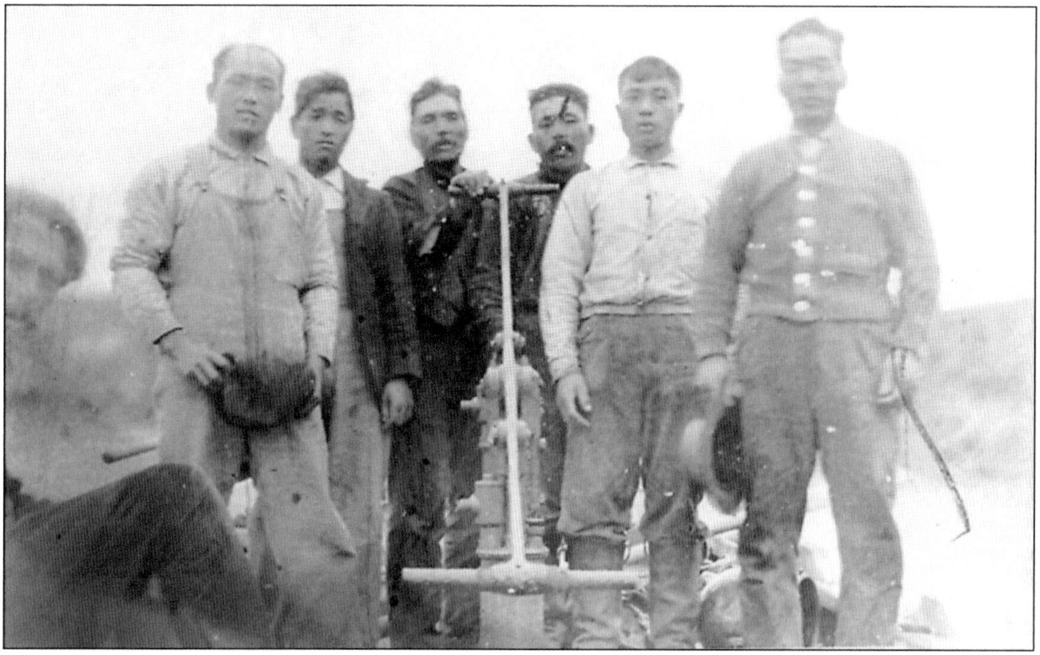

On Board a Dive Boat at Point Lobos, c. 1909. The two men on the left are Chomatsu Kawakamia and Toyomatsu Yamaguchi. In the middle of the boat is the hand pump that produced air for the diver. All the diving gear, including the pump, was imported from Japan. (Kodani family collection.)

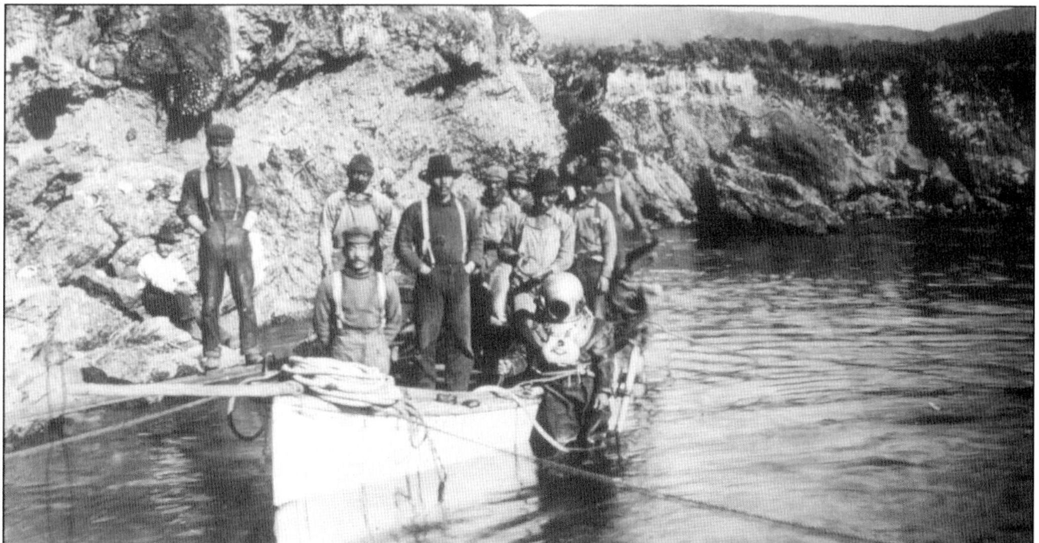

Helmet Divers. Because Monterey Bay is so cold, with an average water temperature of 55 degrees, Kodani sent for helmet divers. The first arrived in 1898. But even for them, the water was too cold. The divers all learned to knit; they would take wool sweaters and tear them apart to make wool underwear to wear under their heavy canvas dive suits. The pump was a key part of the operation, and it had to be taken apart and lubricated every day. The only good lubricating oil to be found in Monterey was olive oil. Divers would complain about the olive smell for the first hour of every dive. (Kodani family collection.)

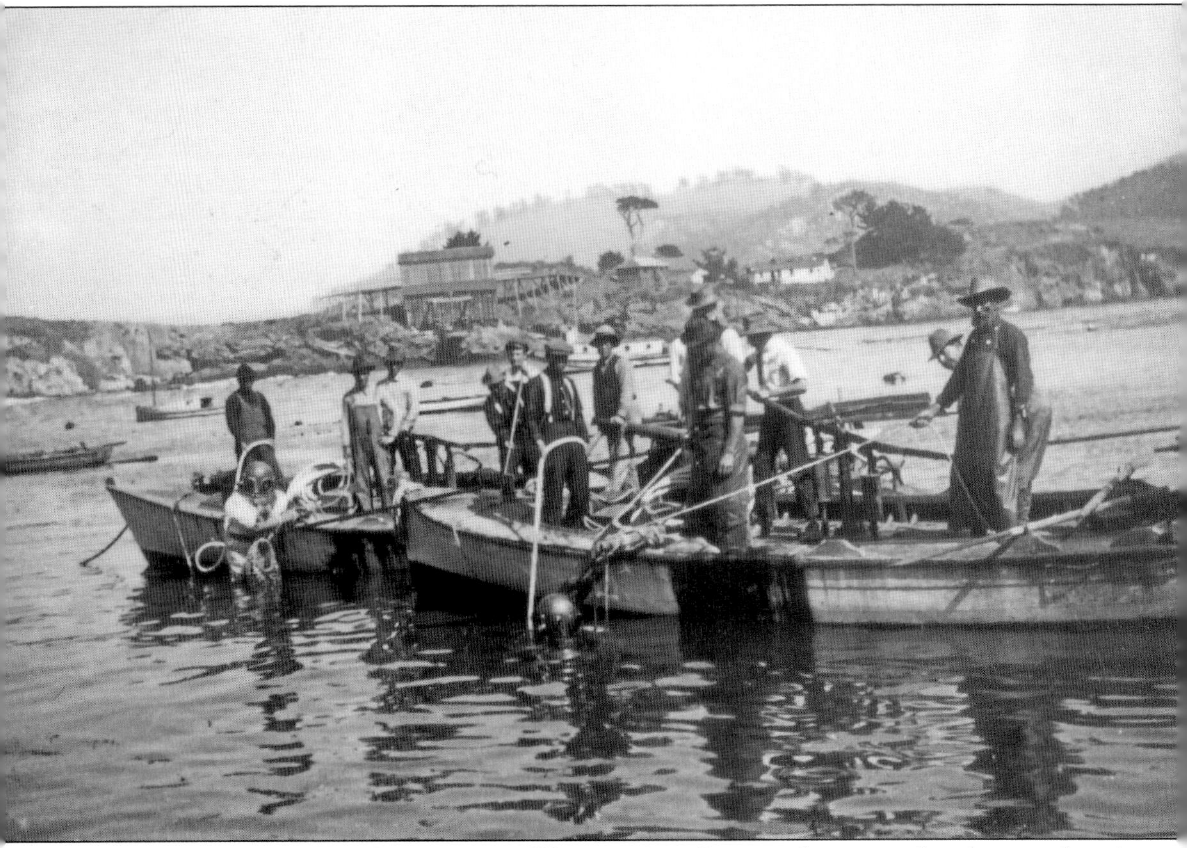

Dive Scene with Two Boats in the Water, 1910. Because the air was hand-pumped to the divers, they were limited to dive no deeper than 20 feet. The deeper the diver went, the harder it was to pump. Sometimes there were four men, two on each side, working the pump. There was a hierarchy on a dive boat. The diver's brother or cousin was usually holding the lifeline, and they always wanted their friends on the pump. (Kodani family collection.)

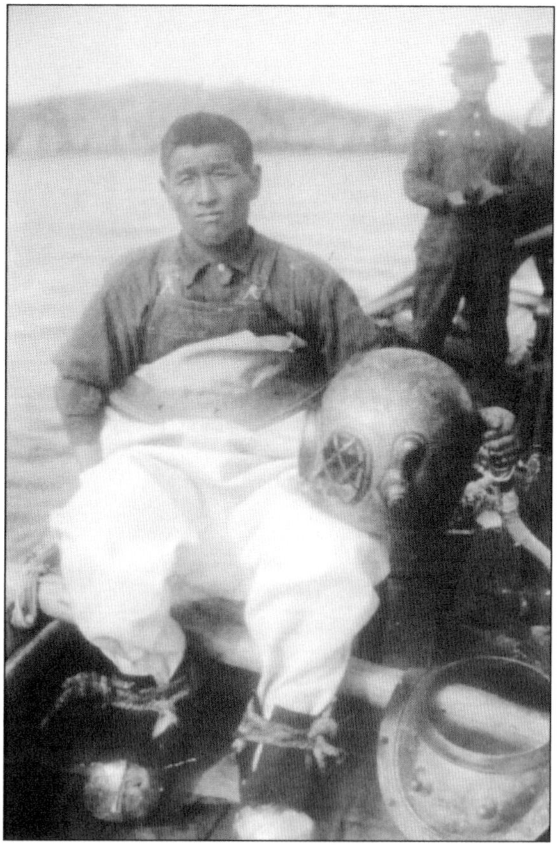

Tajuro Watanabe, 1915. This photograph shows abalone diver Watanabe getting dressed for a dive. Almost all of the abalone divers came to Monterey on a contract. With few exceptions, they returned to Japan. Watanabe was one of the exceptions. (Monterey Library Collection.)

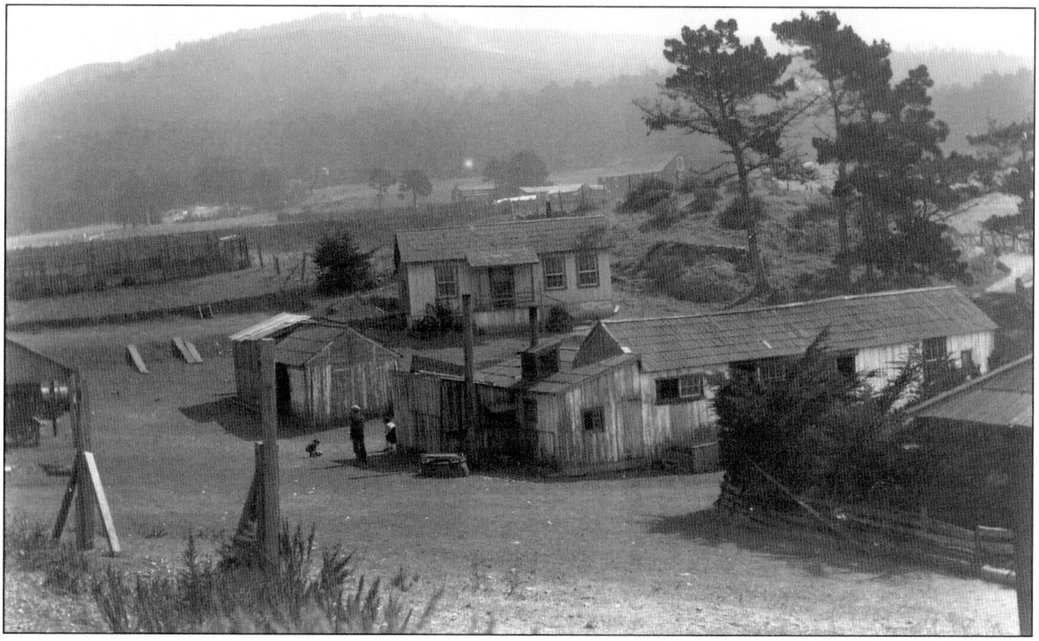

Kodani Village, 1915. This is where the divers and crew lived in Point Lobos. They had all the comforts of home, including a traditional Japanese bath. (Kodani family collection.)

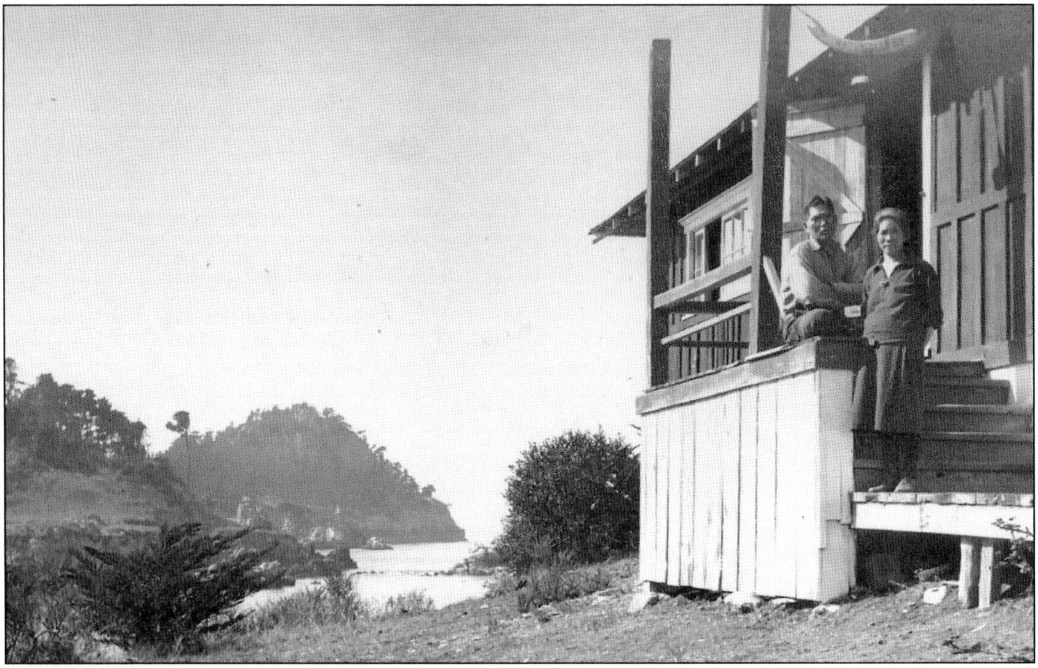

POINT LOBOS HOME, C. 1925. Pictured here are Kodani and his wife, Fuku, on their porch at Point Lobos. (Kodani family collection.)

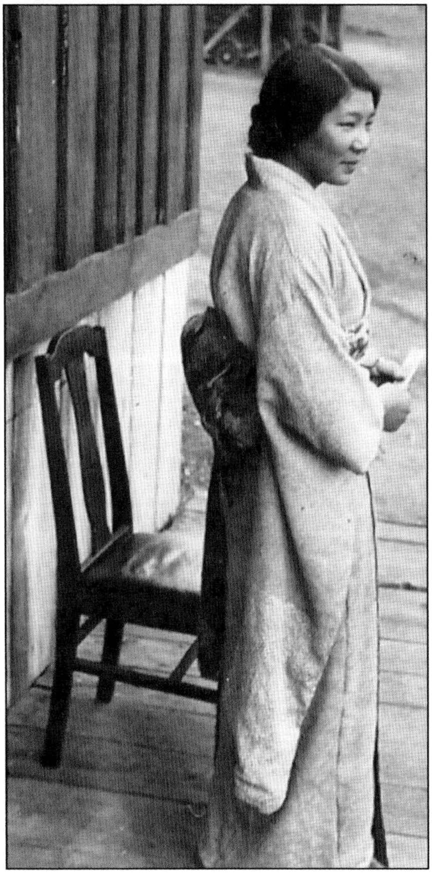

TAKEKO KODANI AT KODANI VILLAGE. Takeko later married into the Tabata family, which owned the Sunrise Market. The market stocked mainly Japanese fresh and packaged foods and fishing supplies. (Kodani family collection.)

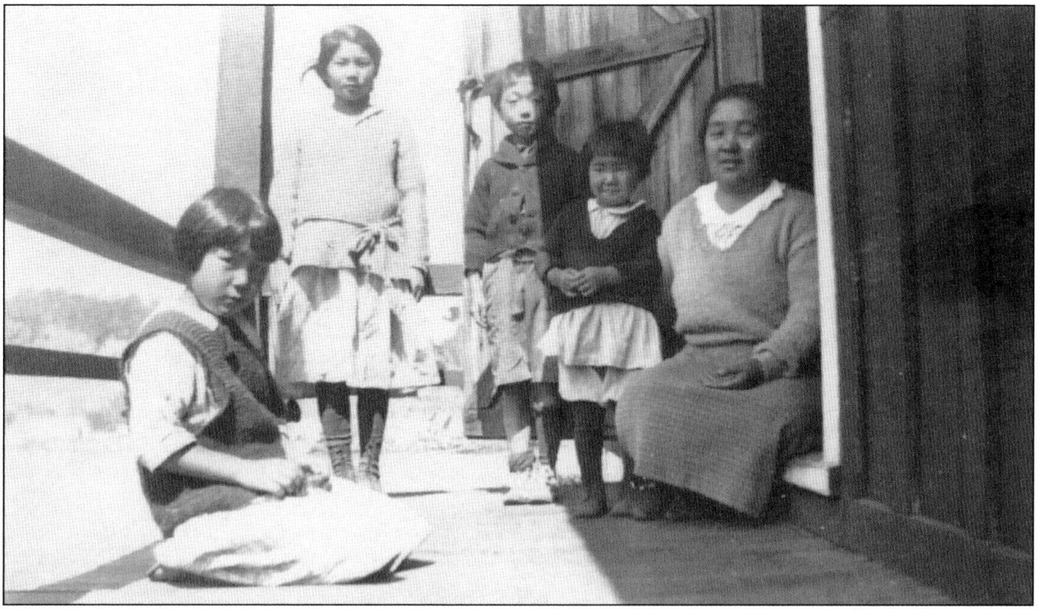

KODANI'S CHILDREN, 1910. The Kodani's children, from left to right, are Takeko, Fusako. Kuniko, and Yoshio. The woman is unidentified. (Kodani family collection)

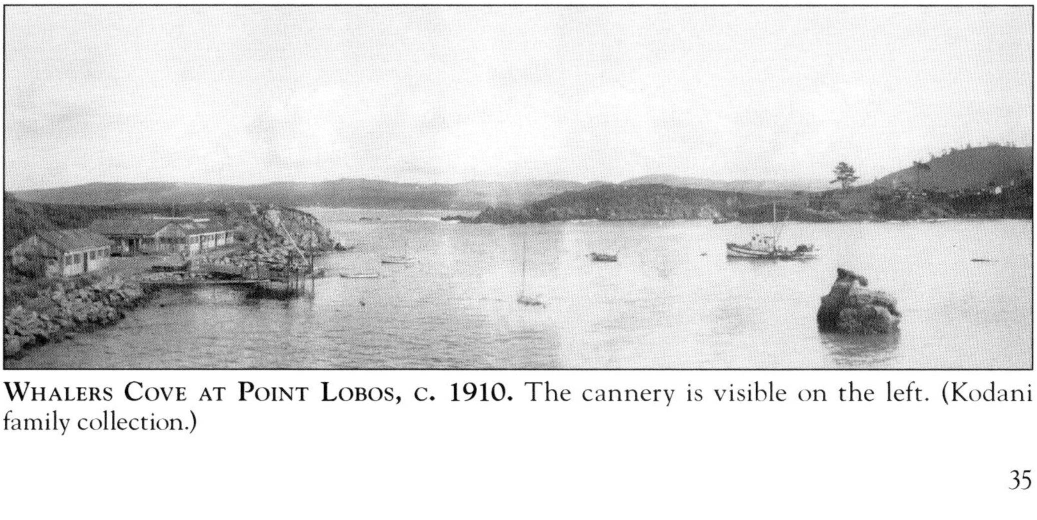

WHALERS COVE AT POINT LOBOS, C. 1910. The cannery is visible on the left. (Kodani family collection.)

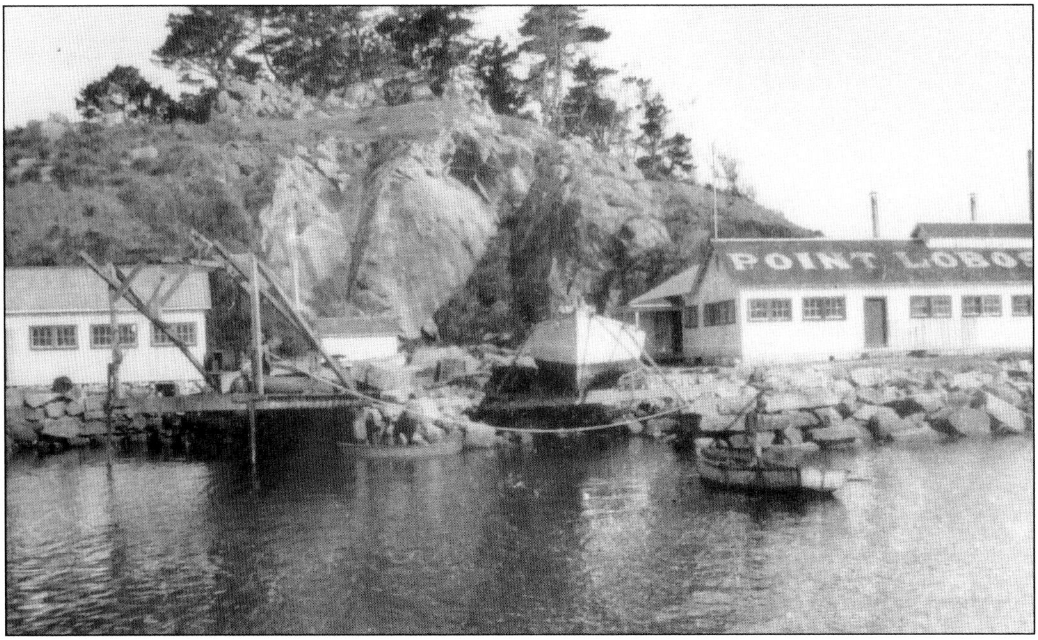

FROM THE COVE AROUND 1915. The cannery is visible in the front. Abalone was originally dried and shipped to Japan, China, and Australia, where there was a large Japanese and Chinese community who would buy it. Early on, abalone was canned primarily for the Japanese market. (Kodani family collection.)

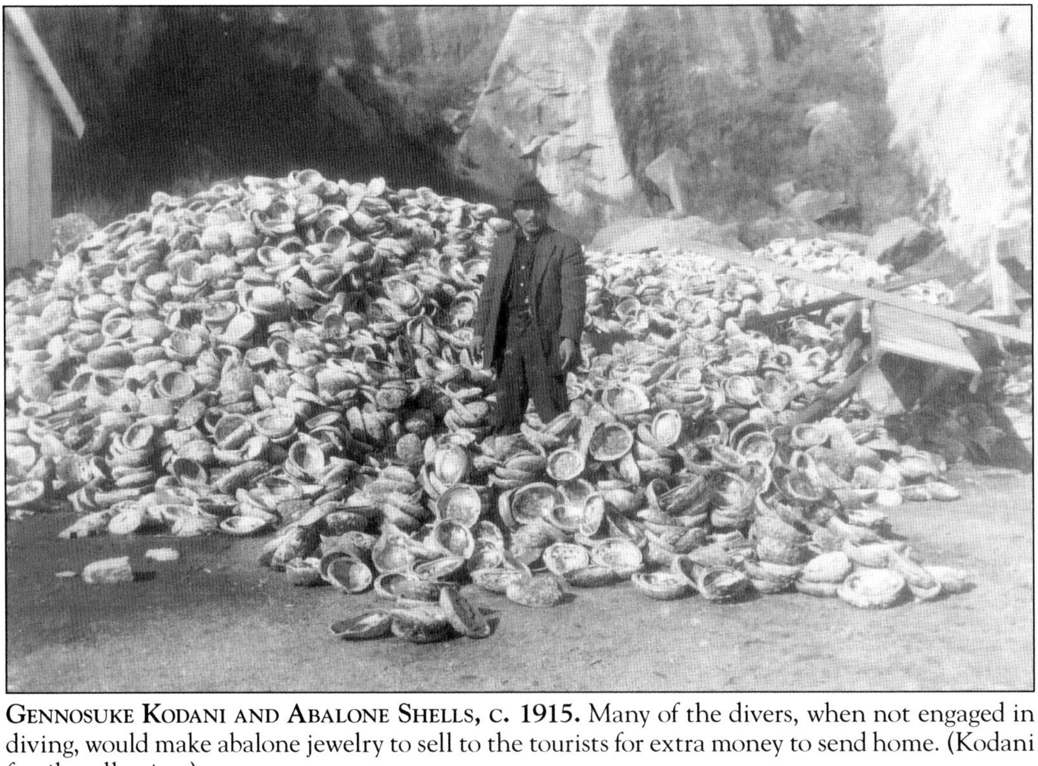

GENNOSUKE KODANI AND ABALONE SHELLS, C. 1915. Many of the divers, when not engaged in diving, would make abalone jewelry to sell to the tourists for extra money to send home. (Kodani family collection.)

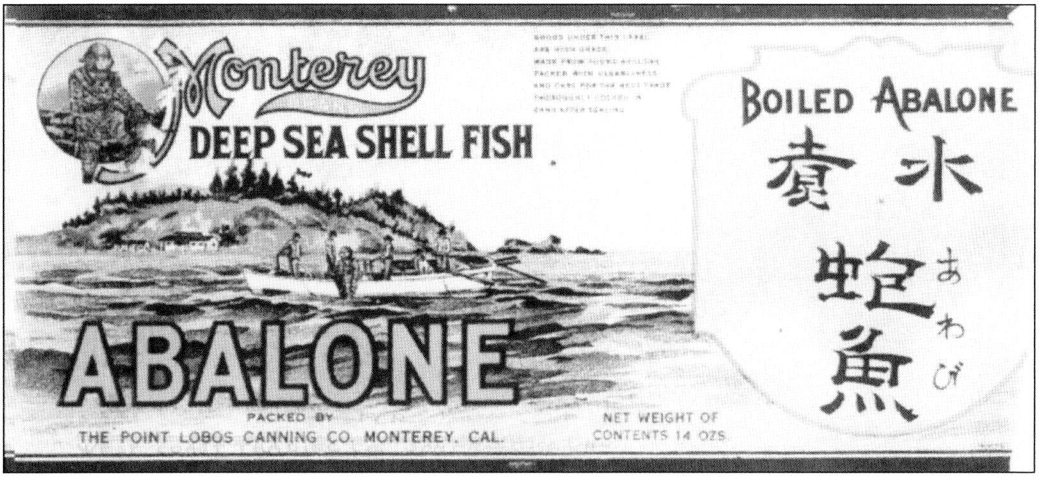

JAPANESE LABEL FOR CANNED ABALONE, C. 1910. In the early 19th century, there was no domestic market for abalone. No one locally knew how to prepare it. The Point Lobos Abalone Company began to can it and sell it to the Japanese community on West Coast and in Japan. (Kodani family collection.)

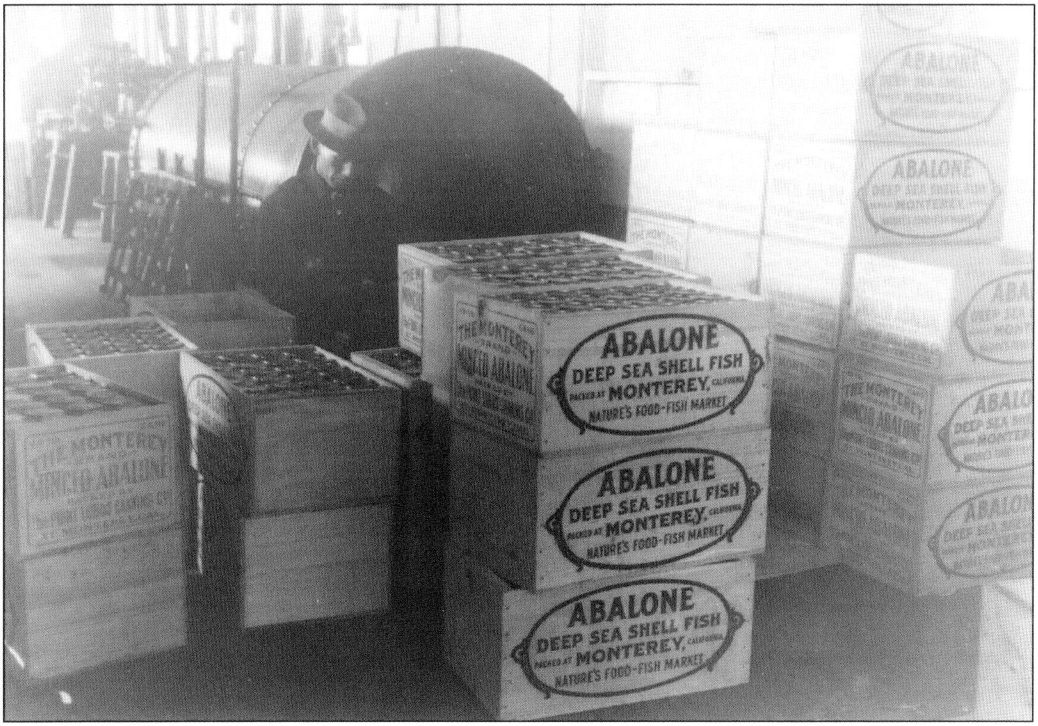

INSIDE THE POINT LOBOS ABALONE CANNERY, C. 1920. The cases of canned abalone are ready to be shipped overseas. Abalone would be removed from the shell, sliced, and put into the cans. It would then be cooked using steam. In 1913, the State of California outlawed the Japanese from exporting abalone out of the state. At that time, there was a very small domestic market for fresh abalone. This California law was seen as a discriminatory effort to restrict competition. (Kodani family collection.)

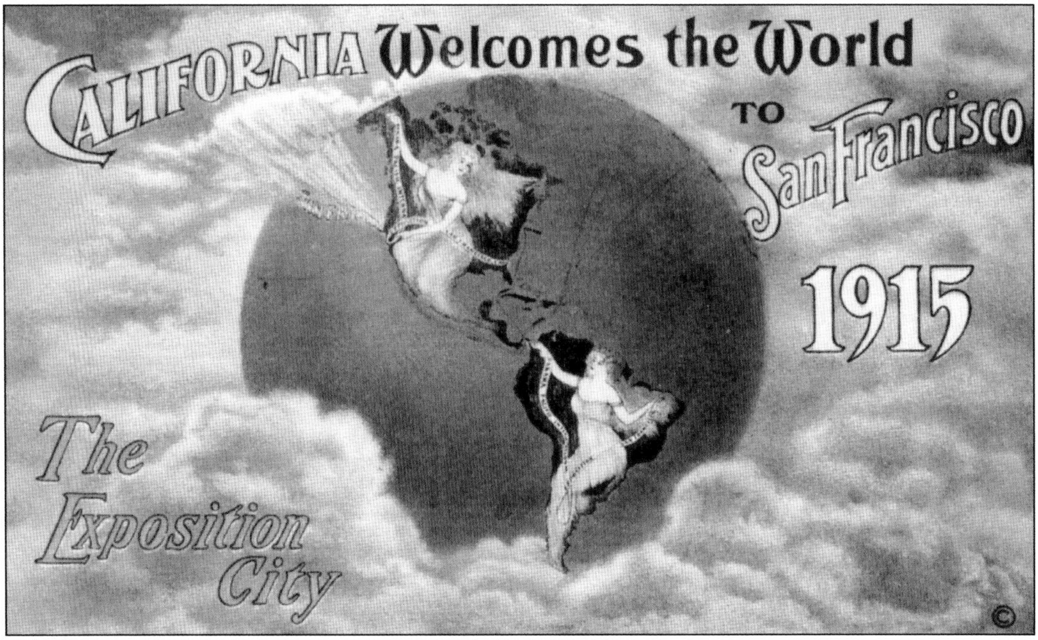

The World's Fair. In 1915, a world's fair came to San Francisco and was called the Panama-Pacific International Exposition. It was a celebration of the opening of the Panama Canal. One building at the fair was dedicated to food, and the Point Lobos Canning Company had a booth there. (Tim Thomas collection.)

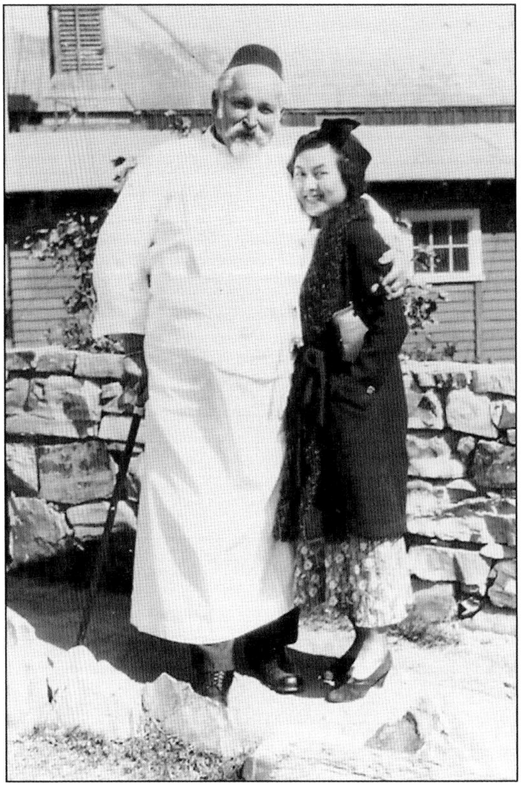

Ernest "Pop" Doelter. In 1906, a German restaurateur named Doelter opened a small restaurant in Monterey. After experimenting with abalone, he learned that the meat had to be tenderized before it could be prepared. He put fresh abalone steaks on the menu, and it became very popular with the local and tourist communities. Pictured here is Pop standing in front of his Monterey restaurant with an unidentified woman. (Kodani family collection.)

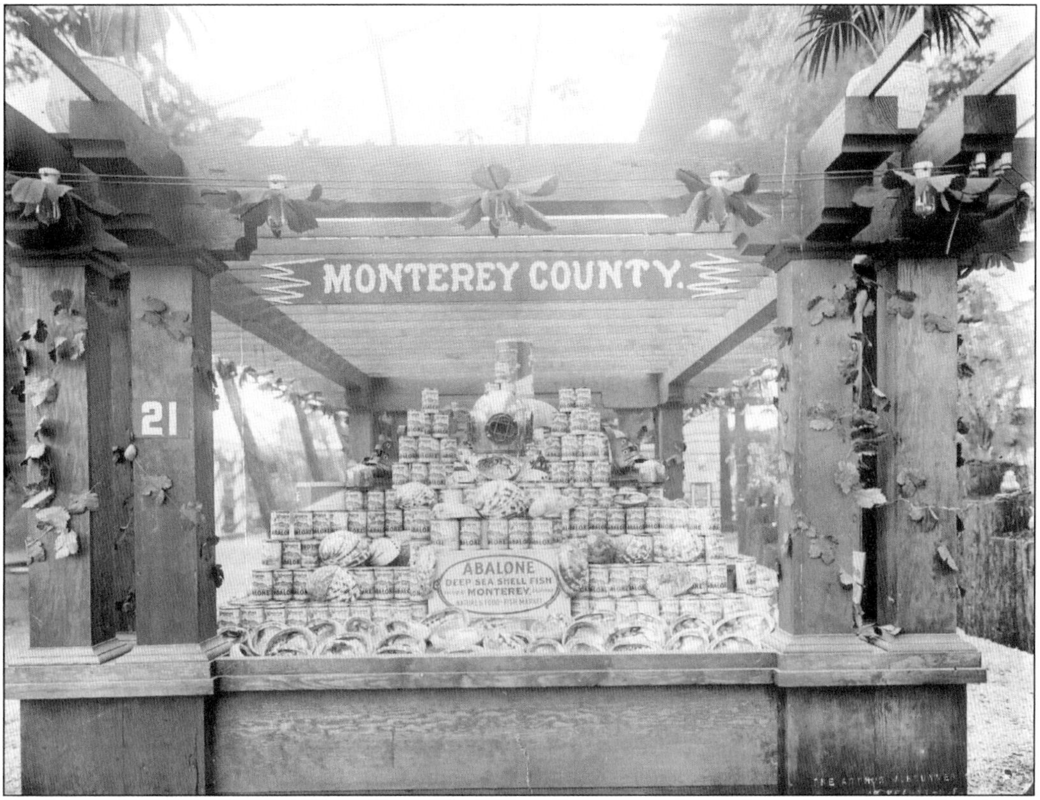

POINT LOBOS BOOTH AT THE WORLD'S FAIR. The Point Lobos Canning Company served fresh abalone to the world at the Panama-Pacific International Exposition, and soon everyone wanted it. This rare photograph shows the Point Lobos booth at the fair in 1915. (Kodani family collection.)

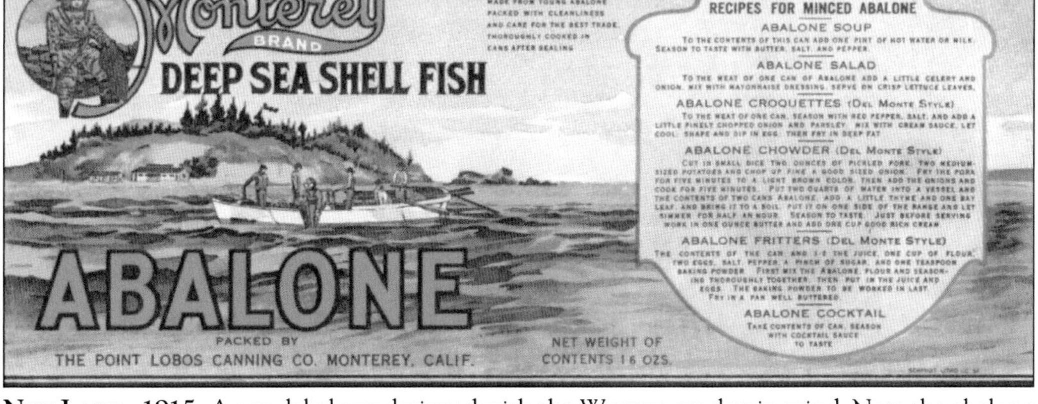

NEW LABEL, 1915. A new label was designed with the Western market in mind. Note the abalone recipes. (Kodani family collection.)

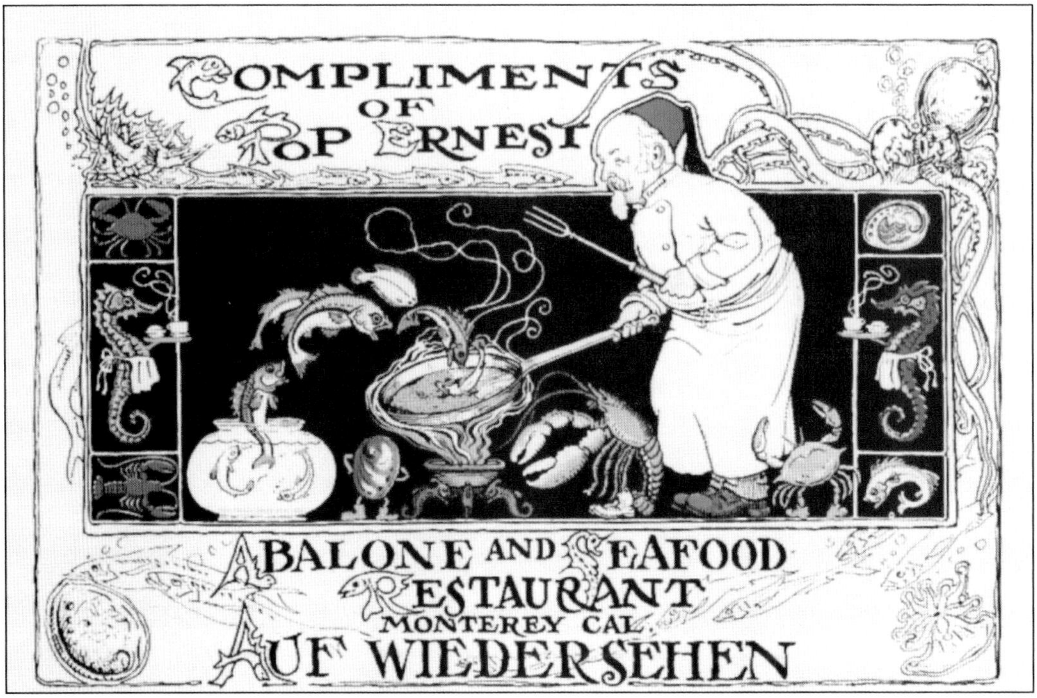

MENU FOR POP'S RESTAURANT, C. 1930. By 1930, Pop Doelter was known as the abalone king. He employed his own Japanese dive crew who catered just to his restaurant. He also brokered abalone to hotels and restaurants all over the western United States. (Pat Sands.)

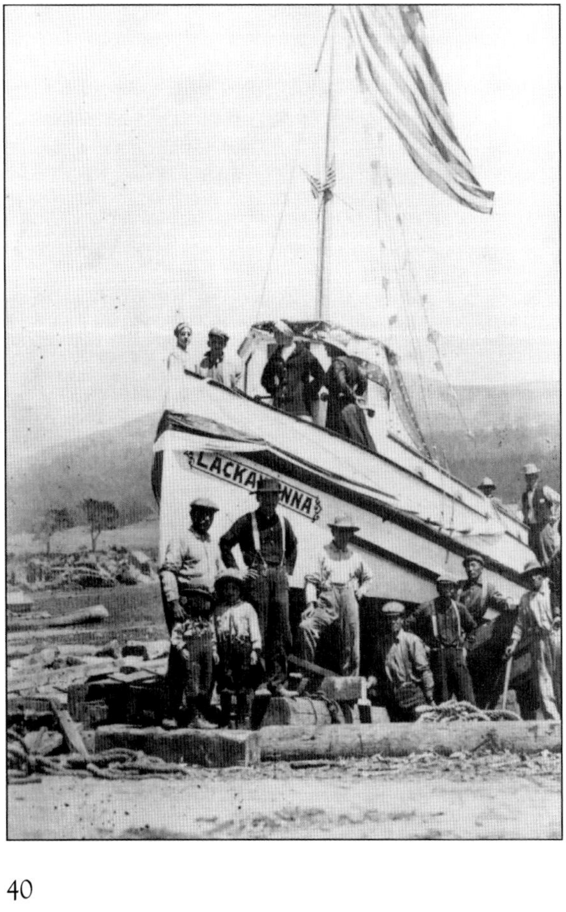

LACKAWANNA, C. 1905. The *Lackawanna* was the Point Lobos Canning Company's first large abalone boat. This ship enabled the company to venture outside of Monterey Bay for abalone. The name refers to a river in Pennsylvania near where A.M. Allan grew up. The boat was named in his honor. (Kodani family collection.)

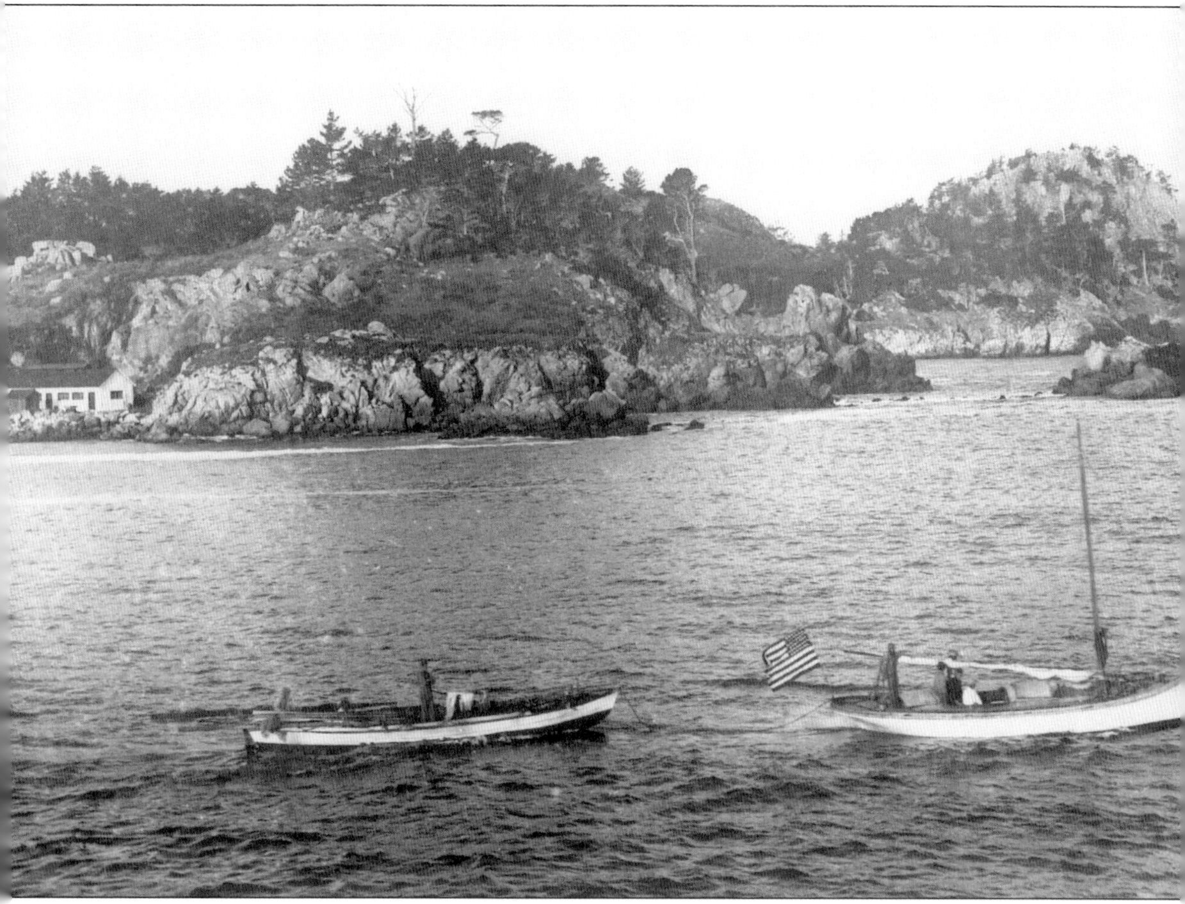

ABALONE DIVE BOATS, C. 1910. Pictured here are two small abalone dive boats in the cove at Point Lobos. Note the American flag. (Kodani family collection.)

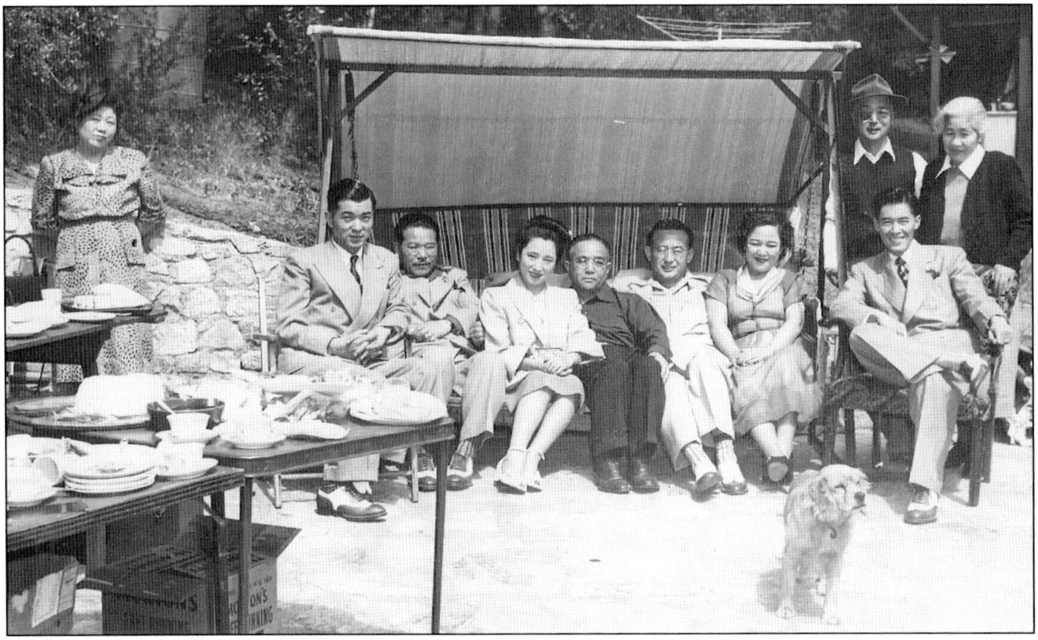

Beach Picnic, c. 1930. Here, the Kodani family and their friends are having a picnic at the beach. (Kodani family collection.)

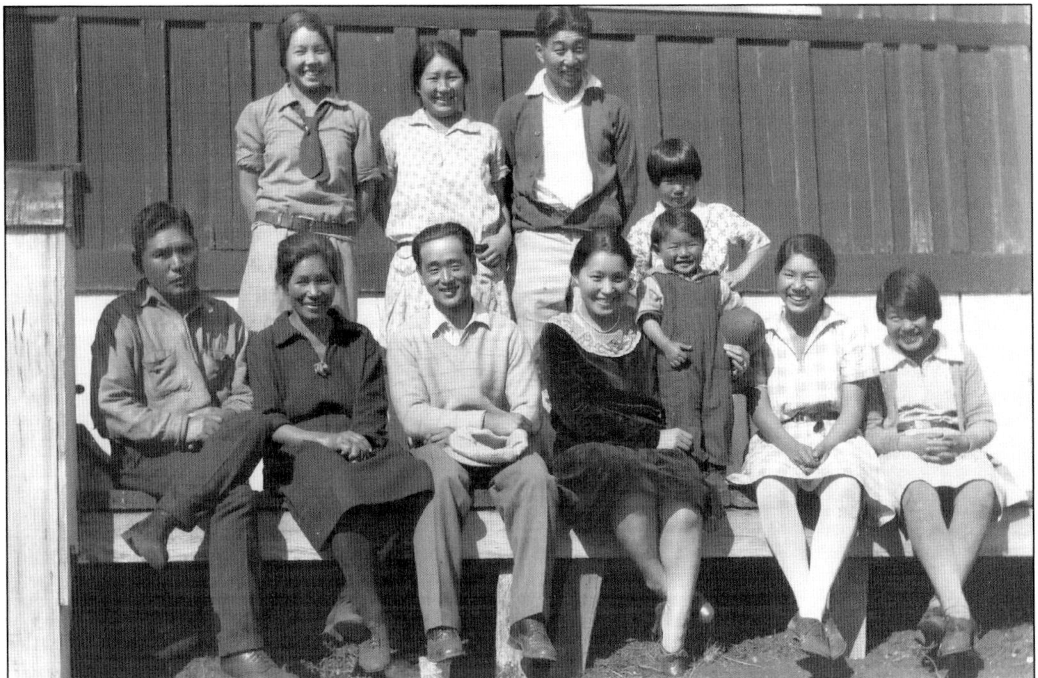

Kodani family at their Home in Kodani Village. In 1924, the United States passed the Asian Exclusion Act. It meant that Japanese and other Asian citizens could no longer immigrate to the United States. Allan was able to negotiate with the US government for permits that allowed the divers, who worked on contracts, to continue to come and dive for abalone. Monterey is the only place where this happened. (Kodani family collection.)

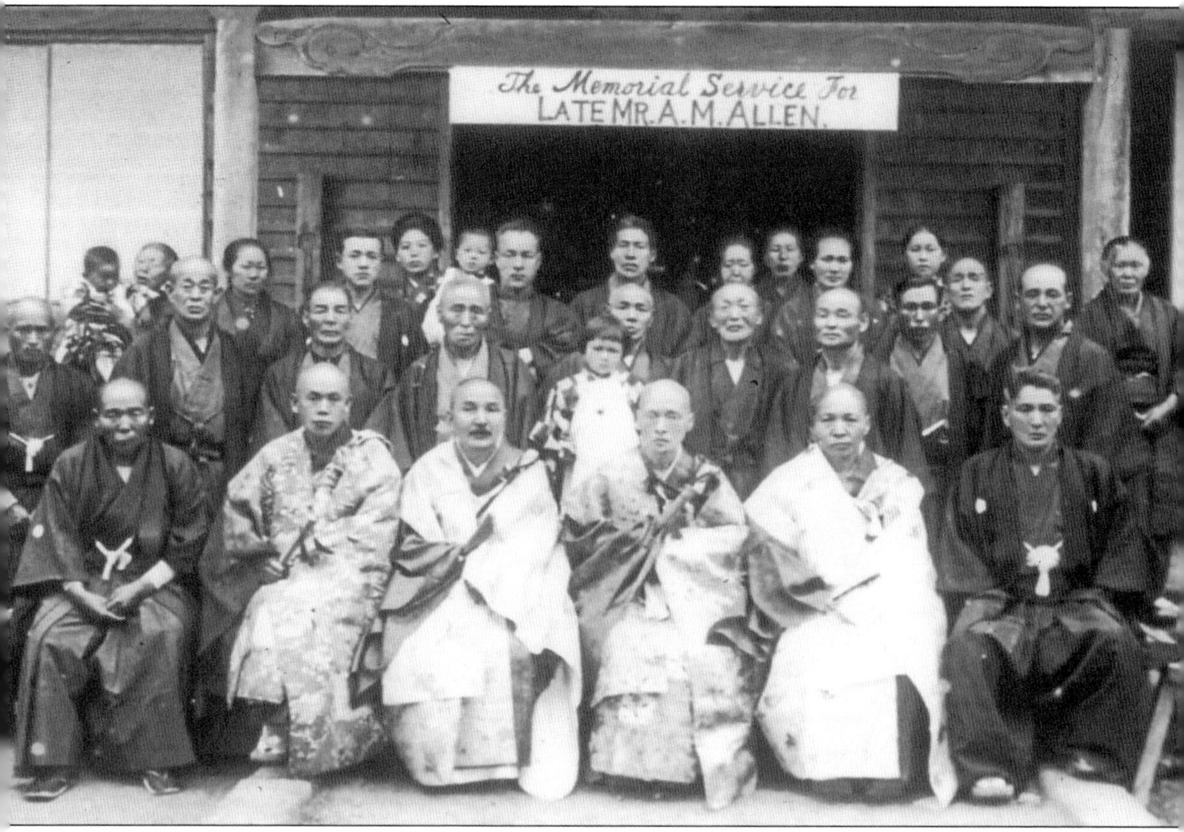

MEMORIAL SERVICE FOR A.M. Allan. Because of A.M. Allan's unfailing friendship and support of Gennosuke Kodani and the fishermen from Japan, a memorial service was held in his honor at the Chosho-ji Temple in Chikura Village, Japan, after his death in April 1930. Nakajiro Kodani can be seen sitting on the far right. Standing right behind Nakajiro is Chomatsu Kawakami. (Toshio Oba collection.)

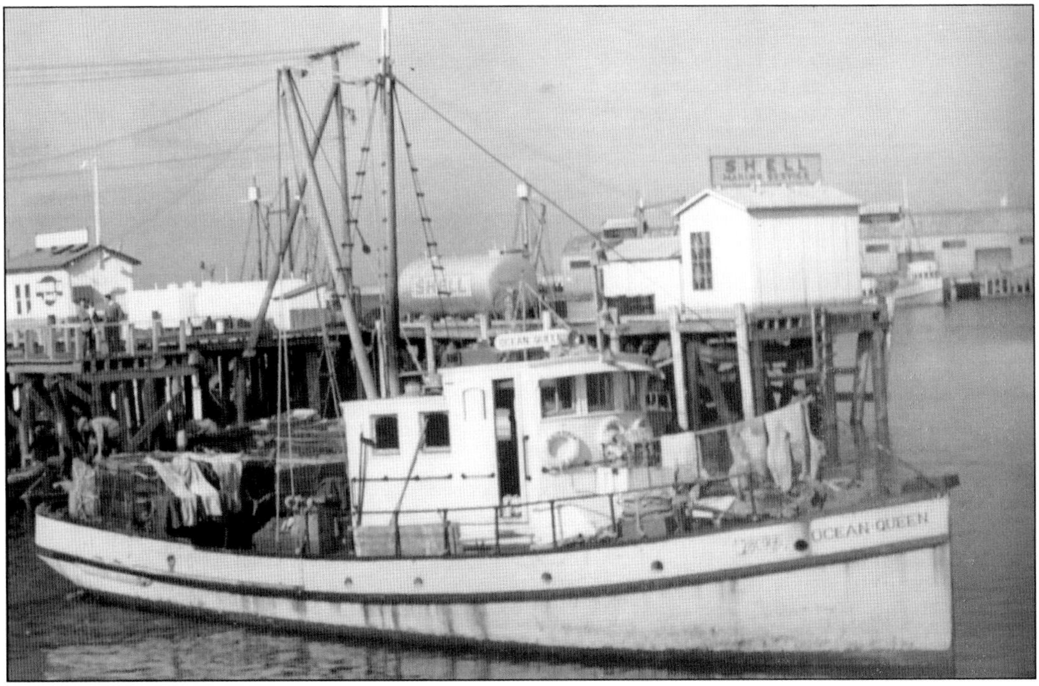

THE *OCEAN QUEEN* AT MONTEREY, 1930. Gennosuke Kodani purchased this boat from the US Treasury Department after it was captured from rumrunners during Prohibition. (George T. Esaki photograph, Jean Esaki and Monterey Library Collection, California History Room.)

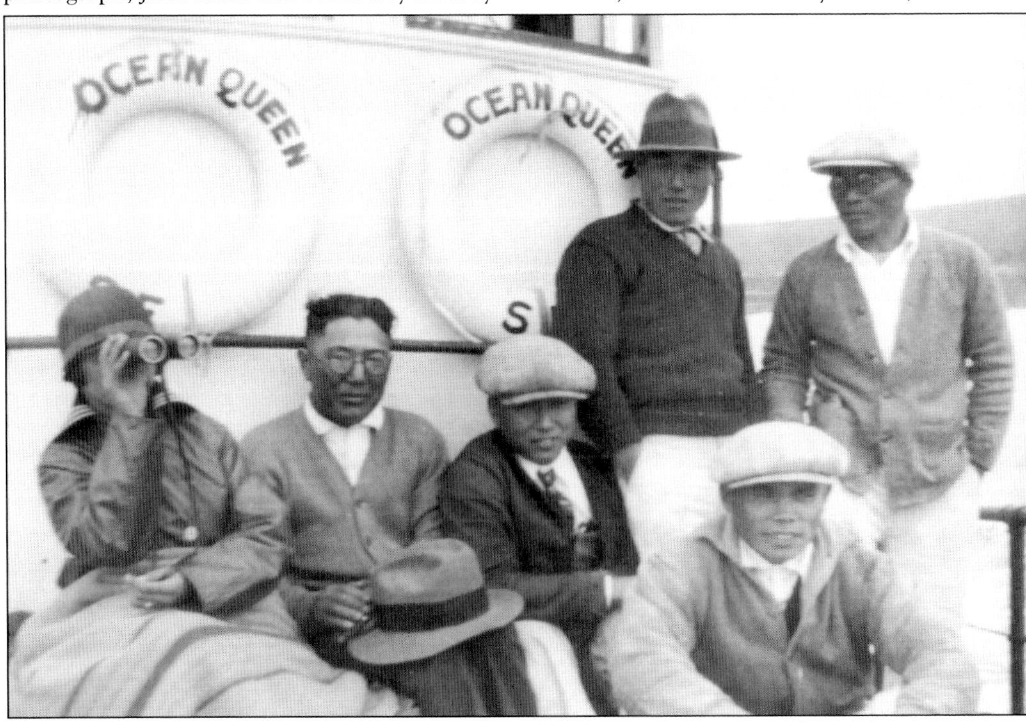

DIVERS AND CREW ABROAD THE *OCEAN QUEEN*, C. 1930. The men are shown here enjoying a rare day off, exploring around Monterey Bay. (Kodani family collection.)

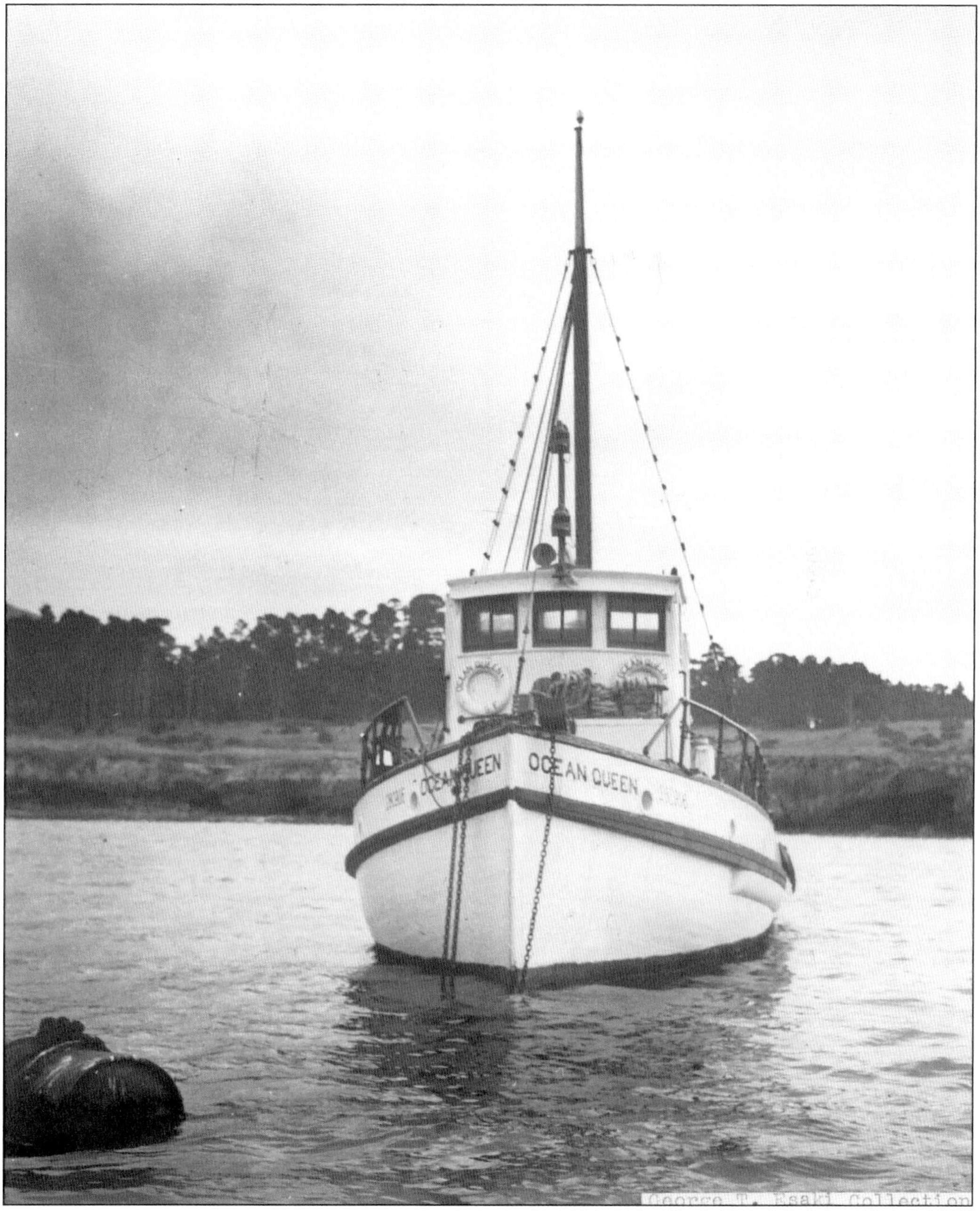

OCEAN QUEEN AT ANCHOR IN THE COVE AT POINT LOBOS. Gennosuke Kodani died at the Carmel Hospital on July 1, 1930, and is buried in Monterey. The Point Lobos Canning Company, the first abalone cannery in California, closed the following year. (Kodani family collection.)

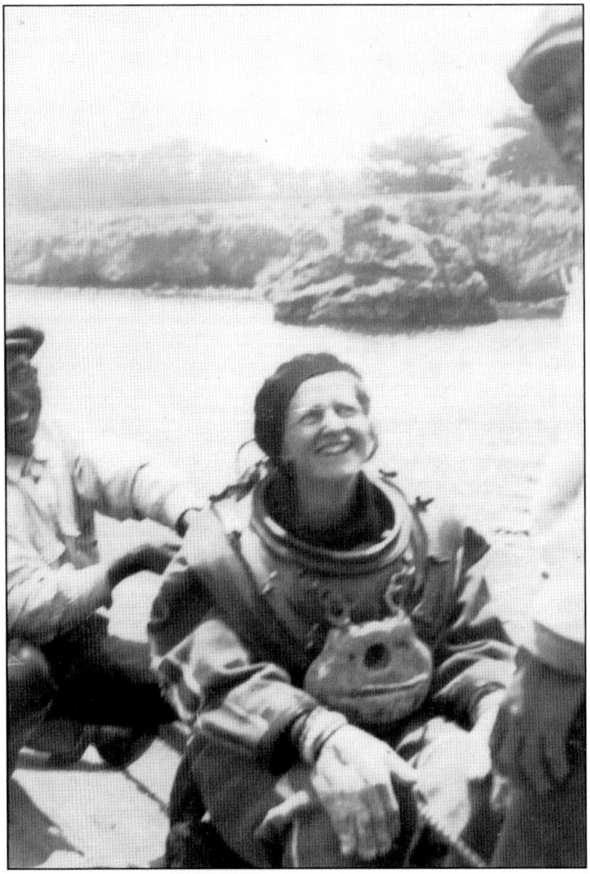

Frances Felin Diving. After the cannery closed, people still went out to the point to dive. Felin, a doctoral candidate in marine biology at the University of California, spent a few days out there diving in the cove in 1932. Note how large the gloves are on her hands. (Kodani family collection.)

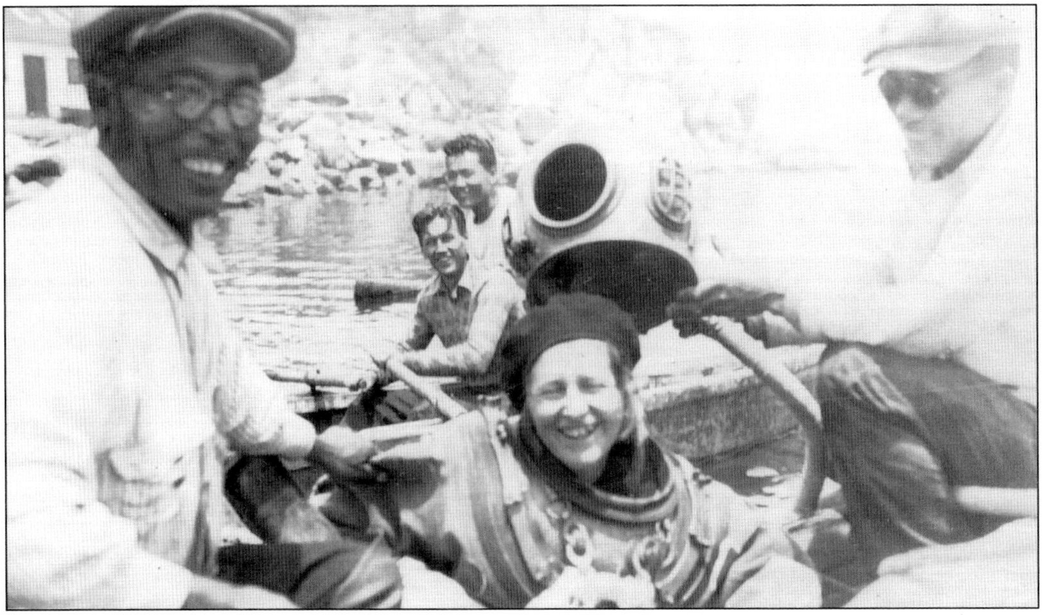

Frances Gets Ready for the Helmet. Here, Felin is getting ready to put on a helmet. The men working with her are part of the Point Lobos dive crew. (Kodani family collection.)

Three

FARMS AND BUSINESSES WORKING THE LAND

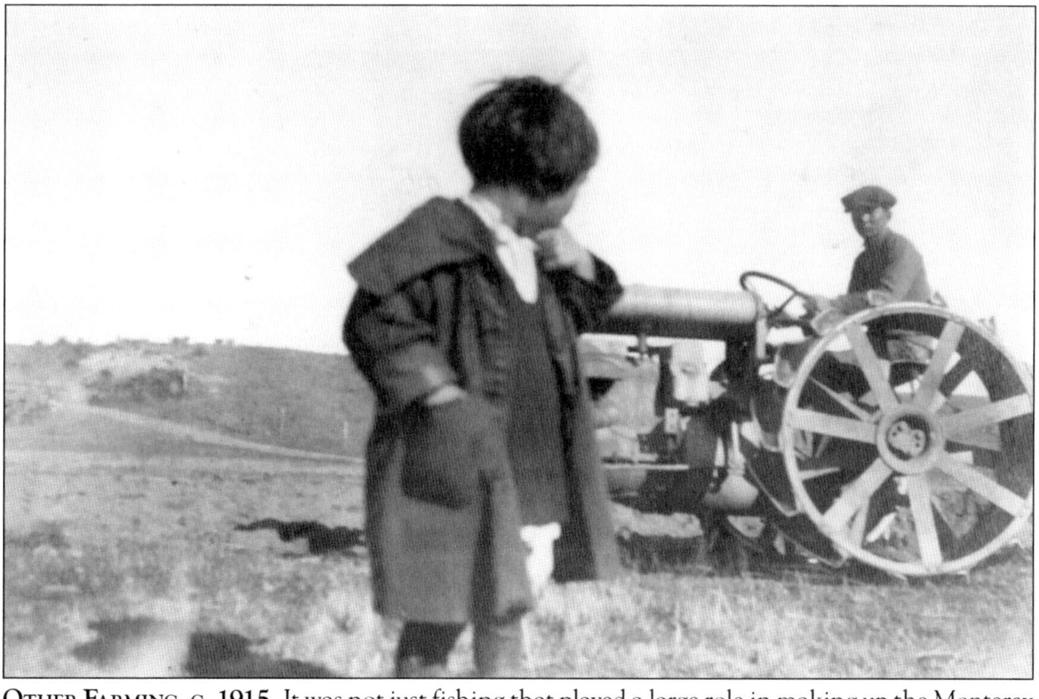

OTHER FARMING, C. 1915. It was not just fishing that played a large role in making up the Monterey Japanese community. There were also small farms south of Carmel, Carmel Valley, and later in Seaside. (Kodani family collection.)

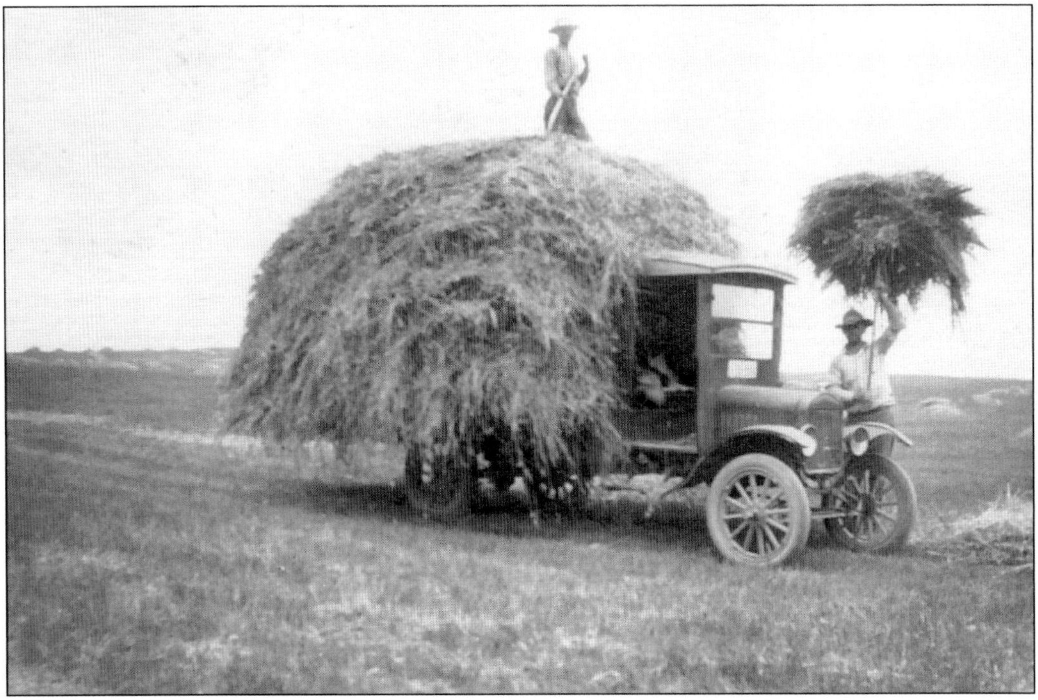

A Hay Truck, c. 1915. One of the early farmers in the Carmel Valley was Kumahiko Miyamoto, who came to Monterey in June 1900. He was the first to grow artichokes in the valley. No one wanted them, so he had to give them away. Later, he taught people how to eat them. The hay truck is not on Miyamoto's farm. (Kodani family collection.)

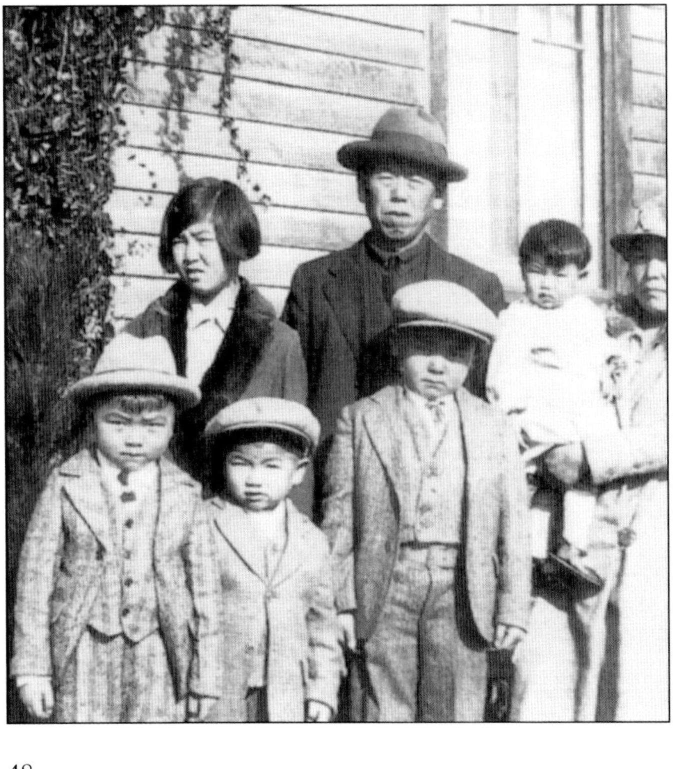

The Tanaka Family, c. 1930. Pictured are, from left to right, (first row) George, Frank, William, and Yee, holding Tomoe; (second row) Kayomi and Koichi. (Monterey Library Collection.)

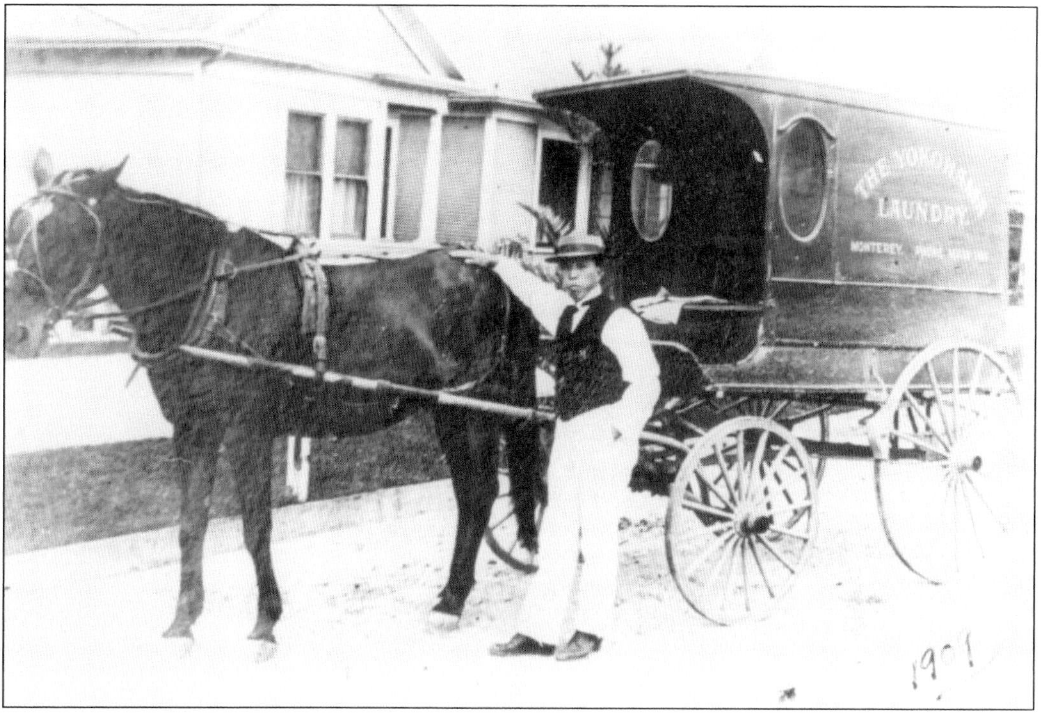

Setsuji Kodama in 1909. Here, Setsuji is standing next to his delivery wagon for the Takasayashi family's Yokohama Laundry Company in Monterey. Setsuji, along with his wife, Fujiko, first came to the Monterey Peninsula in 1914 from the Hiroshima Prefecture. They both were very involved with the community and were highly respected. (George Kodama and Monterey Public Library, California History Room.)

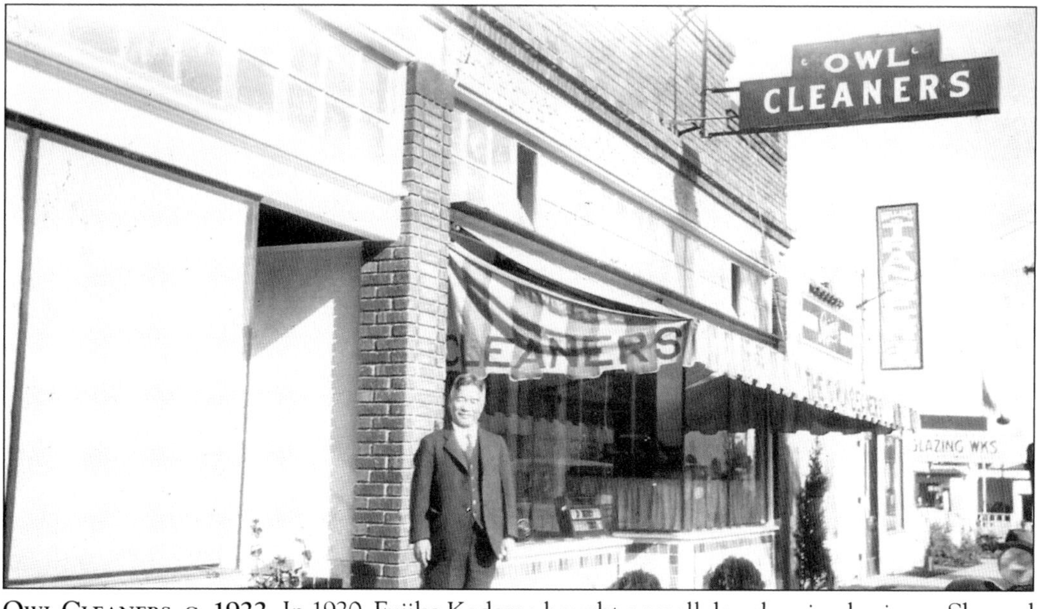

Owl Cleaners, c. 1922. In 1920, Fujiko Kodama bought a small dry-cleaning business. She and her husband, Setsuji, opened the Owl Cleaners, the first Japanese dry cleaner on the Monterey Peninsula. (Kodama family collection.)

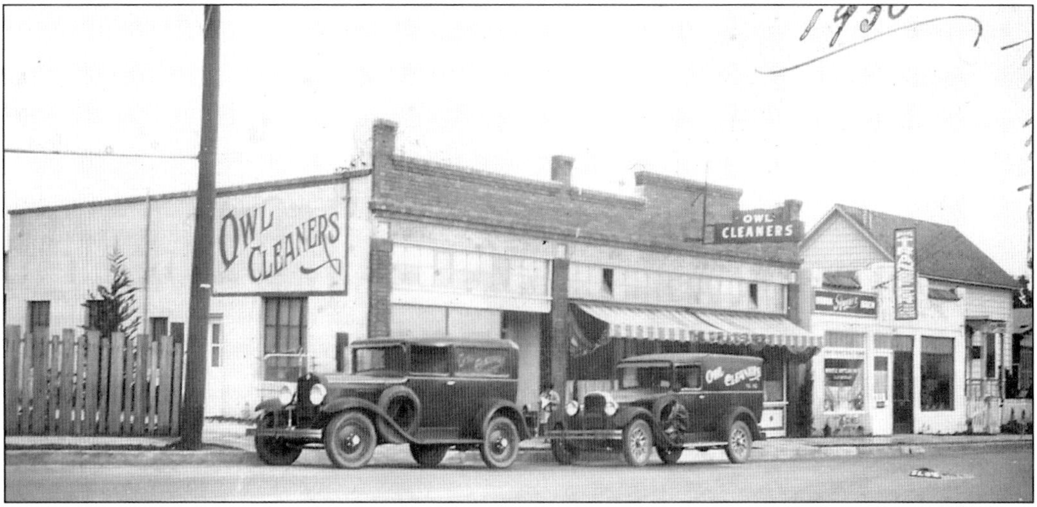

OWL CLEANERS. The Kodama family cleaners moved into a new store in Monterey in 1929. Although the store did general dry-cleaning, it specialized in cleaning hats and gloves. In those days, all the men wore hats, and the ladies wore gloves. (Kodama family collection.)

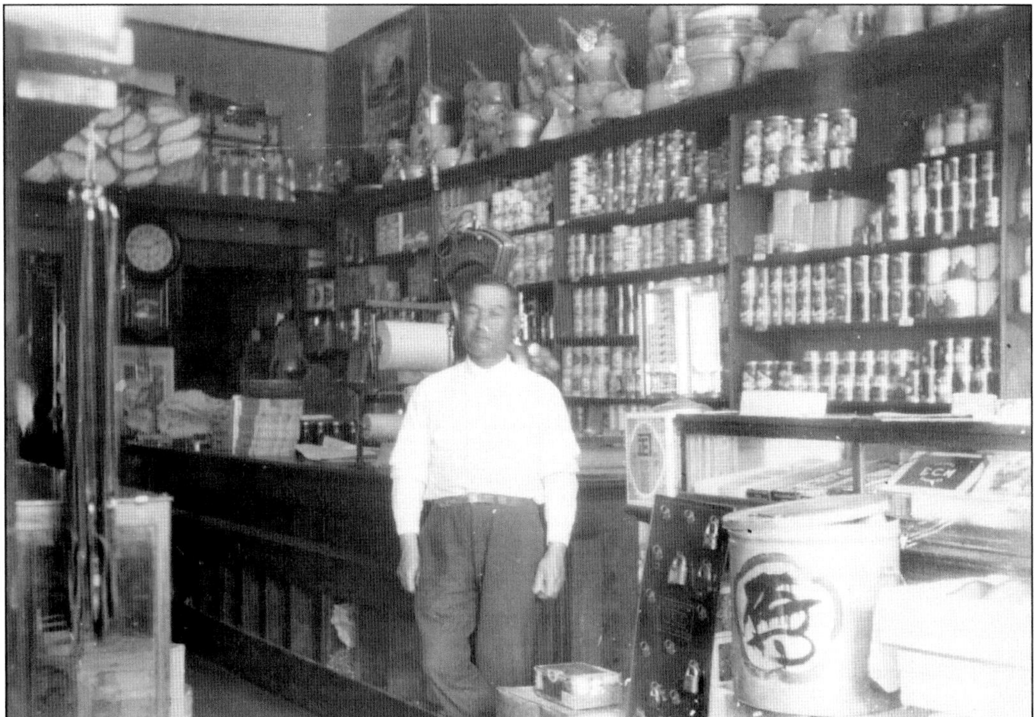

SUNRISE MARKET MONTEREY, C. 1933. There was every kind of store one could imagine, from dry goods that catered to the Japanese community to fish markets that catered to everyone. At the Sunrise Market, one could get special food that reminded one of home. There were also Uchida's Dry Goods, the Bath House, Japanese barbers, shoe and radio repairmen, and even Suyama Shoe and Candy Store. There was something for everyone. Tonosuke Esaki, business partner in the Sunrise Grocery on Washington Street, Monterey, poses in the store. (George Esaki photograph, Jean Esaki and Monterey Public Library, California History Room.)

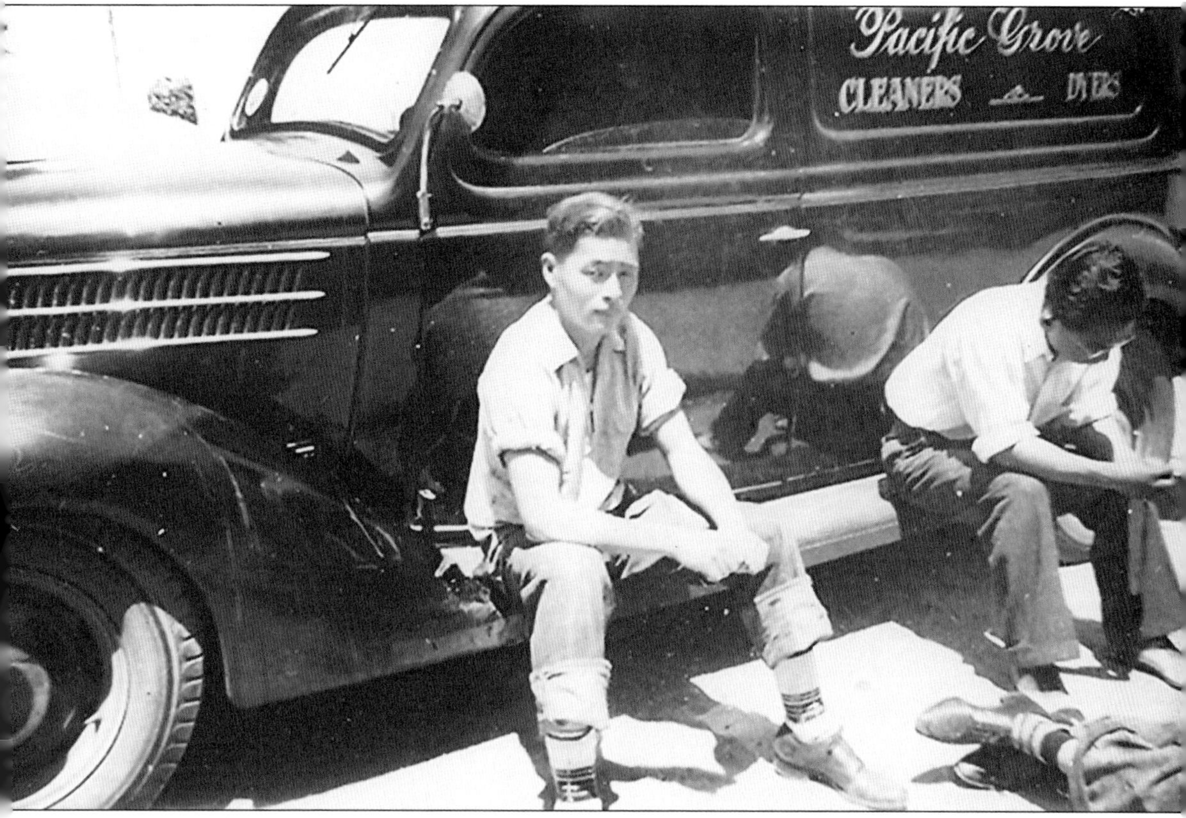

PACIFIC GROVE CLEANERS DELIVERY TRUCK, C. 1940. This photograph shows Mickey Ichiuji (left) and an unidentified coworker taking a rest after making deliveries. (Ichiuji family collection.)

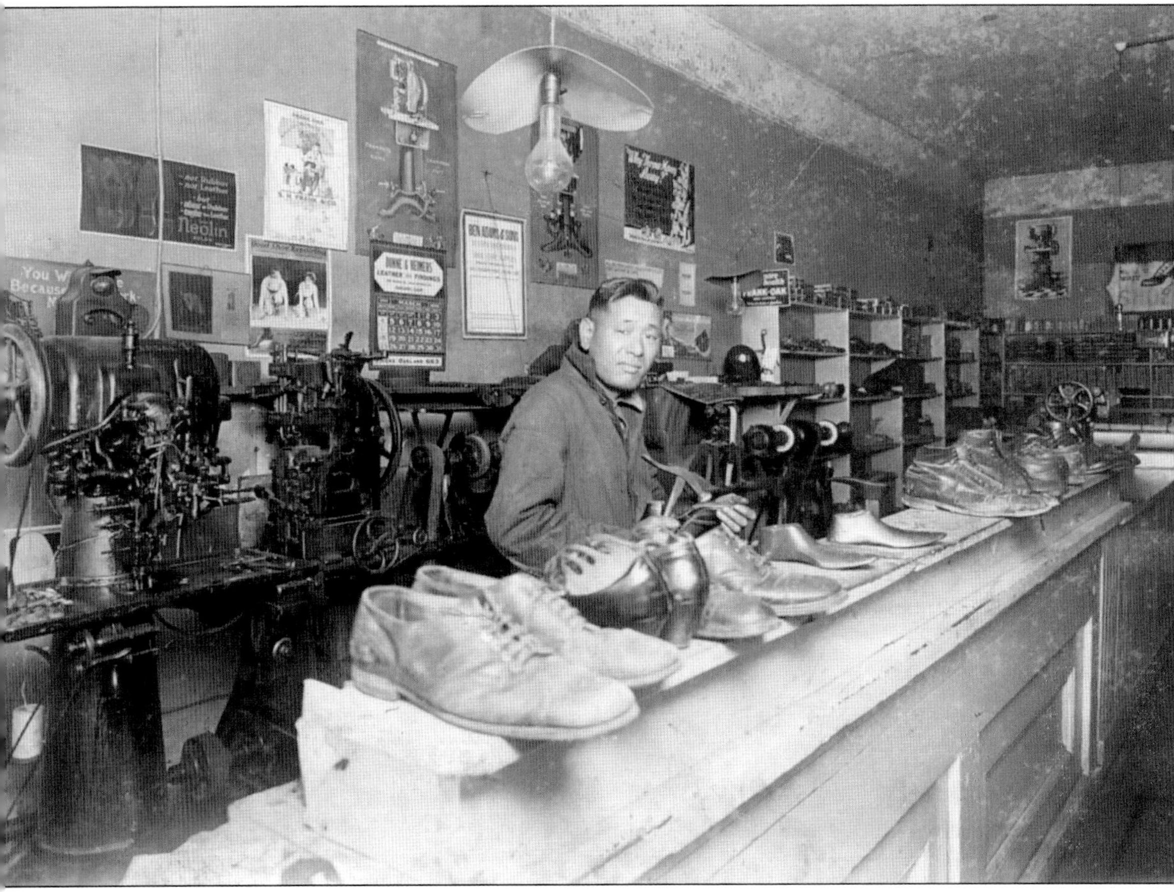

Kikujiro Ichiuji, Repairing a Shoe, c. 1925. Ichiuji immigrated to the United States in 1906, when he was just 16 years old. He came from the Shimane Prefecture. He originally worked in the nursery business, but he always held a fascination with repairing shoes and opened his first shop in Pacific Grove in 1919. He named his store the Grove Shoe Hospital. (Ichiuji family collection.)

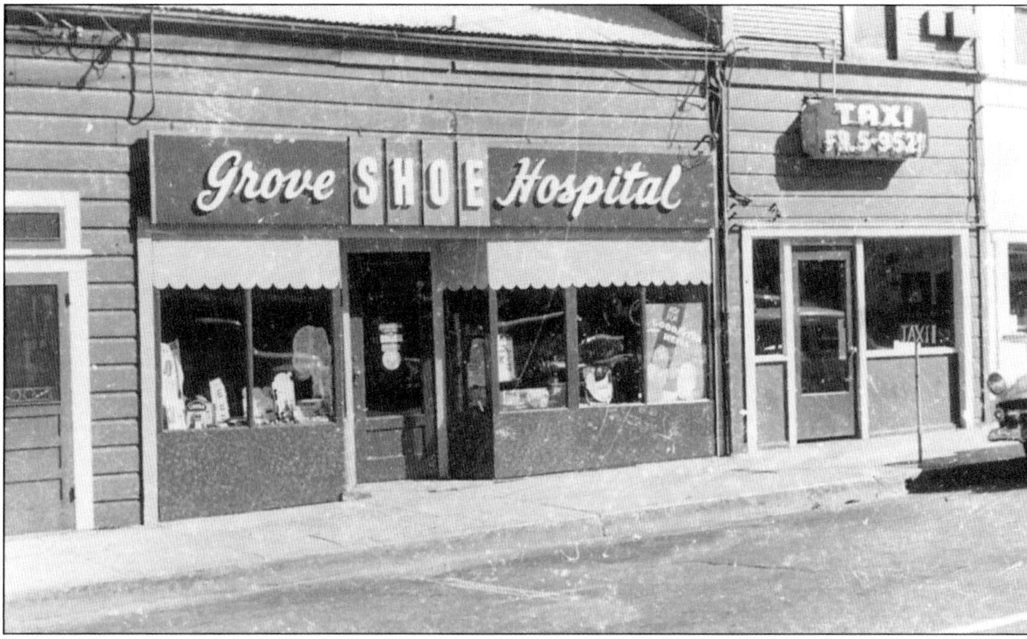

The Grove Shoe Hospital in Pacific Grove, c. 1925. Before Kikujiro Ichiuji came to the Monterey Peninsula, he spent some time in Seattle, where he fell in love with shoe repair. One day in 1919, he heard there was a small shoe repair business for sale in Pacific Grove; he jumped at the chance and bought it. (Ichiuji family collection.)

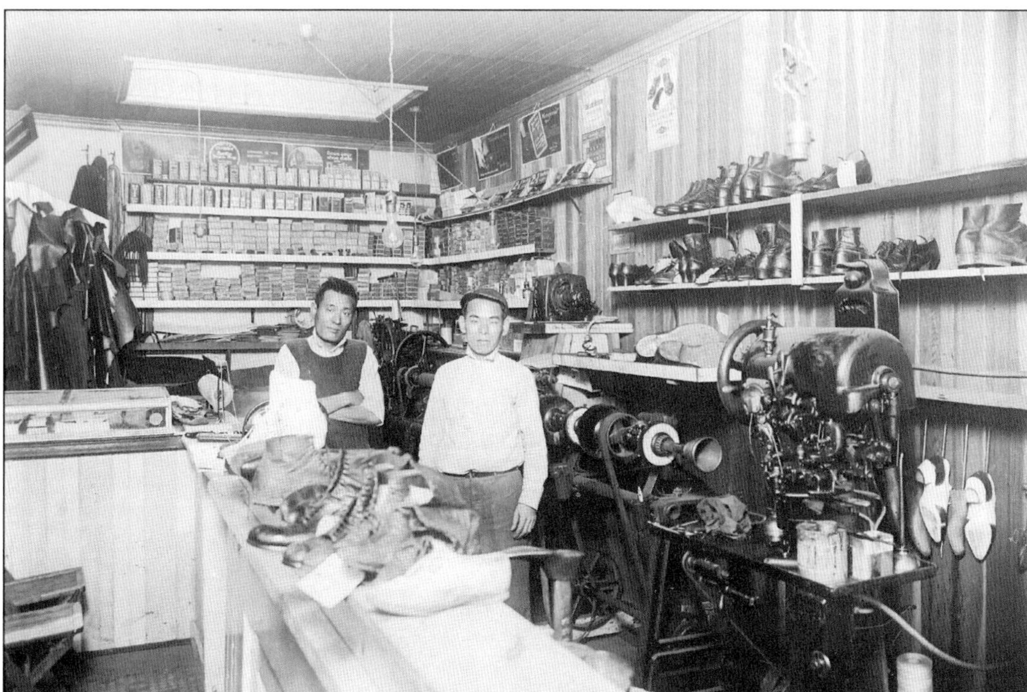

Inside the Second Ichiuji Shoe Hospital, c. 1930. The Ichiuji family had another shoe store, run by Kikujiro's son Mickey (right), seen here with his father. (Ichiuji family collection.)

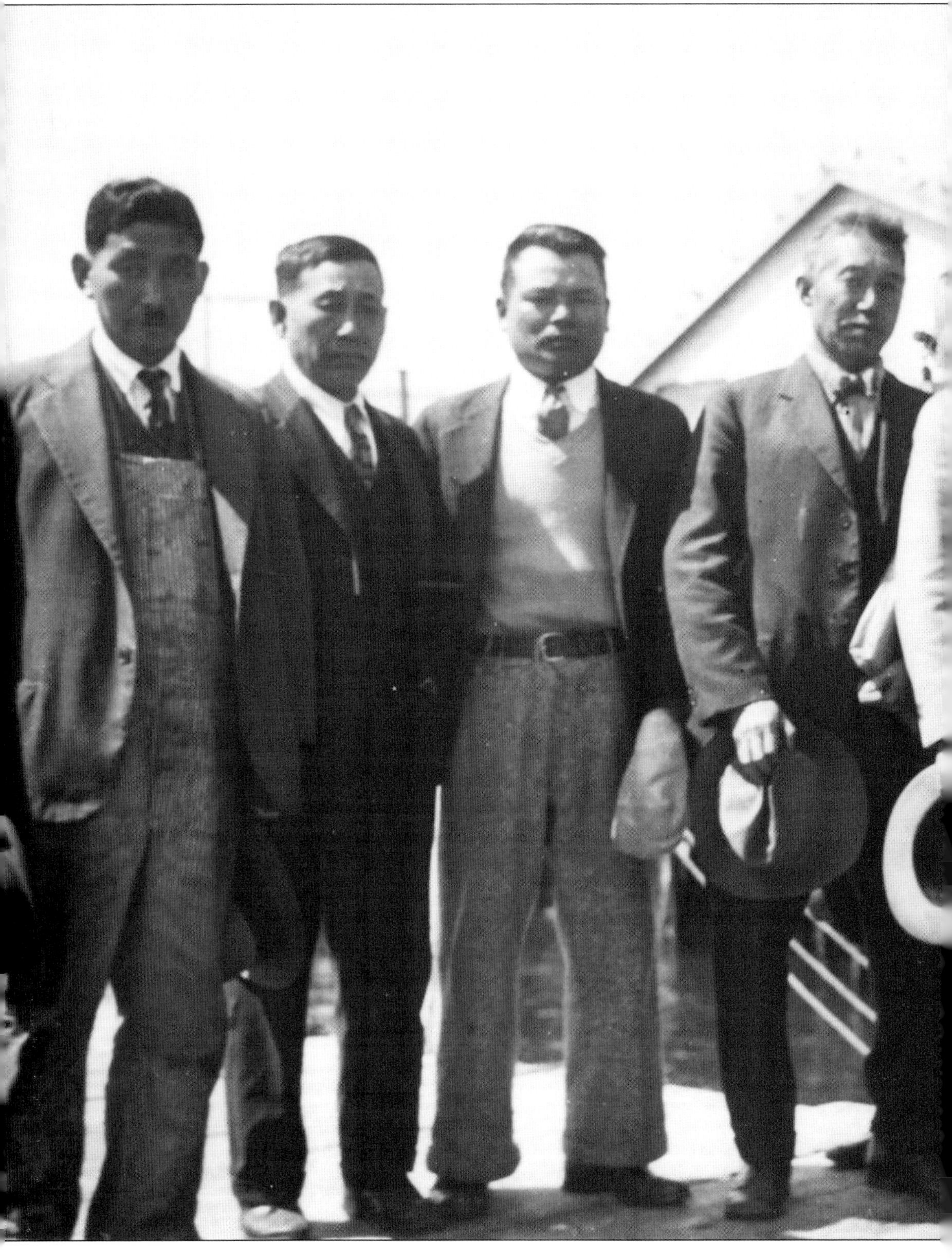

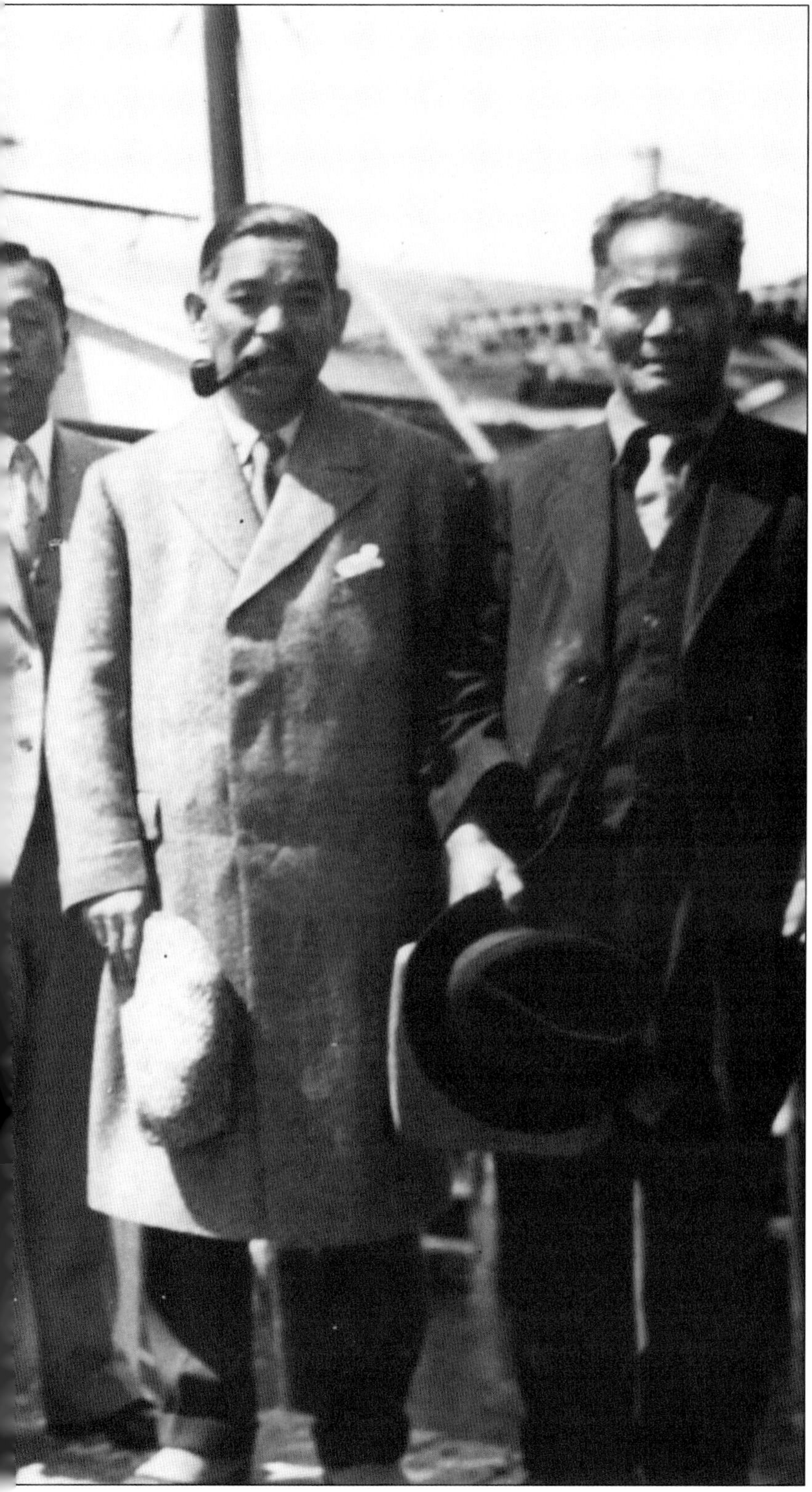

MONTEREY JAPANESE BUSINESSMEN NEAR THE MONTEREY WHARF, C. 1925. On the far left in the coveralls is Unosuke Higashi, who was the owner of Hagishi's Fish Company. Junichi Oda is third from left. (Kodama family collection.)

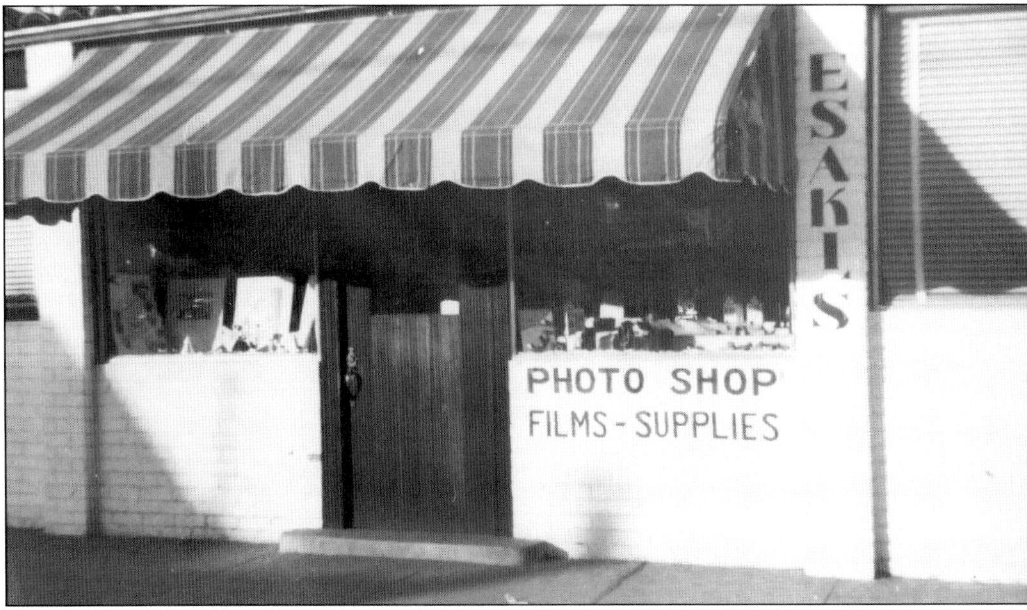

ESAKI'S PHOTO SHOP, 275 EAST FRANKLIN STREET, CHRISTMAS 1947. George Esaki and wife, Jean, started their photography business right after World War II. George later moved his business to Alvarado Street. (Jean Esaki and Monterey Public Library, California History Room.)

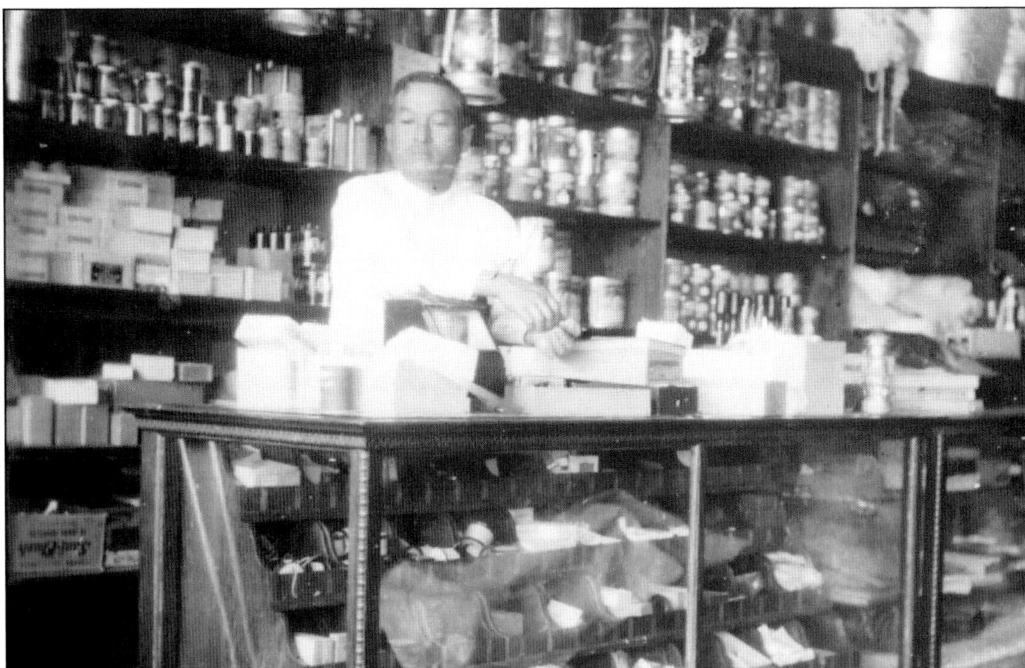

ESAKI FAMILY, C. 1950. The Esakis were very active with the Monterey Japanese community. Besides photographing many of the activities, George also was the leader of Boy Scout Troop 47, which produced three Eagle Scouts. George is seen here behind the counter of Esaki's Photo on Alvarado Street on November 27, 1953. (Jean Esaki and Monterey Public Library, California History Room.)

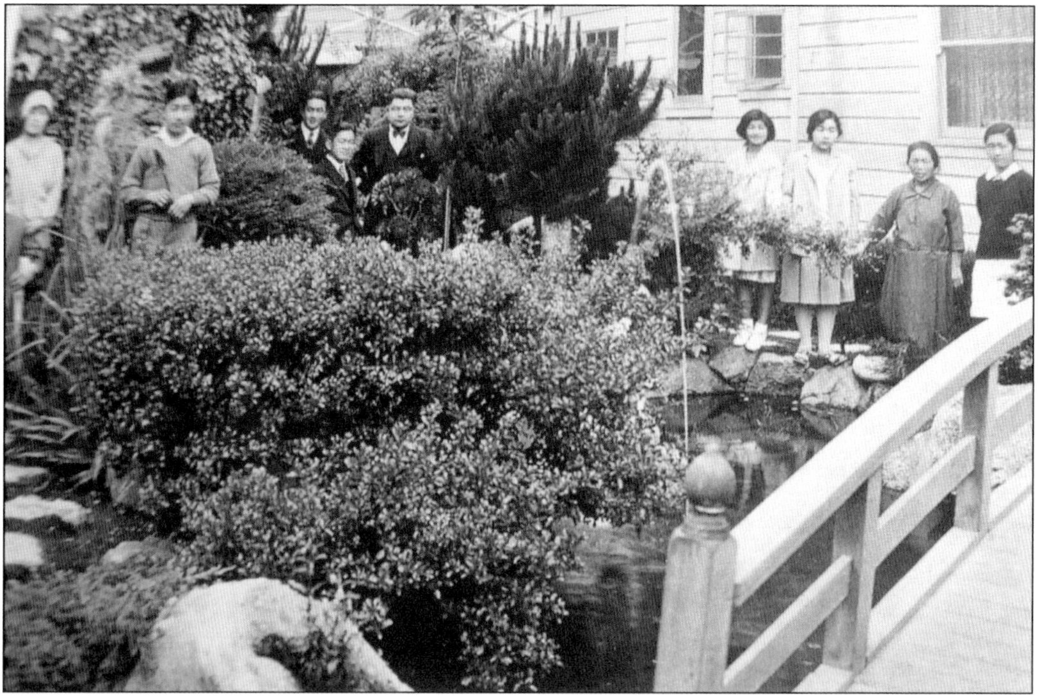

The Hagishi Family, c. 1925. Besides being in the fish business, the Hagishi family also ran a traditional Japanese hotel near the Monterey Wharf. This hotel catered mainly to Japanese fishermen who were coming to Monterey to fish sardines. It also had a restaurant serving excellent Japanese food that was favored by the entire Monterey community, including Caucasians. Many newly married couples had their wedding photographs taken in the Hagishi family hotel's garden. (Hagishi family collection.)

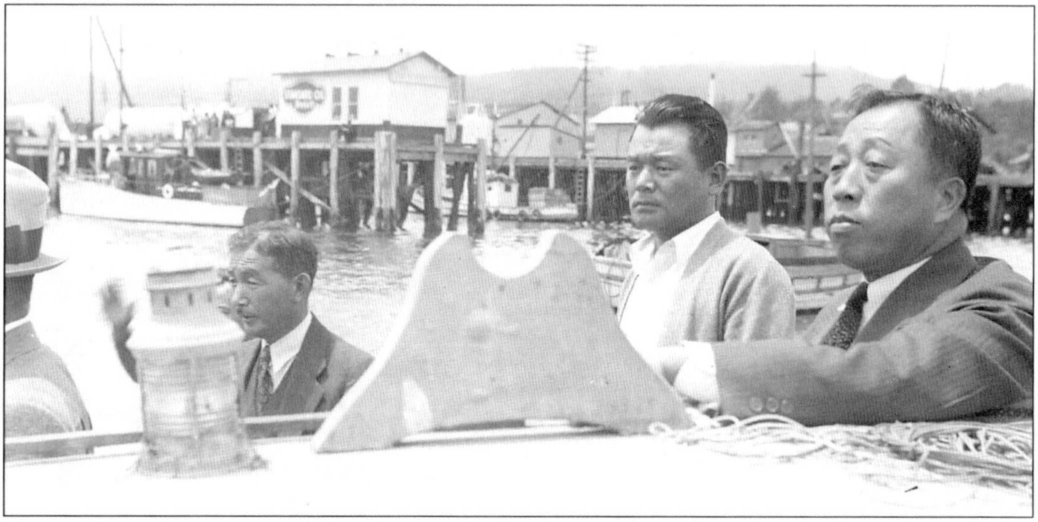

The Monterey Wharf, c. 1930. The wharf was an important place for the Monterey Japanese community. Prior to World War II, 80 percent of the businesses on the Monterey Wharf, from abalone processors to fish markets, were Japanese-owned. Pictured are Ikutaro Takigawa (left), of the Coast Abalone Processors; Junichi Oda (center), of the Western Whole Fish Company; and Setsuji Kodama, who was a community leader. (Kodama family collection.)

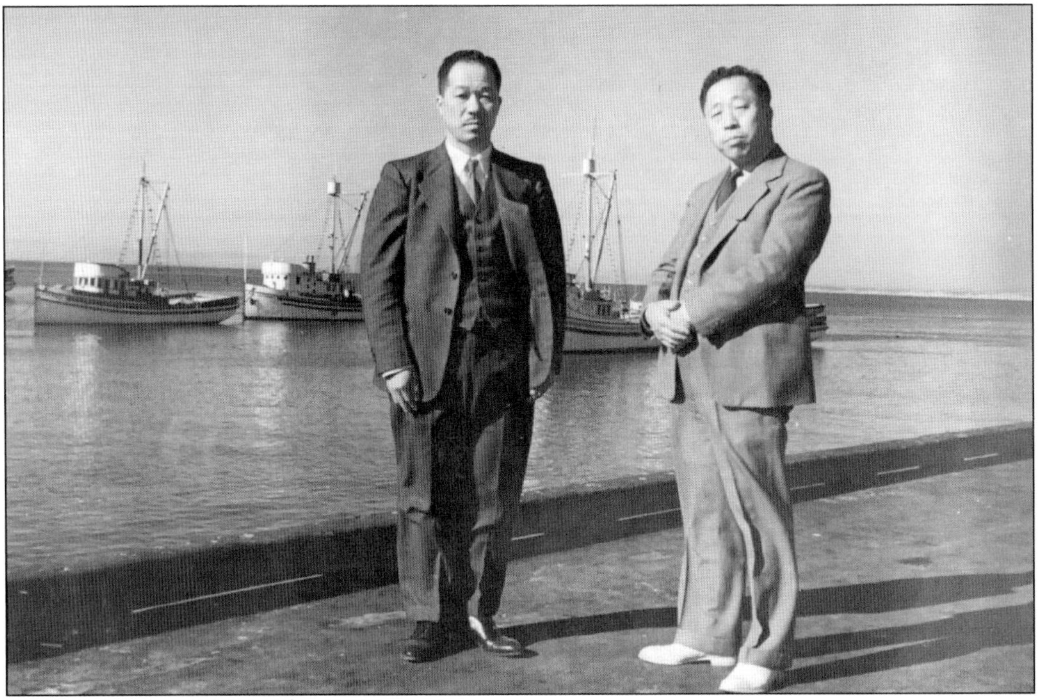

Sardine Boats, c. 1930. Before going into the dry-cleaning business, George Kodama's family was in the fish business. His father, Setsuji Kodama, originally had a wholesale fish market in Sacramento called Capitol Fish. George (right) eventually moved to Monterey in 1914 and was a partner in a wholesale fish business. In the background are three Monterey sardine boats. The man on the left is unidentifed. (Kodama family collection.)

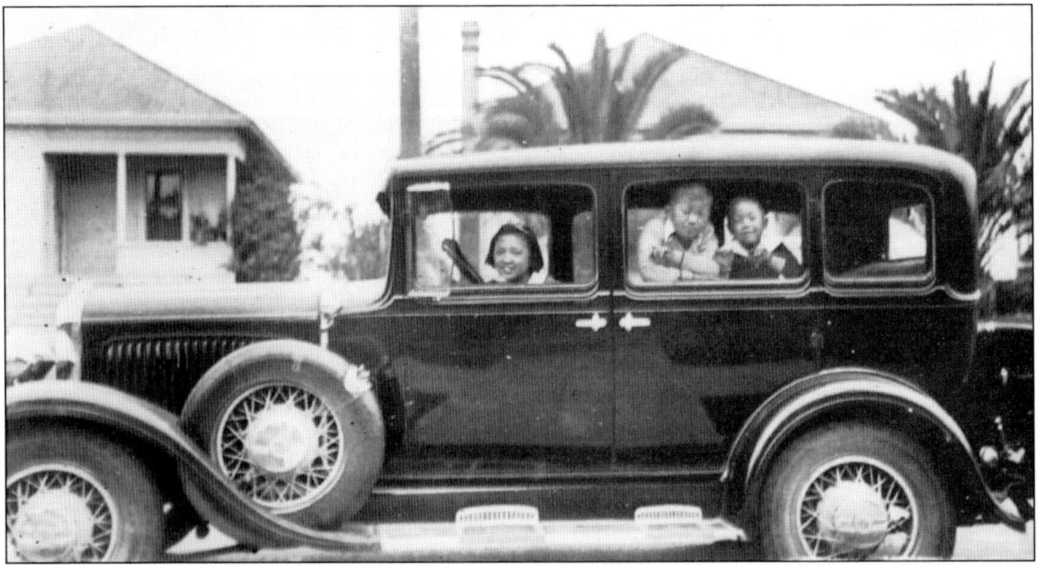

Kodoma's Children, c. 1930. Pictured here are George Kodama's children playing in the family car. (Kodama family collection.)

Four

Sports

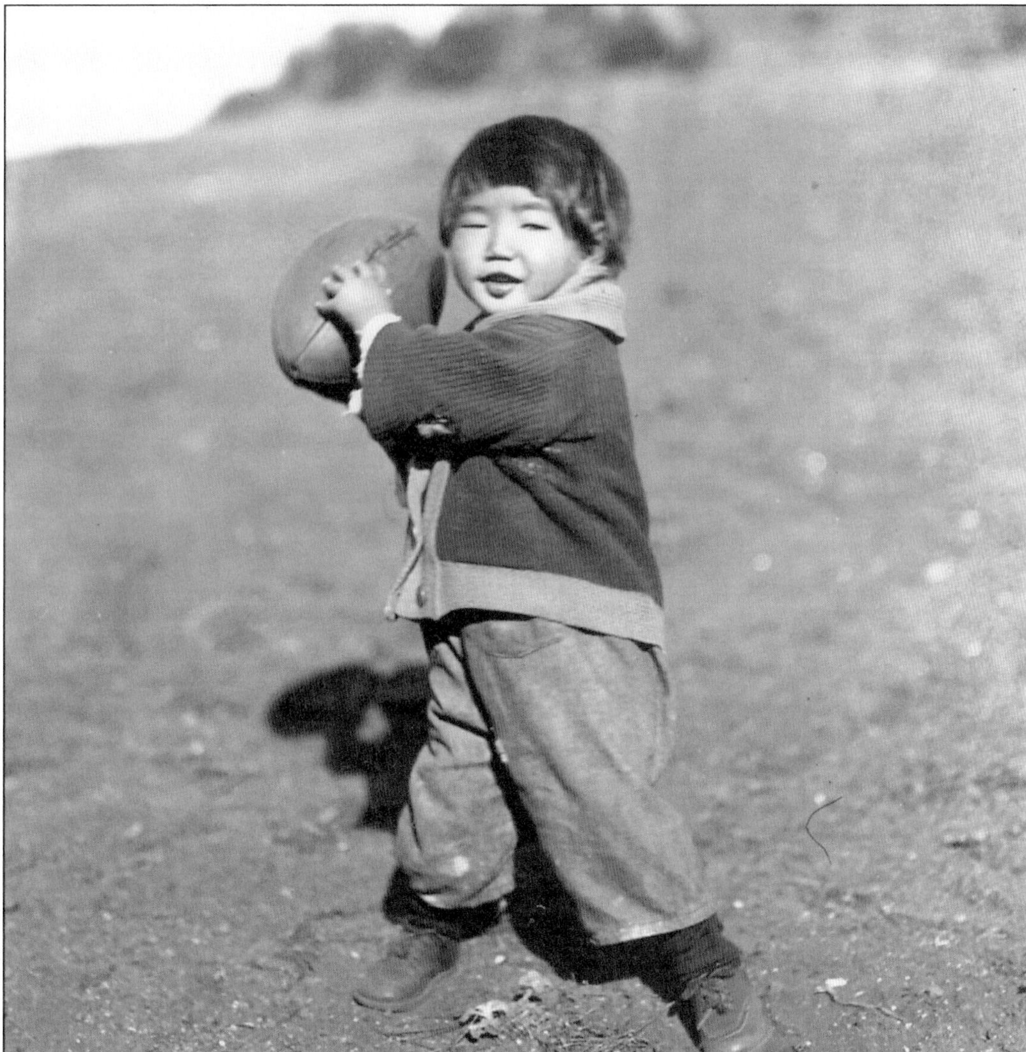

Play Ball! Here is Fumiko Kodani pictured around age 5 at Point Lobos. (Kodani family collection.)

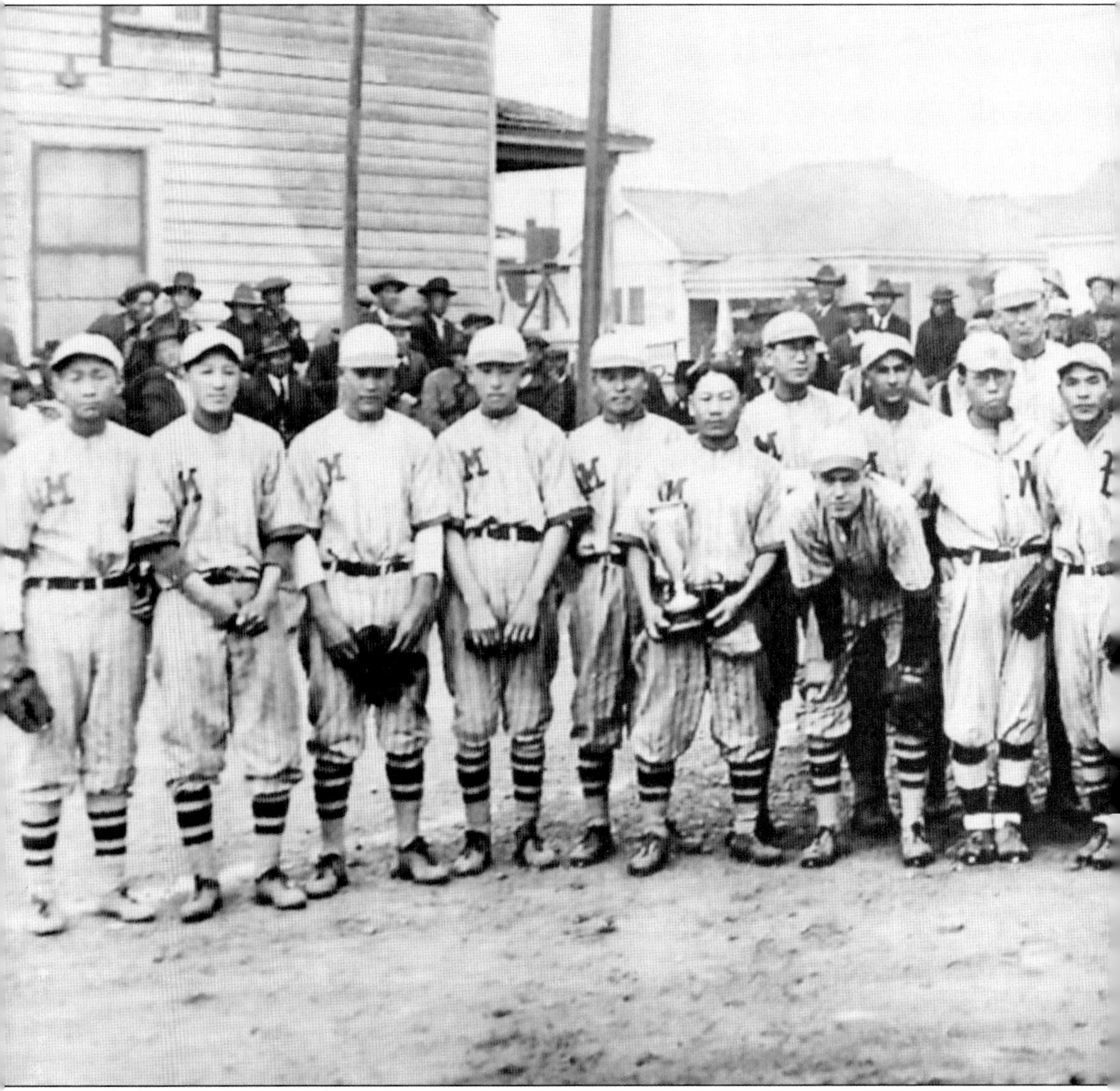

The Monterey Minatos. This 1923 group photograph shows the Monterey Minatos and the Watsonville Kasei after a championship game. Baseball was first introduced to Japan in the early 1870s by American educator Horace Wilson. Roy Hattori, who played with the Monterey Minatos,

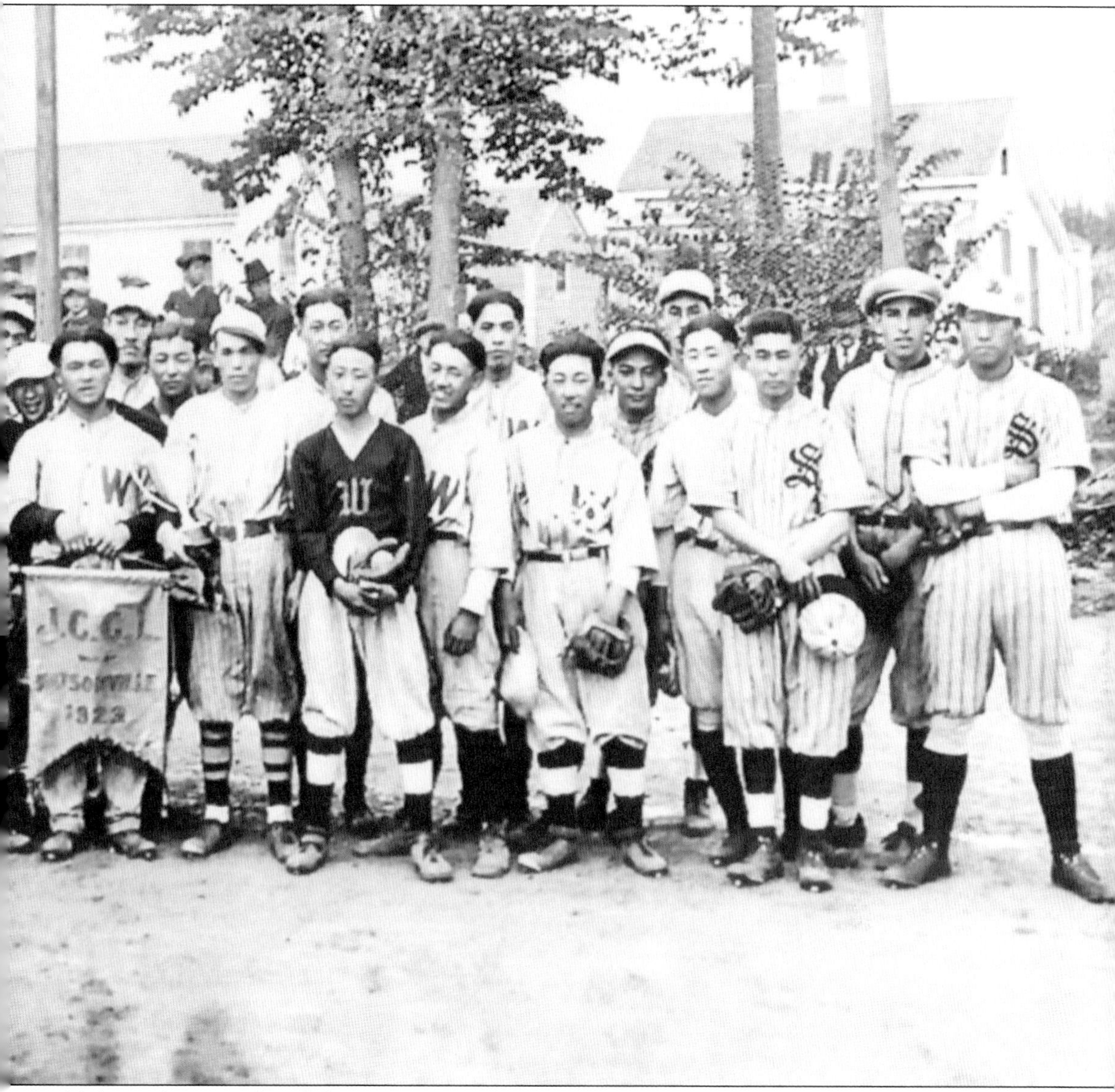

told the author, "We loved the game. Our fathers loved it, too. They loved baseball before coming to the United States." (Oda family collection.)

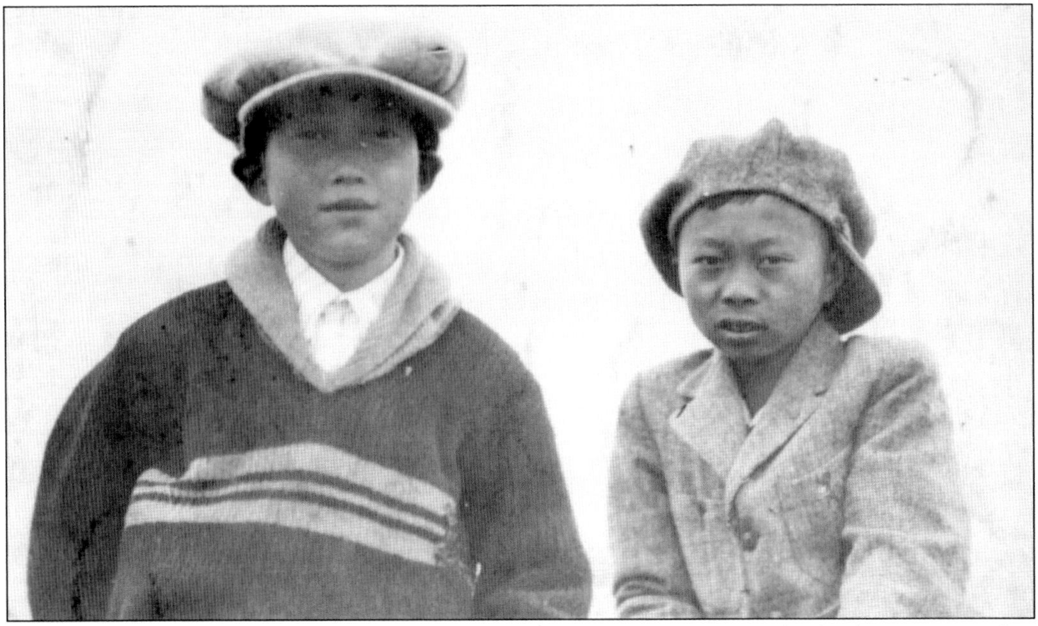

Dreaming of the Big Leagues. These two boys dreamed of playing in the big leagues someday. Sports were a unifying activity, not just for the Japanese but also for all of Monterey. They all played together, both Japanese and Sicilian kids. Often, the boys would learn each other's languages before they spoke English. In the local ballpark, one might hear a Japanese kid speaking Sicilian and a Sicilian kid speaking Japanese. (Kodani family collection.)

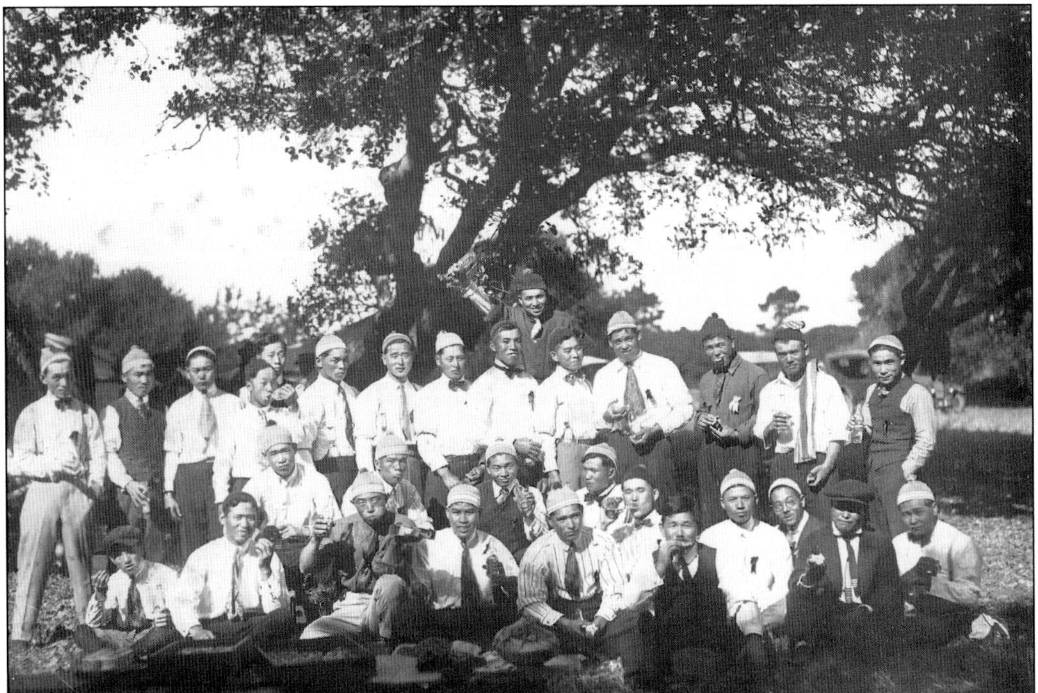

These Guys are Ready to Play Ball, c. 1915. This is an early group photograph of a Japanese community picnic. (Oda family collection.)

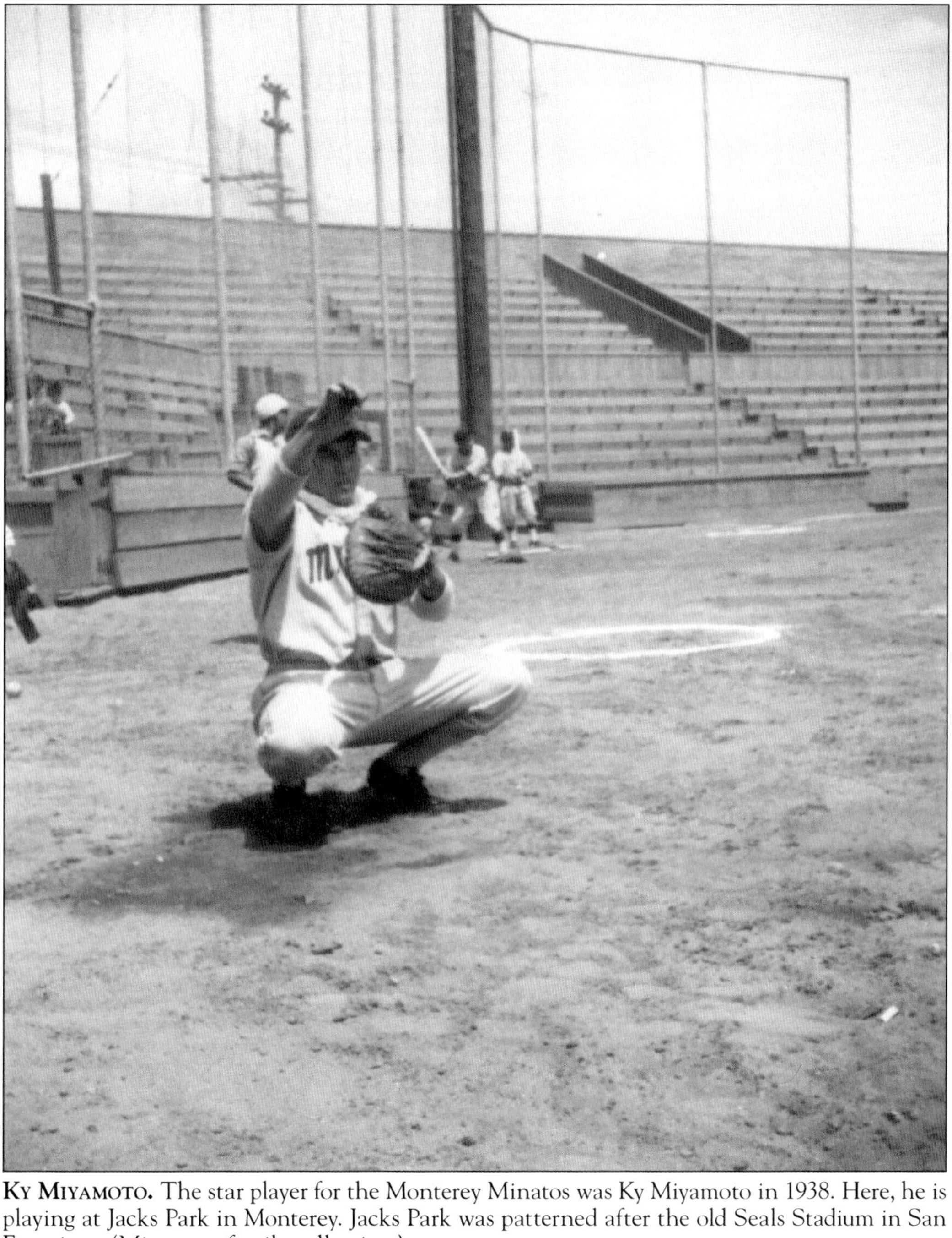

KY MIYAMOTO. The star player for the Monterey Minatos was Ky Miyamoto in 1938. Here, he is playing at Jacks Park in Monterey. Jacks Park was patterned after the old Seals Stadium in San Francisco. (Miyamoto family collection.)

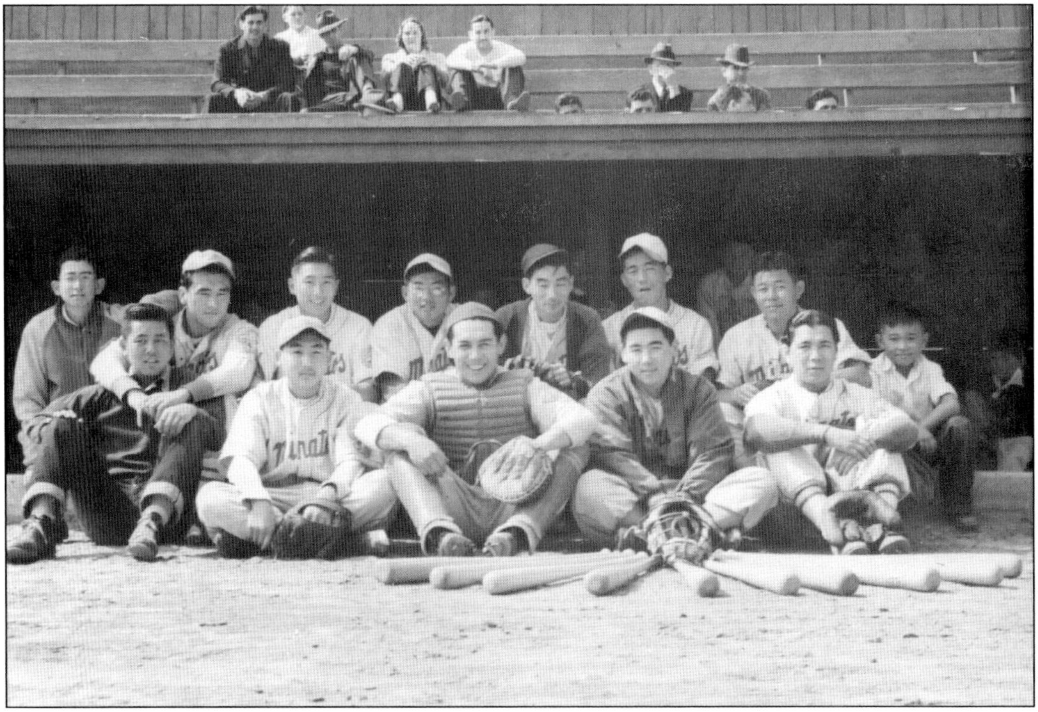

THE MONTEREY MINATOS AFTER WINNING THE 1935 4C2A CHAMPIONSHIP. The Minato Athletic Club was formed in the late 1920s to give young Japanese men a chance to participate in athletics. The name *minato* means "port, harbor, or bay." (Miyamoto family collection.)

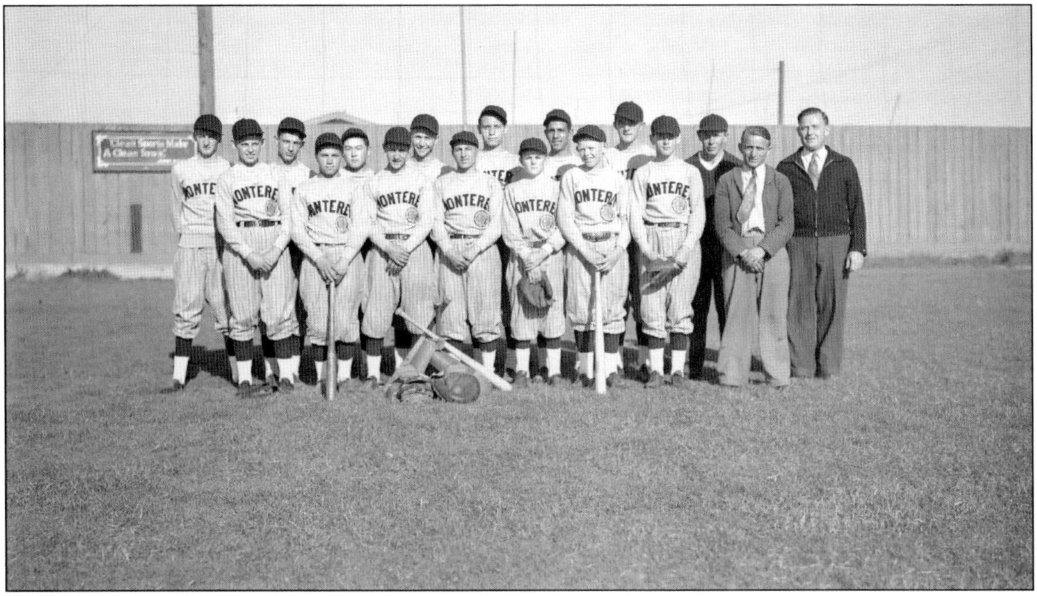

MONTEREY HIGH SCHOOL BASEBALL TEAM, C. 1930. Frank Manaka, whose family came to Monterey in 1916 to fish, was a star pitcher on the Monterey team. In the early 1920s, he saw Joe DiMaggio play at Jacks Park. Frank thought, "If Joe DiMaggio, son of a fishermen, can be a baseball player, then why can't Frank Manaka, son of a fishermen, be a baseball player?" Frank's father had other ideas, and Frank became a fisherman. (Monterey Library Collection.)

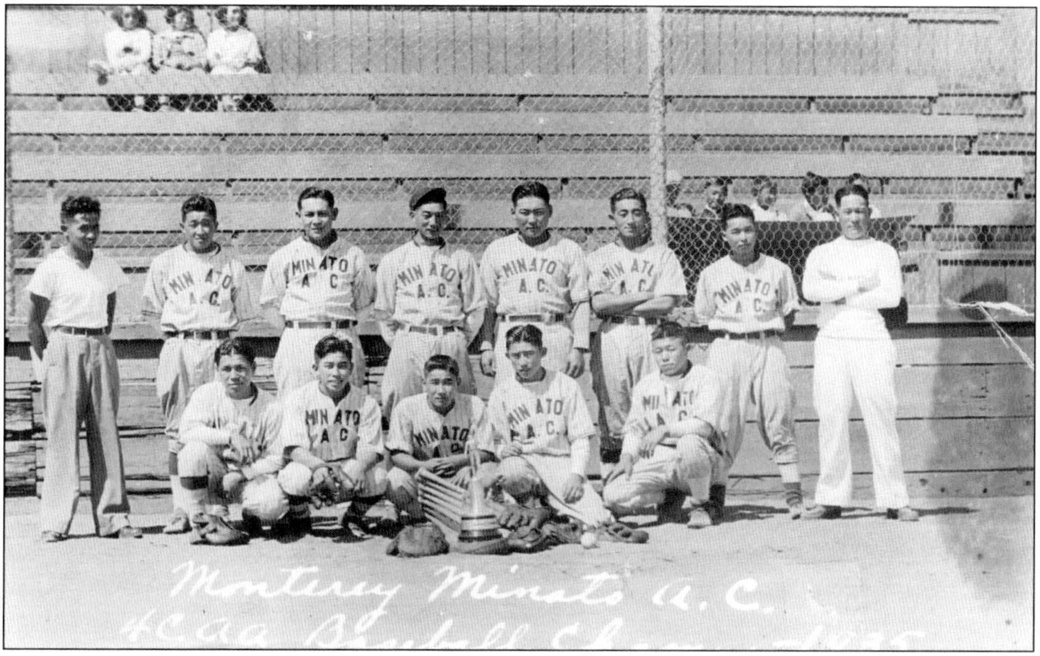

The Minatos, c. 1935. Maya Miyamoto said of the Minato Athletic Club, "We traveled all through Northern and Southern California. We'd ride to games in the back of old Model T trucks with sideboards and canvas tops. On the way home, we'd sleep in the back." Identified in this photograph are, from left to right, (first row) Roy Hattori, Masami Higashi, and James Takigawa (second, third, and fifth from left); (second row) Yo Tabata and James Tabata, later owner of Sunrise Grocery (second and sixth from left). (George Kodama and Monterey Public Library, California History Room.)

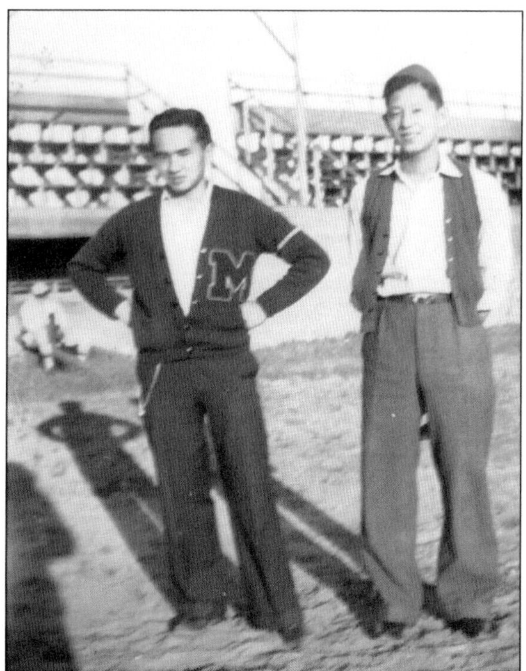

Two Minato Players. Pictured here are Mum Tani (left) and Tom Seito around 1935. (Miyamoto family collection.)

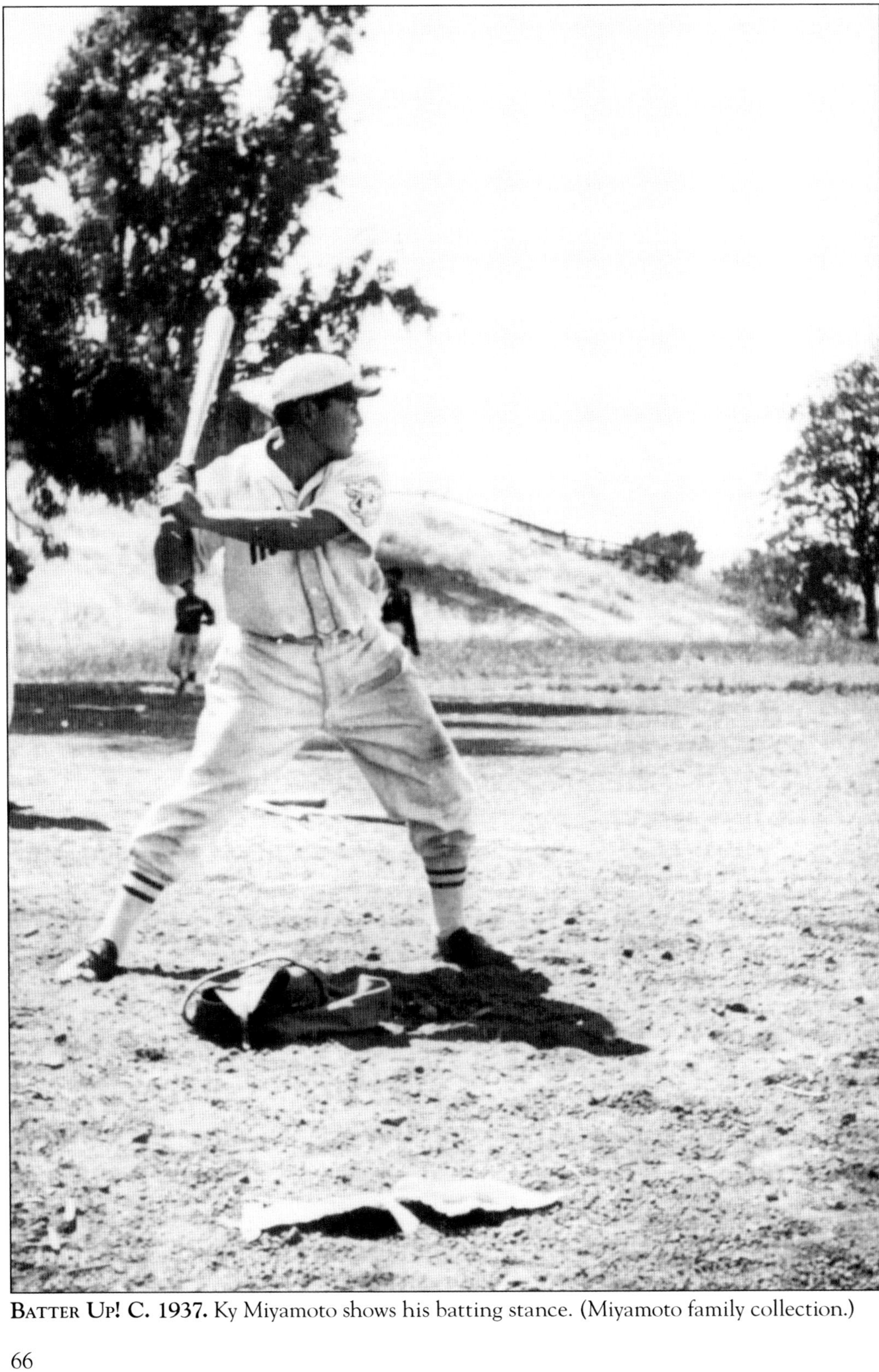

BATTER UP! C. 1937. Ky Miyamoto shows his batting stance. (Miyamoto family collection.)

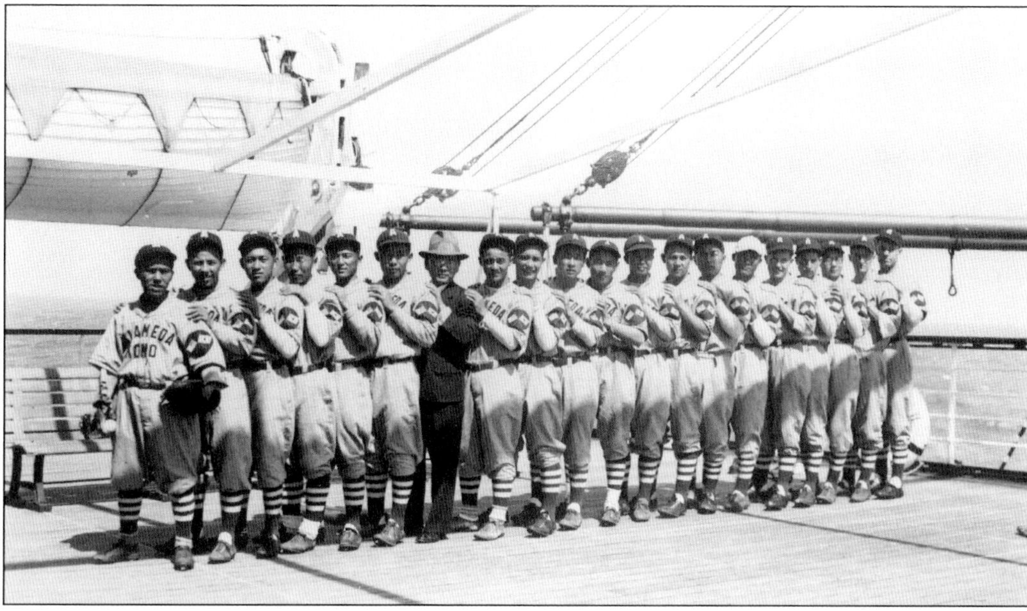

Kono All-Stars. In 1937, Ky Miyamoto was picked to play with the California Kono All-Stars, a group of Japanese baseball players from Northern California who traveled to Japan, Korea, and Manchuria to play baseball. Here, they are onboard a ship in San Francisco about to depart. During the three-month tour, the Kono All-Stars won 40 of their 60 games. (Miyamoto family collection.)

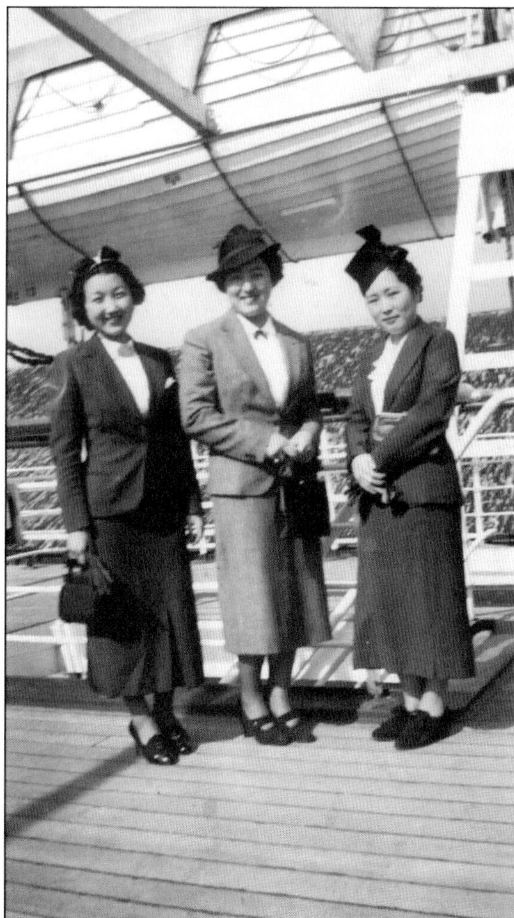

The Players' Mothers Came to Say Good-Bye. Pictured are Grace Fujino (left), Yoshi Higuchi (center), and Kimiko Higashi. (Miyamoto family collection.)

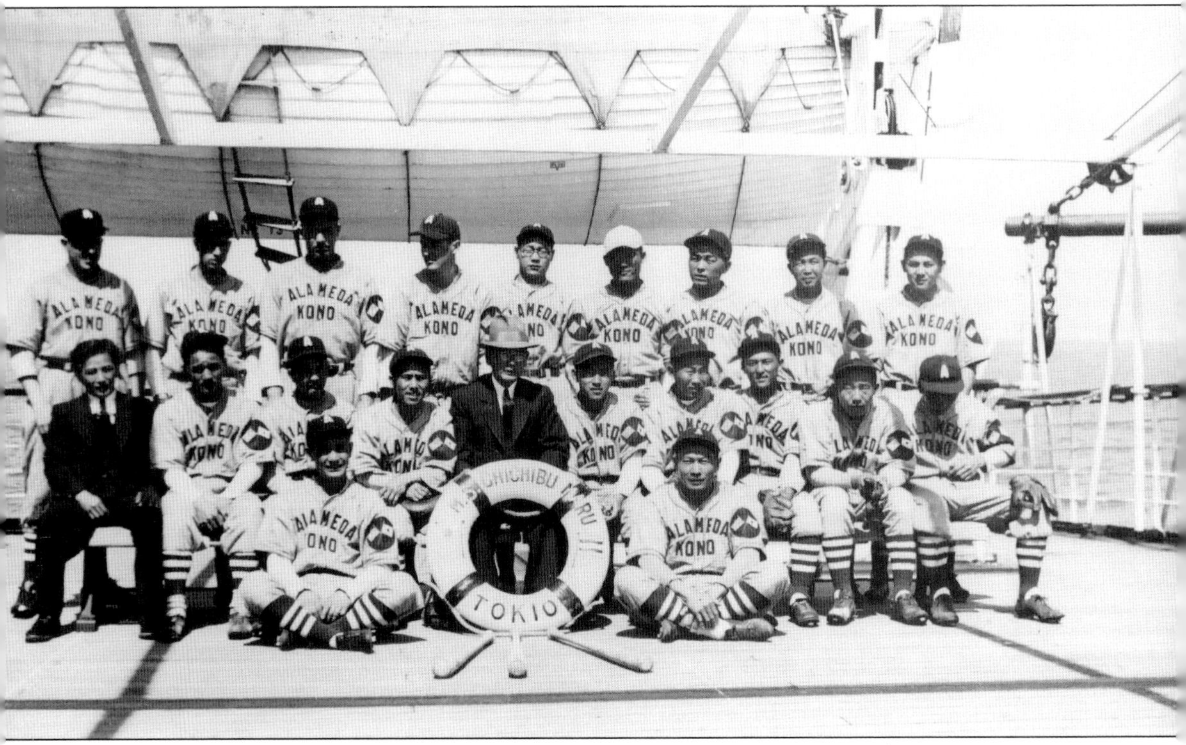

THE KONA ALL-STARS ONBOARD THE SHIP *CHICHIBU-MARU*. Upon arrival in Japan, Ky Miyamoto wrote, "Just arrived in Yokahama. Docked about 7:00 p.m. last night. Had a wonderful trip but I guess the sea isn't for me as I got seasick all the way to Honolulu." (Miyamoto family collection.)

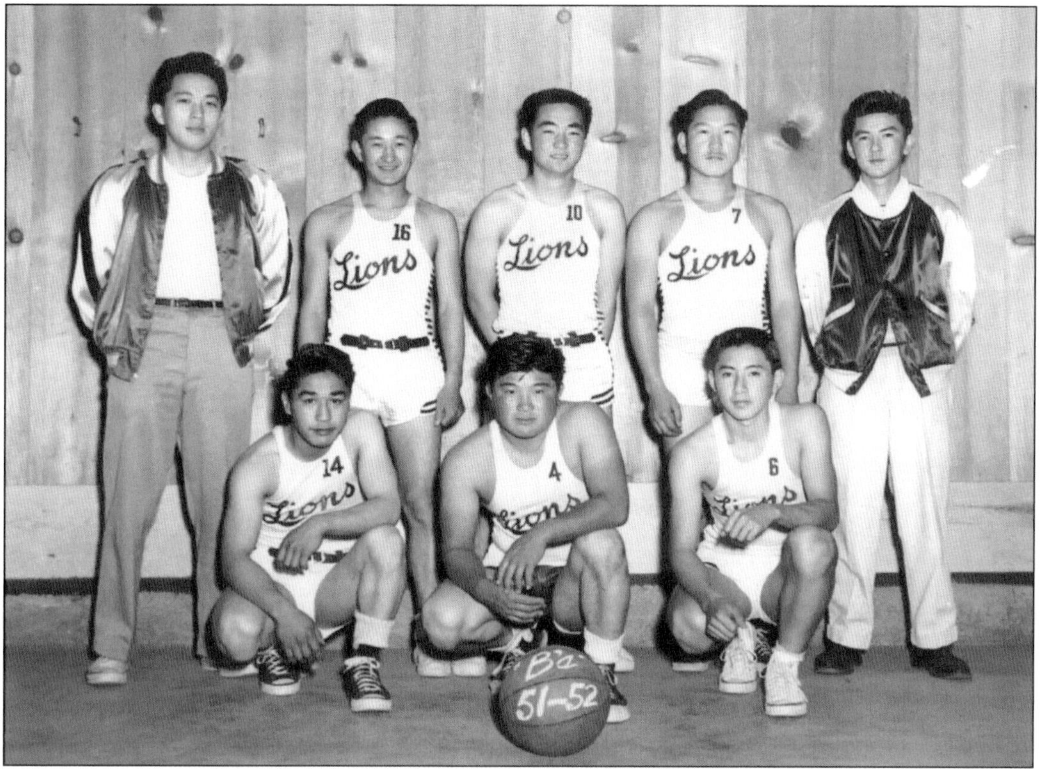

MINATO BASKETBALL. Basketball was a favorite sport for both Japanese men and women. Identified in this team photograph are (first row, from left) Frank Uyeda and Waco Shintani; (second row) George Kodama (left) and Ben Omoto (right). The Takigawa and Esaki families operated a fish-processing plant in a two-story building in New Monterey near Cannery Row. The upstairs became a makeshift gym for the Minato basketball and judo teams. (Miyamoto family collection.)

THE MINATO LIONS 1938 CHAMPIONSHIP TEAM. Pictured, from left to right, are (first row) Jim Tobata, John Gota, George Izsaki, ? Yotabata, and Jim Takigawa; (second row) ? Oyster, Ky Miyamoto, coach Roy Hughes, Kaz Oka, and Archie ?. (Miyamoto family collection.)

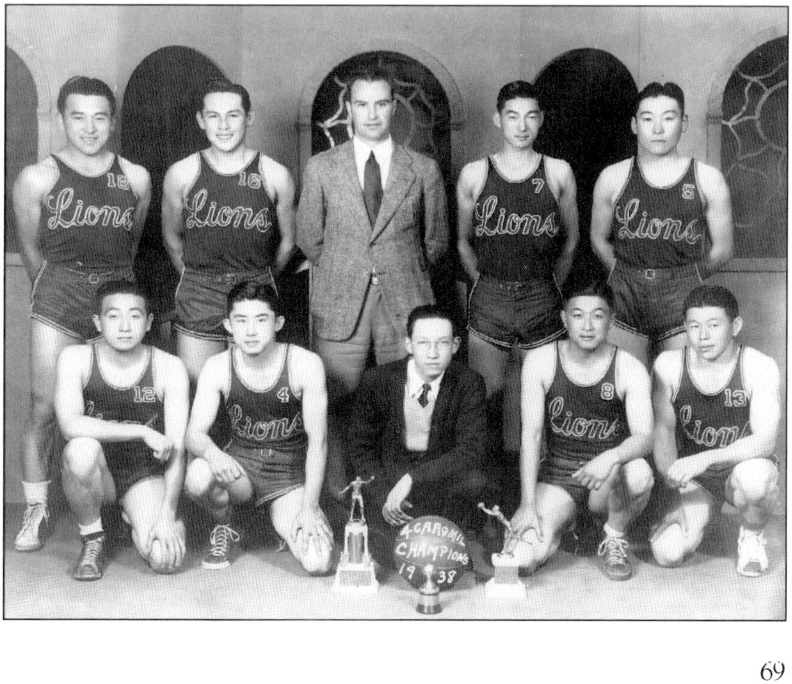

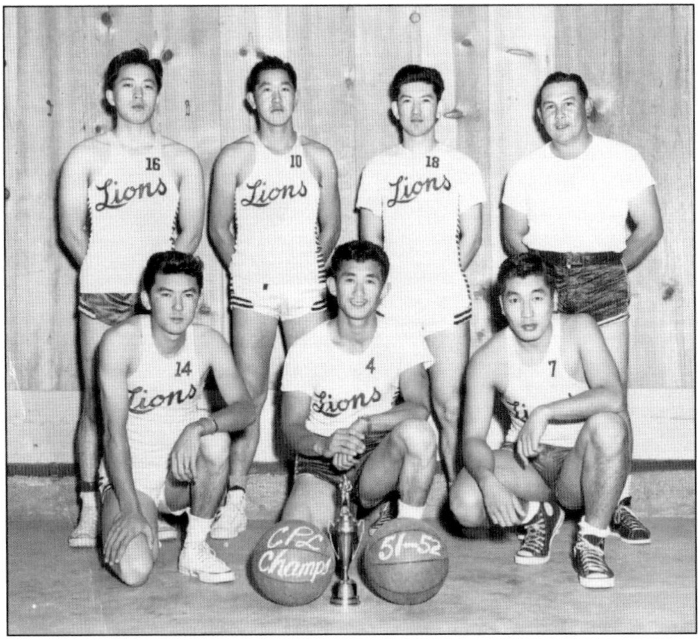

The Minato Character. Monterey historian David Yamada said of the Minato teams, "The Minato members developed character that carried over their everyday lives in the Monterey community. If you look around the Japanese community on the Monterey Peninsula today, it is not surprising to see so many of the current leaders are associated in some way with the two generations of athletes who excelled with the Monterey Minatos." Pictured are the 1951–1952 Minato Lions. (Miyamoto family collection.)

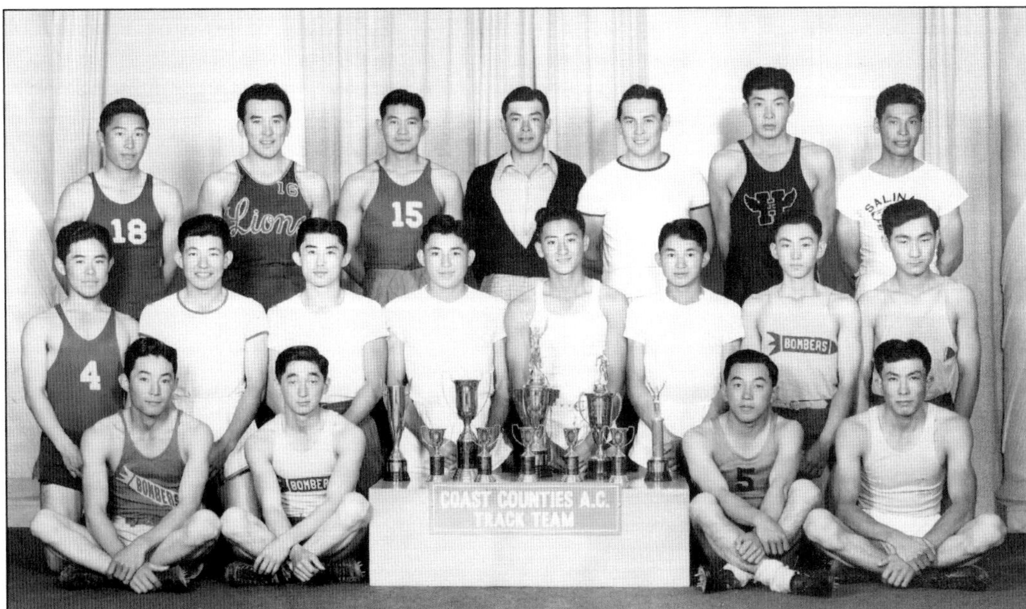

Minatos Track and Field. The Minatos also had a track-and-field team. In 1934, the team won the 4CAA Track and Field title in Hollister. The team won the 880-yard and mile runs, the 120 low hurdles, the discus, the pole vault, shot put, and football throw. The team traveled throughout the state, competing and winning against the best athletes in Northern California. This photograph is of the Minato's championship in the 1938–1939 Stockton Invitational. (Miyamoto family collection.)

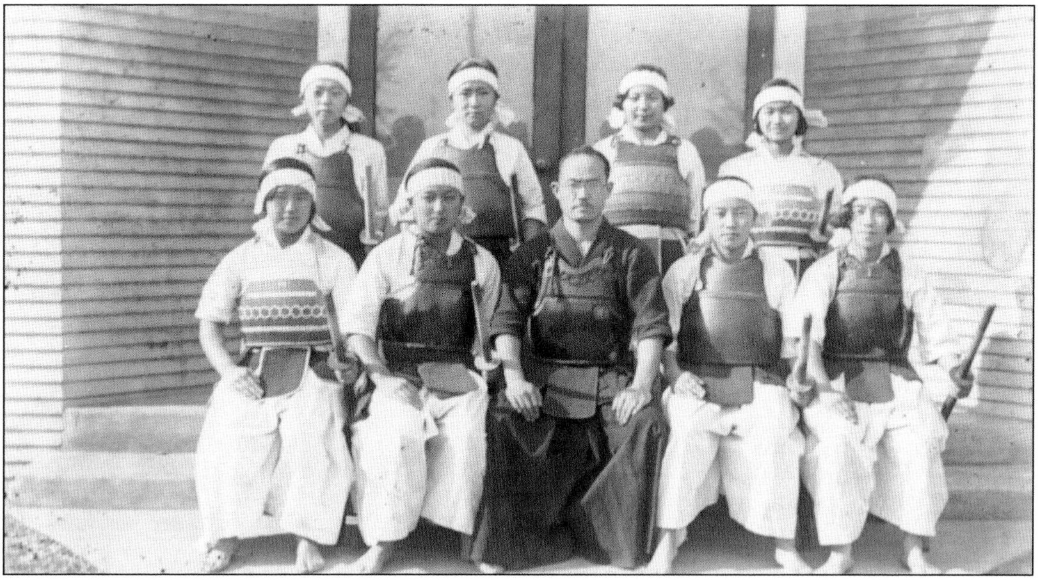

KENDO FENCING TEAM, C. 1930. This is an early kendo fencing team in front of the JACL Hall. Identified in this image are Sachi Higuchi-Oka and Nobkuo Higashi Takigawa (second row, left and second from left) (George Kodama and Monterey Public Library, California History Room.)

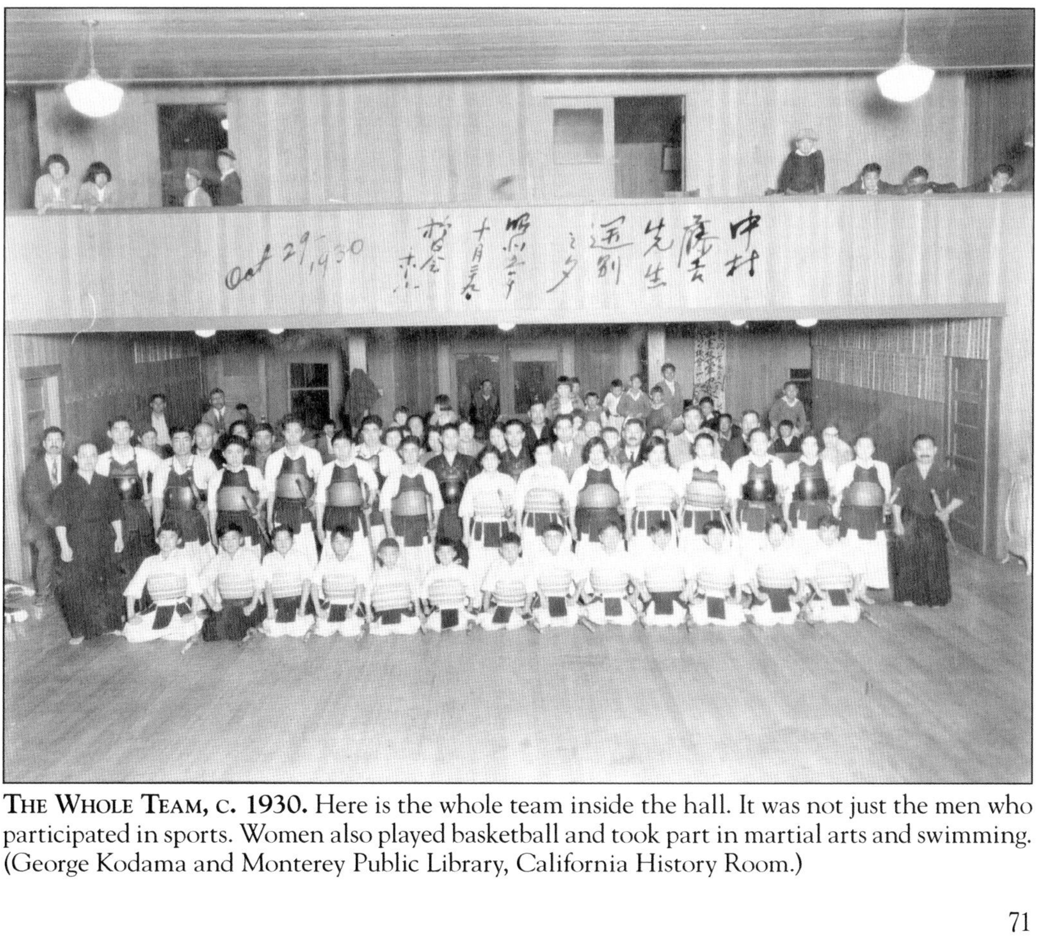

THE WHOLE TEAM, C. 1930. Here is the whole team inside the hall. It was not just the men who participated in sports. Women also played basketball and took part in martial arts and swimming. (George Kodama and Monterey Public Library, California History Room.)

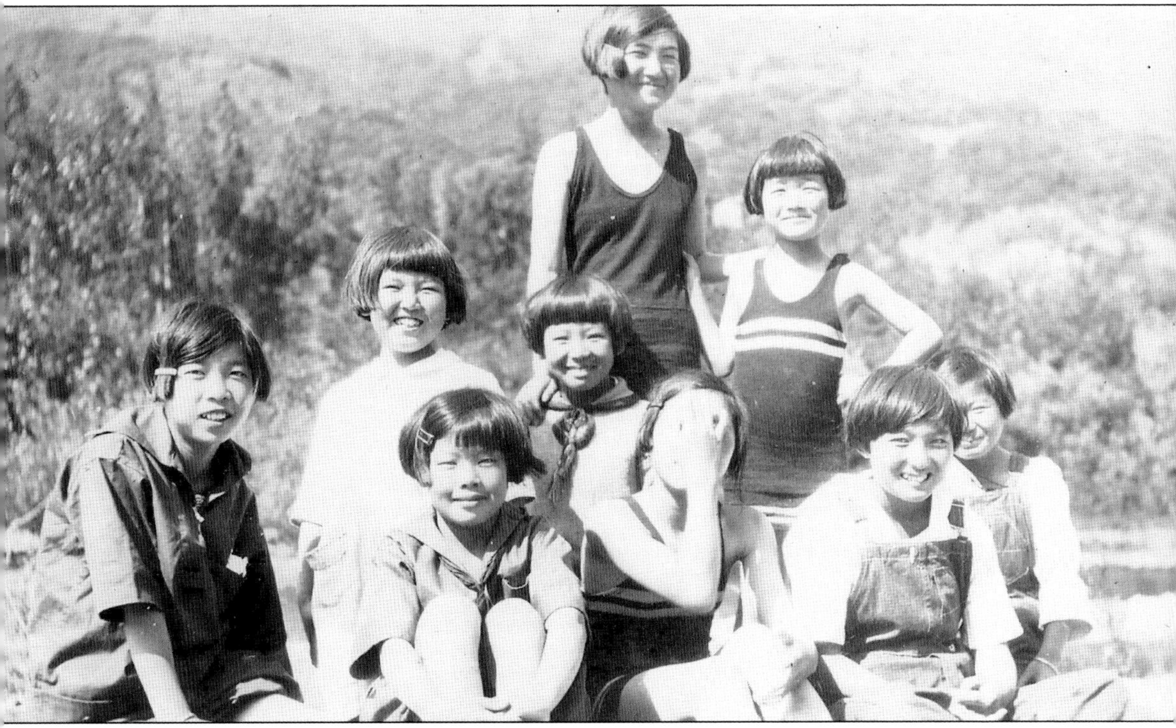

Let's Go Swimming! Here is a group of girls getting ready to go swimming around 1925. (Kodani family collection.)

Five

Royal Visits from Home

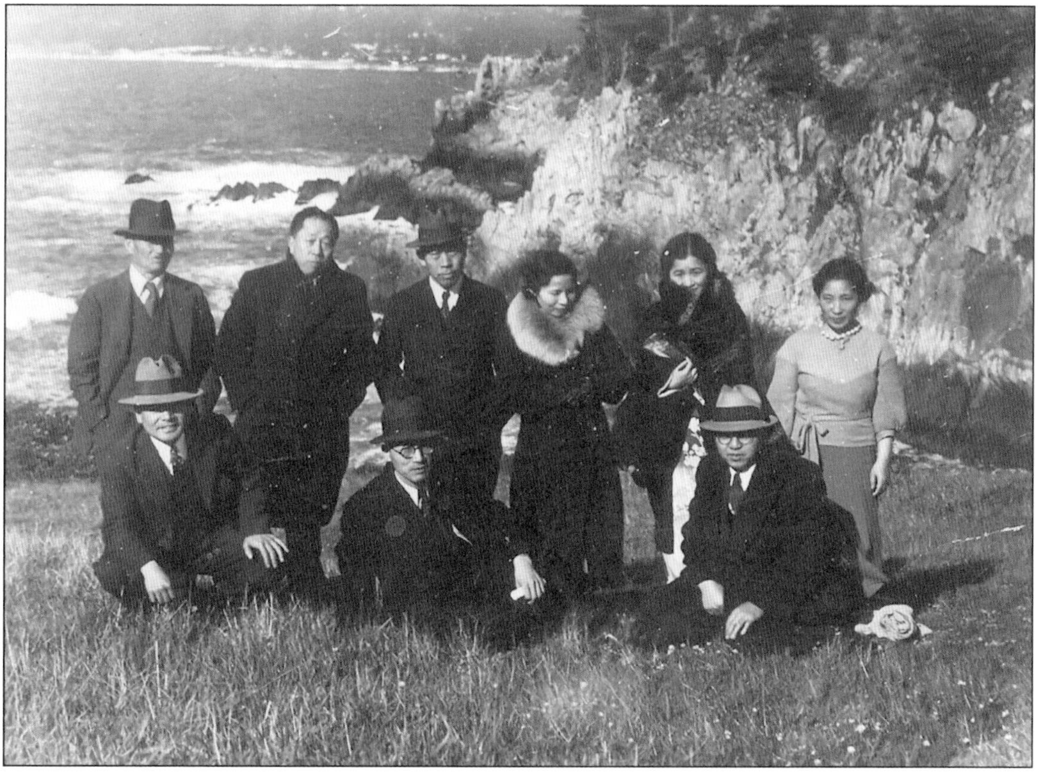

Community Picnics in Point Lobos, c. 1931. Picnics were (and are still) a big part of the Monterey Japanese community. These events are held every year at various locations around the Monterey Peninsula. Pictured are Monterey Japanese community leaders at Point Lobos for the visit of and picnic for Prince and Princess Asaka in 1931. (Kodani family collection.)

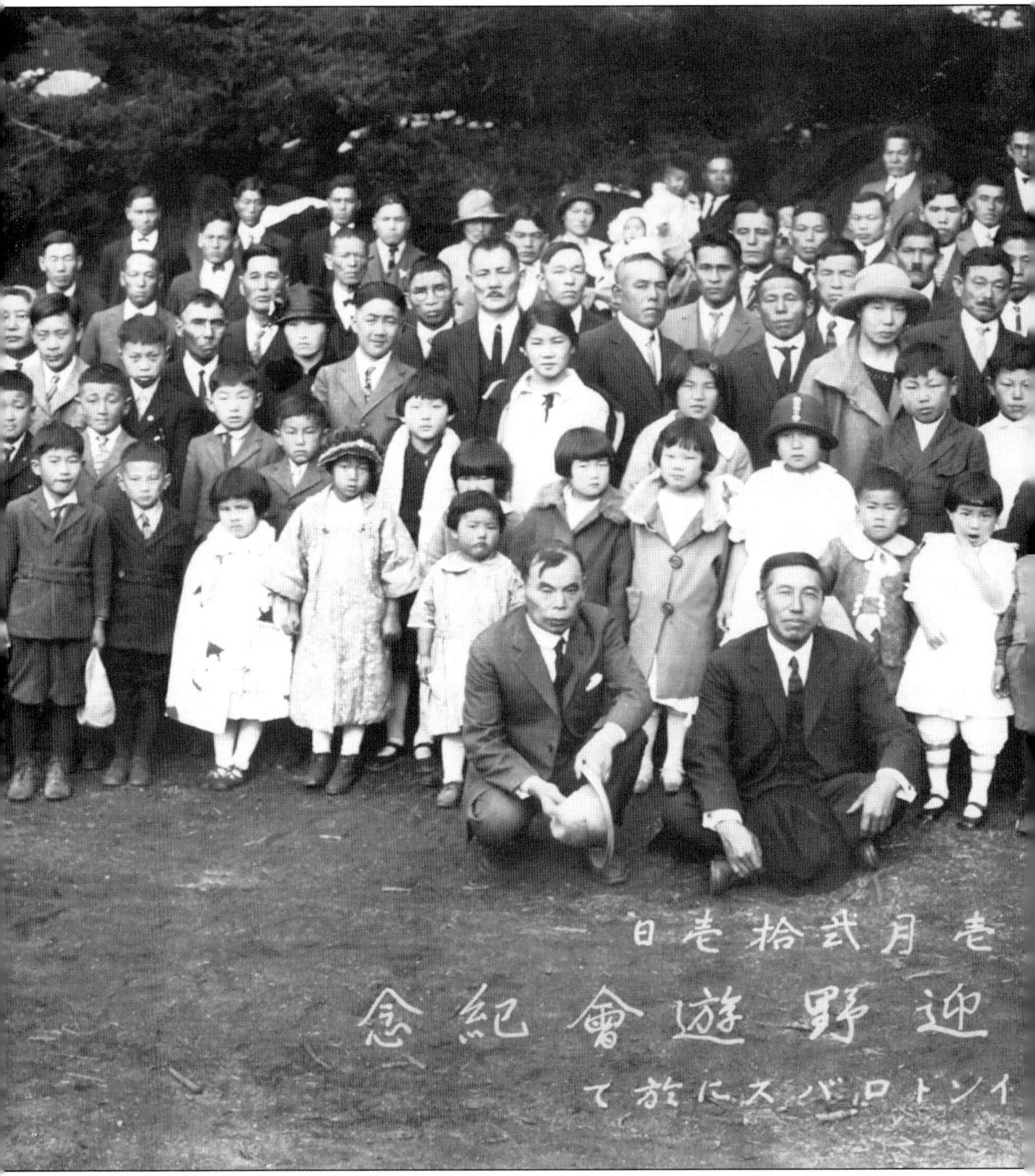

The Japanese Imperial Prince and Princess. In 1925, Prince and Princess Asaka of Japan visited Monterey. This photograph shows the local community coming out to welcome them to Point Lobos, where a picnic was held in their honor. In May 1931, His Imperial Highness Prince

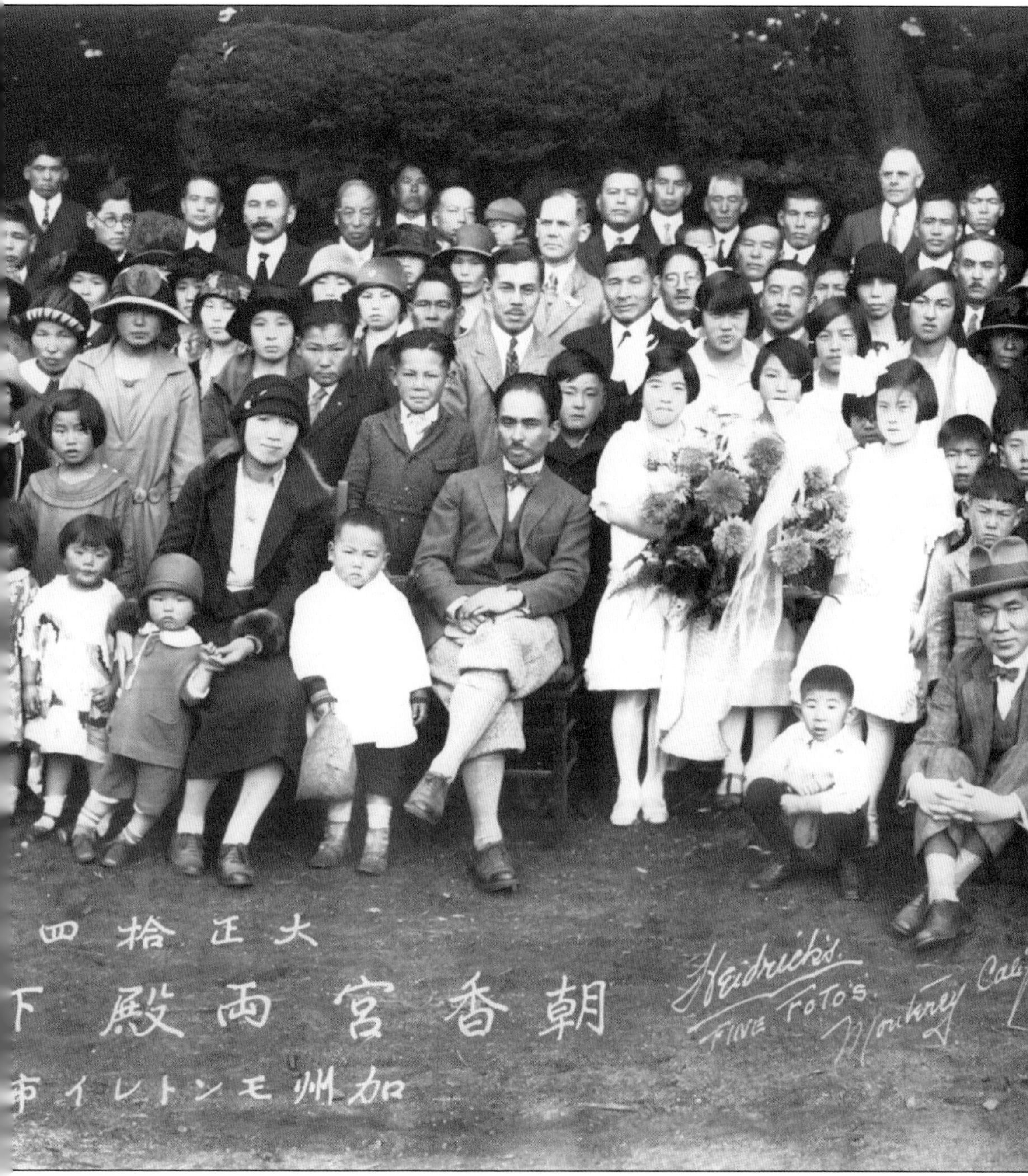

Takamatsu and his wife, Princess Kikuko, also visited Point Lobos when they were on their honeymoon world tour. (Larry Oda family collection.)

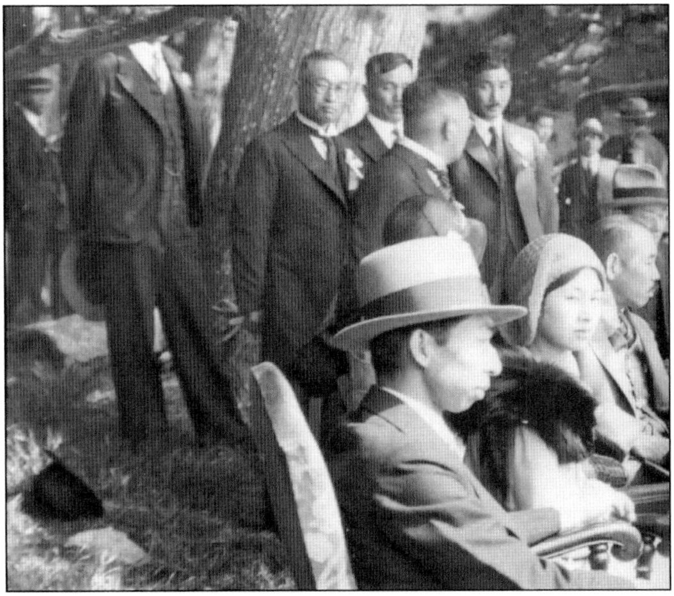

Royal Newlyweds. Again, Monterey's Japanese community came together and held a welcoming picnic at Point Lobos for the royal newlyweds. While in Monterey, the prince (foreground in hat) and princess (right) stayed at the very elegant Hotel Del Monte, but the picnic was held outdoors at Point Lobos because Monterey looked so much like Japan, which would allow the royal highnesses to feel at home. And they reportedly did. (A.C. Heidrick photograph, George Kodama and Monterey Public Library, California History Room.)

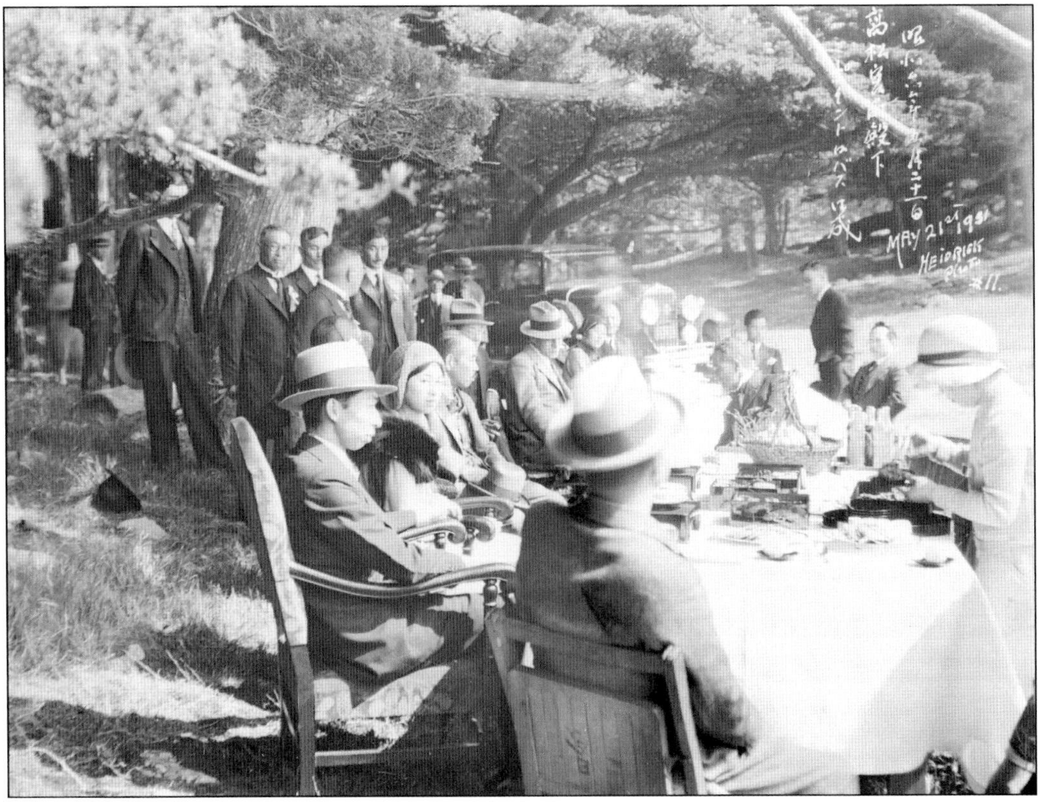

Bento Boxes. Special bento boxes were made of Monterey pine and inlaid with abalone shells. These were presented as gifts to the prince and princess. Everything was thought of—from the food to serve to the tables, chairs, and tablecloths—except a privy for the princess. After much embarrassment, an acceptable facility was made in the all-male divers' bunkhouse. (A.C. Heidrick photograph, George Kodama and Monterey Public Library, California History Room.)

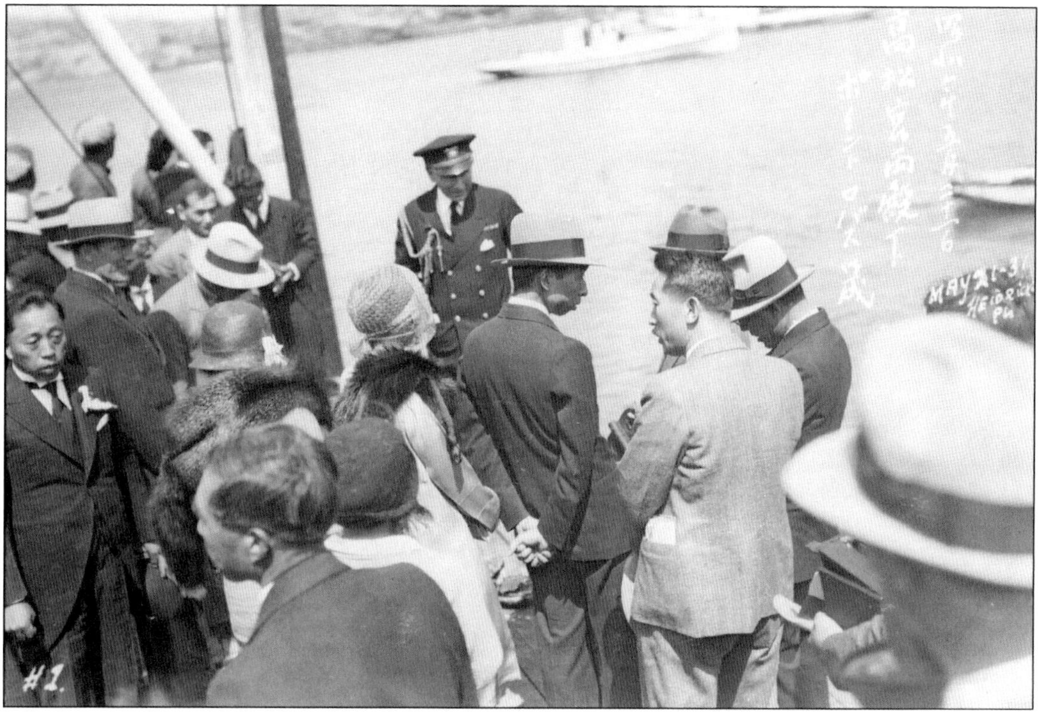

ABALONE-DIVING DEMONSTRATION. Because Prince Takamatsu (center, in hat with hands clasped behind back) had an interest in marine biology, a special abalone-diving demonstration was performed in front of the Point Lobos Cannery. (Monterey Library Collection.)

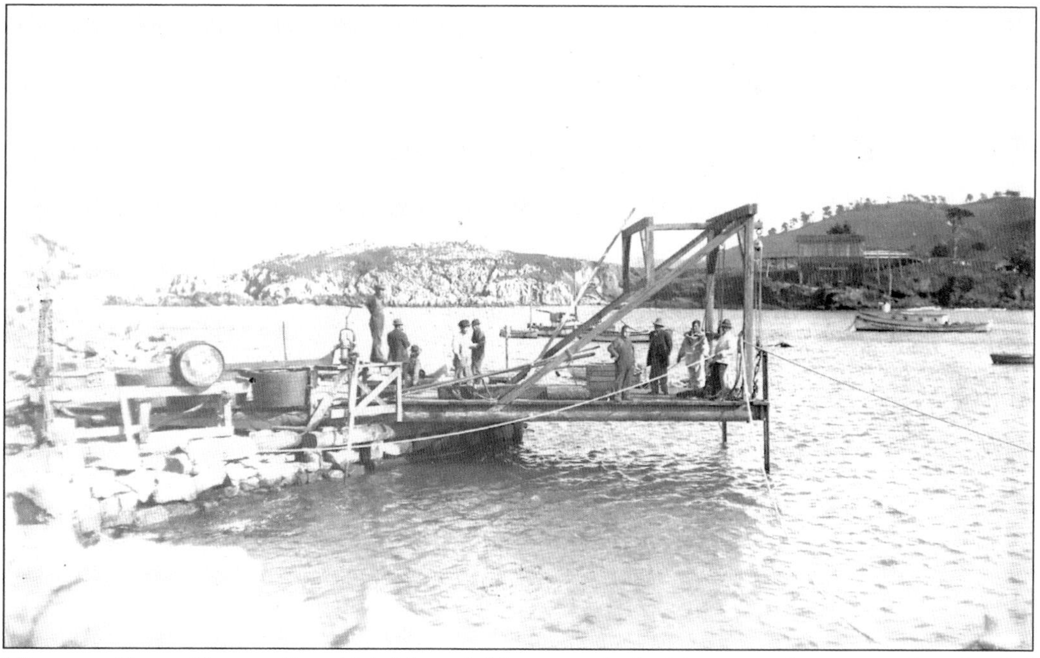

WHALERS COVE. Here, a diver (third from left) gets ready for his imperial guests at the wharf of Whalers Cover. Others in the photograph are associated with the Point Lobos Canning Company and are there to assist the diver in dressing and with air support. (Kodani family collection.)

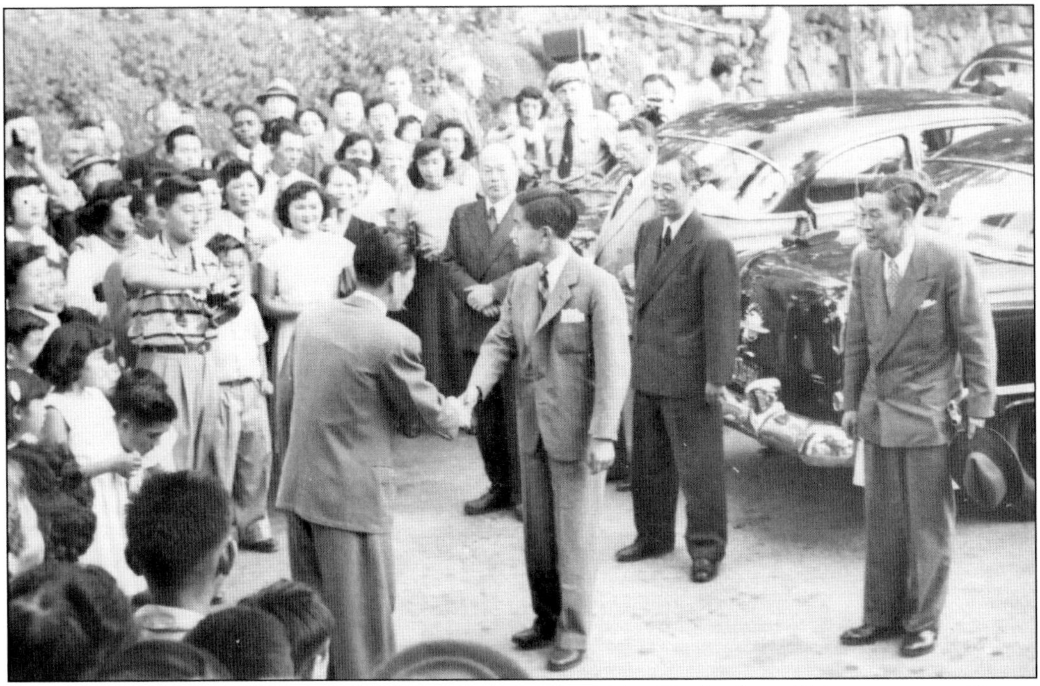

MONTEREY LEADERS GREET ANOTHER ROYAL VISITOR IN 1952. The leaders of Monterey greet Crown Prince Akihito (on right, shaking hands), who is now the emperor of Japan. He is also a marine biologist by training. (Jean Esaki and Monterey Public Library, California History Room.)

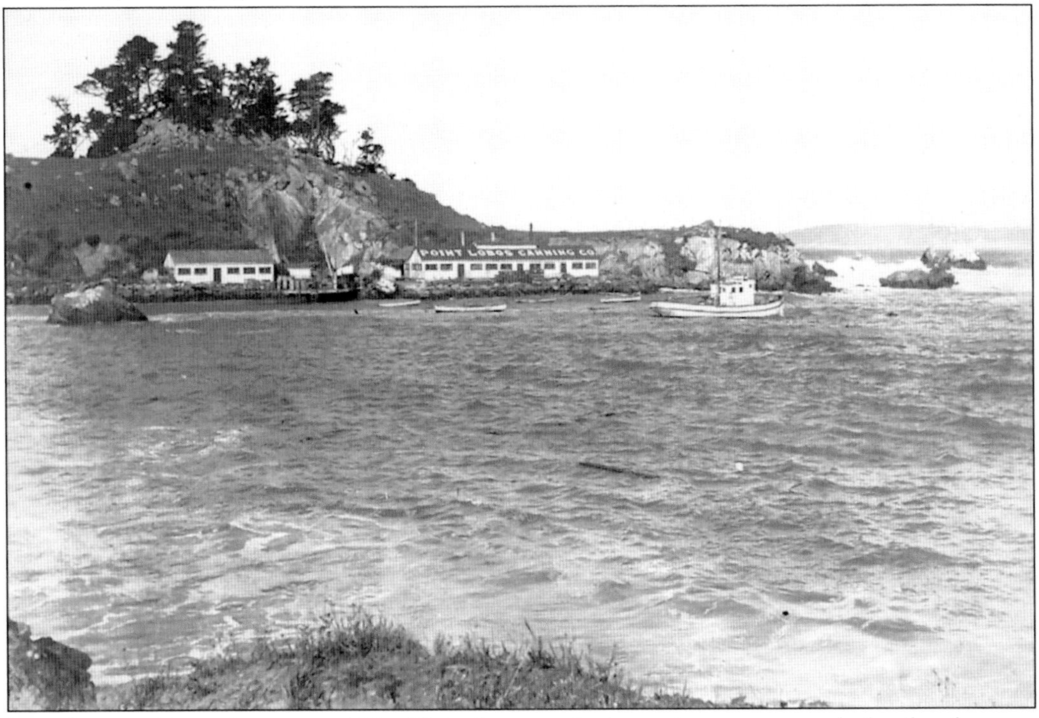

THE COVE AT POINT LOBOS, C. 1931. This photograph shows the cannery and wharf at the cove in Point Lobos. (Kodani family collection.)

Six

Spiritual Matters

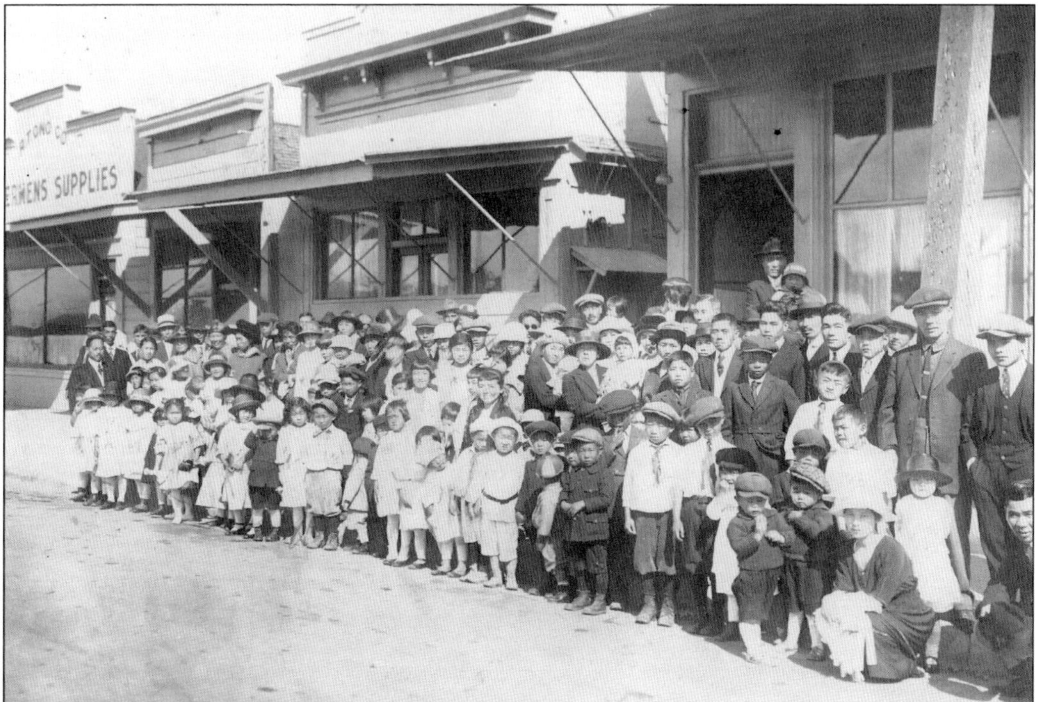

Religion and the Japanese Community in Monterey. Although it is said that religion does not play a central role for the Japanese, it did play a large role for the Japanese community in Monterey. The Monterey Peninsula Presbyterian Mission was established in 1908 in Carmel Valley. As this photograph shows, the church moved to Washington Street, right in the heart of Monterey's Japantown, in 1912. The building on the left is R.T. Ono Company, Fishing Supplies. (Matsuyama family collection.)

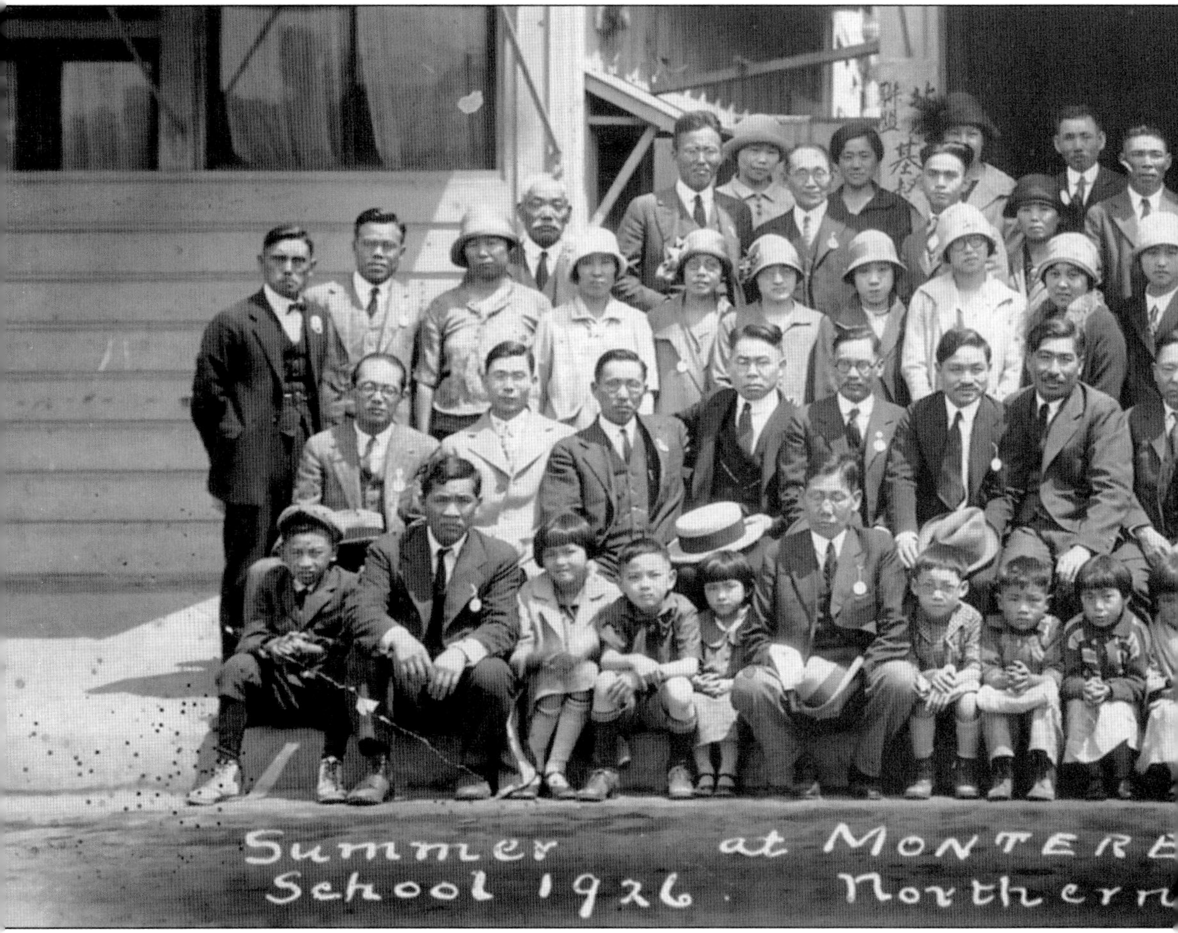

Japanese Church Federation Summer School. This photograph shows the Japanese Church

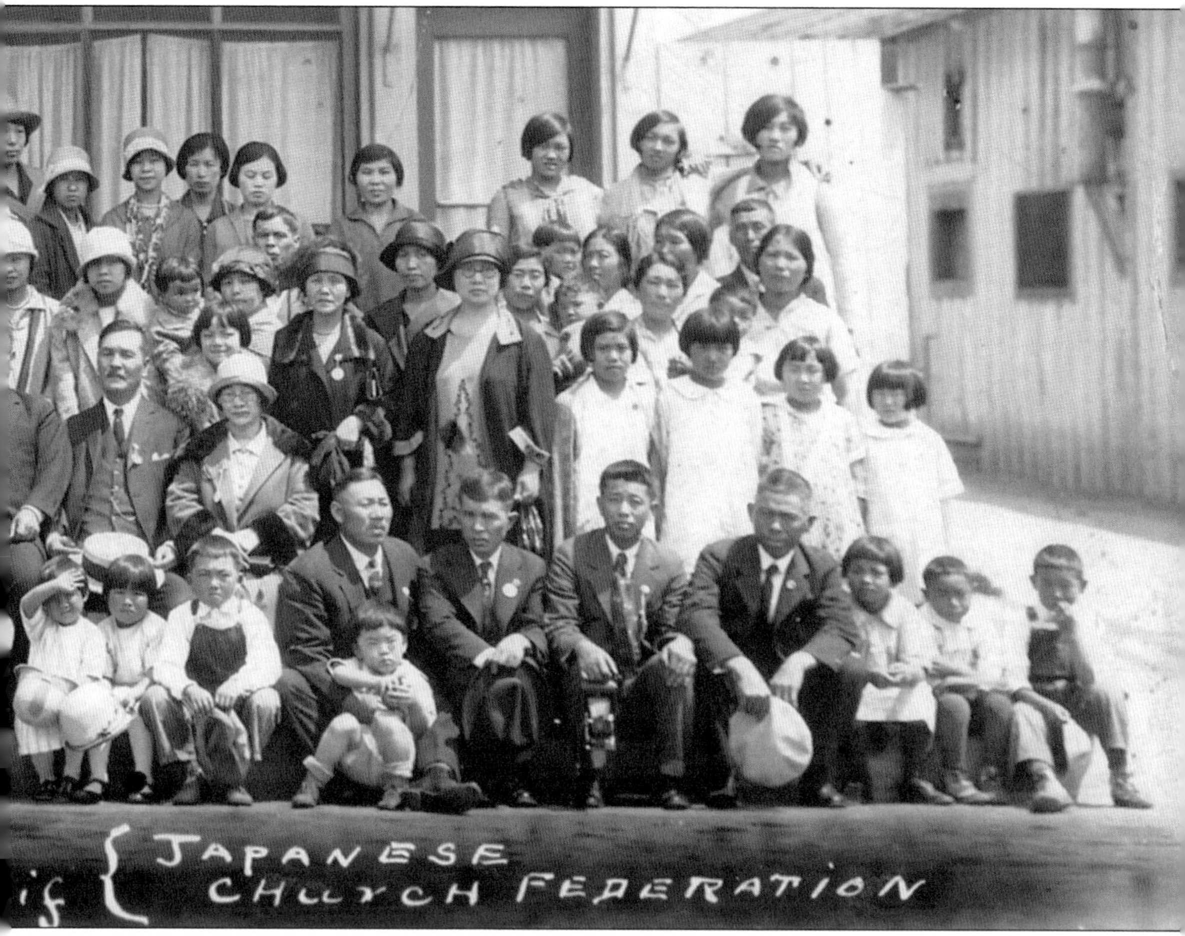

Federation Summer School for religious studies in 1926. (Matsuyama family collection.)

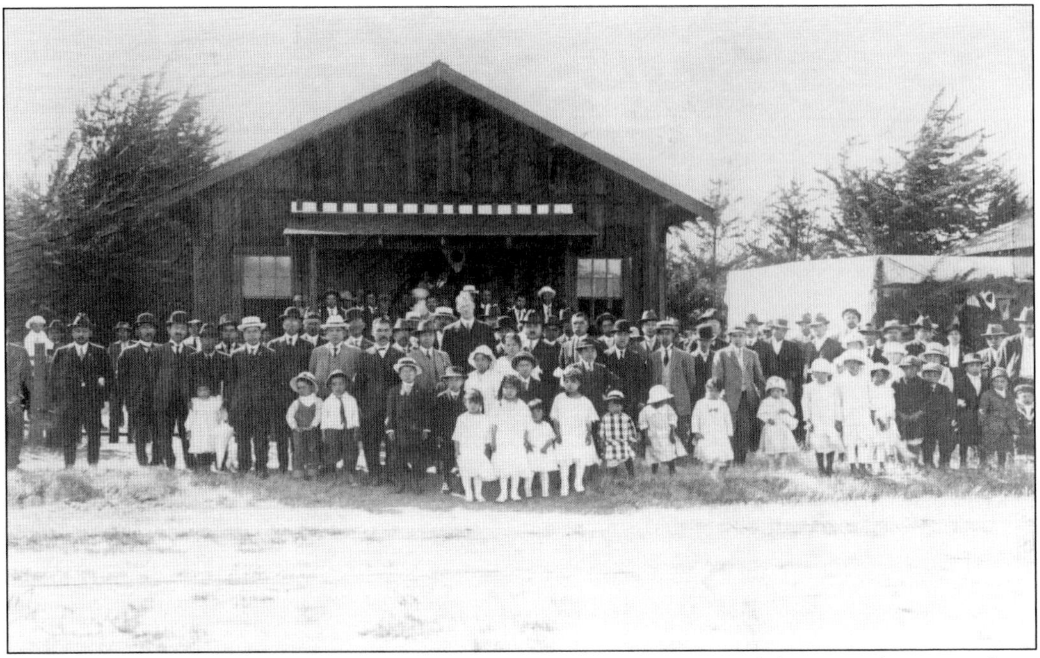

Early Presbyterian Mission in Carmel Valley, c. 1910. Many of the Isseis first came here with their Buddhist or Shinto beliefs but quickly converted to Christianity. The Presbyterian Mission Church originally met in a private home in Carmel. This Carmel chapel was dedicated in 1911. (Matsuyama family collection.)

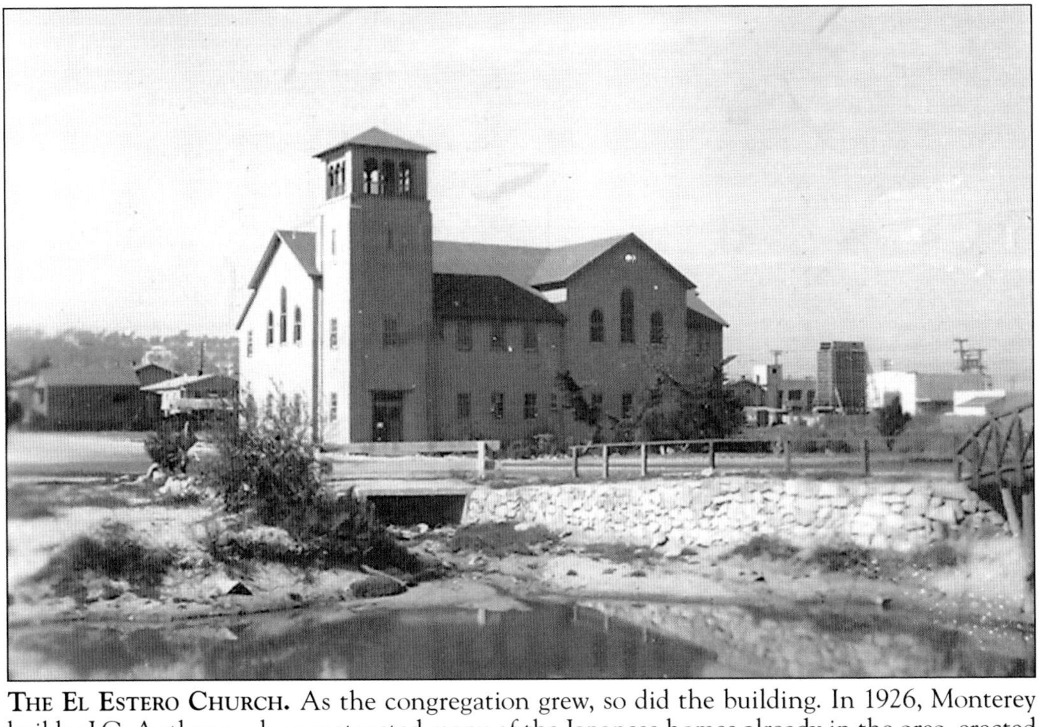

The El Estero Church. As the congregation grew, so did the building. In 1926, Monterey builder J.C. Anthony, who constructed many of the Japanese homes already in the area, erected this new home for El Estero Church. (Matsuyama family collection.)

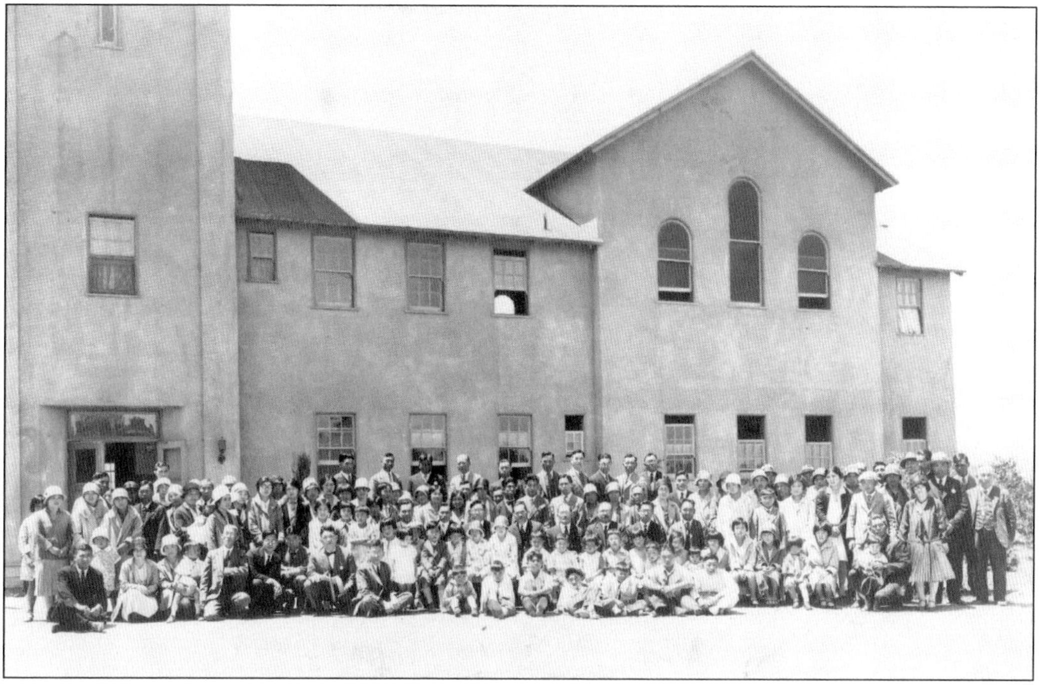

THE WHOLE CONGREGATION. Here, the entire membership poses in front of the newly built church. (Matsuyama family collection.)

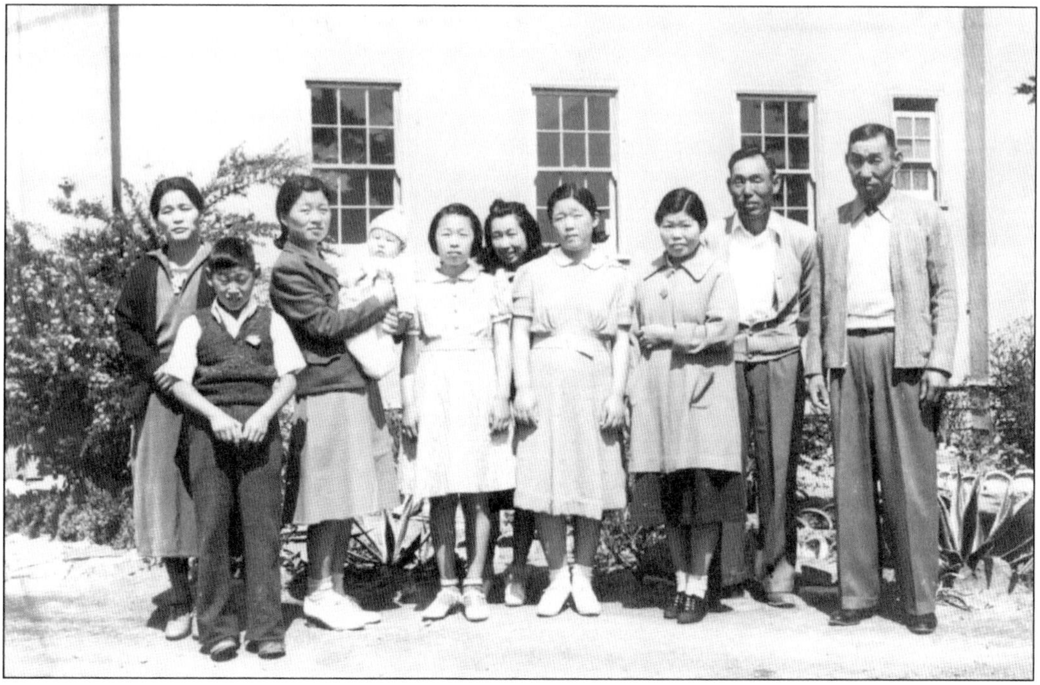

A FAMILY GETTING READY FOR CHURCH. The El Estero Church still plays an important part on the lives of the Monterey Japanese. It has always sponsored a variety of different events for every age of members and nonmembers alike. (Matsuyama family collection.)

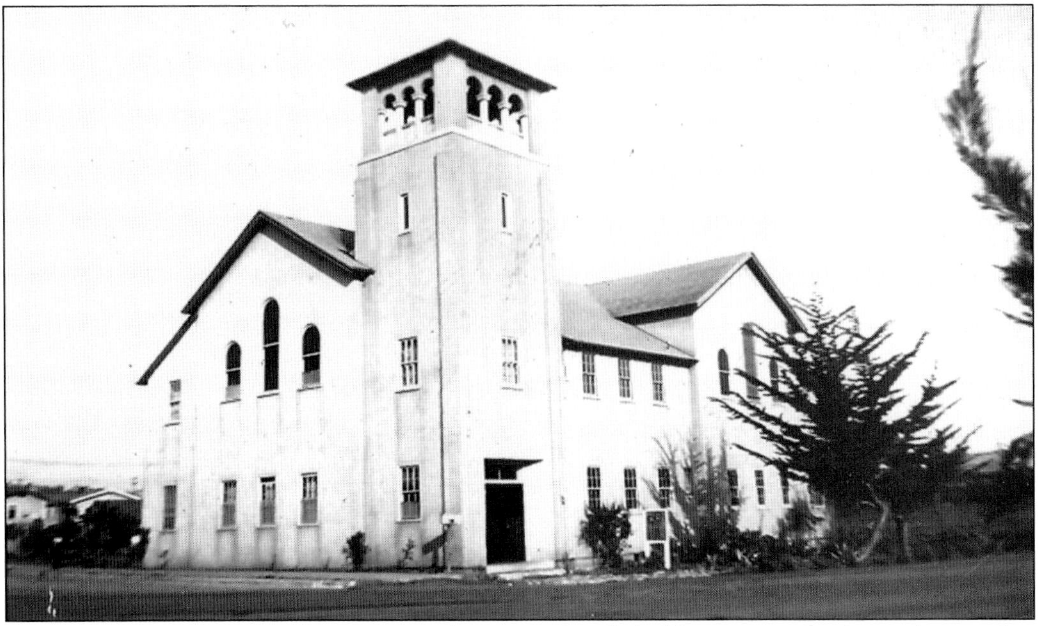

ANNUAL SALMON DINNER. Every year, El Estero Church holds an annual salmon dinner that attracts people from all over the Monterey Peninsula. It first started in 1926 and was held on the first Friday in June. At that time, the majority of the congregation was made up of fishing families, so the men would catch the salmon and do most of the cooking and serving. (Matsuyama family collection.)

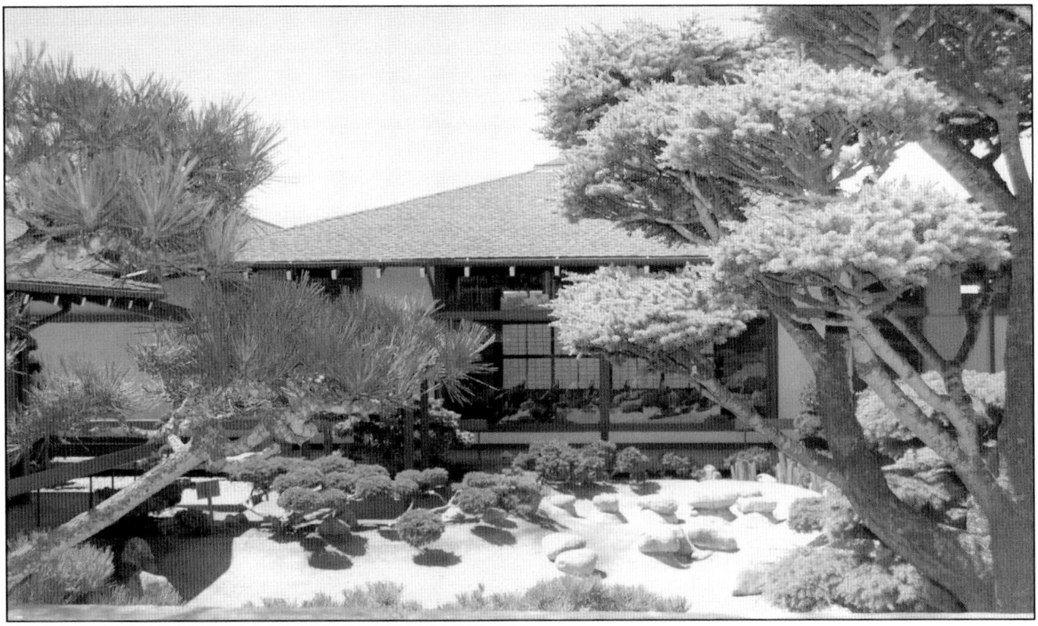

MONTEREY PENINSULA BUDDHIST TEMPLE. Before 1956, there were no Buddhist temples on the Monterey Peninsula. For over 30 years, services were held in the JACL Hall. Finally, on June 6, 1965, the first Buddhist temple was dedicated in Seaside. On June 13, 1976, it burned to the ground. The Japanese community pulled together, and a second temple was dedicated less than a year later. (Kodama family collection.)

Seven

THE MONTEREY JAPANESE AMERICAN CITIZENS LEAGUE

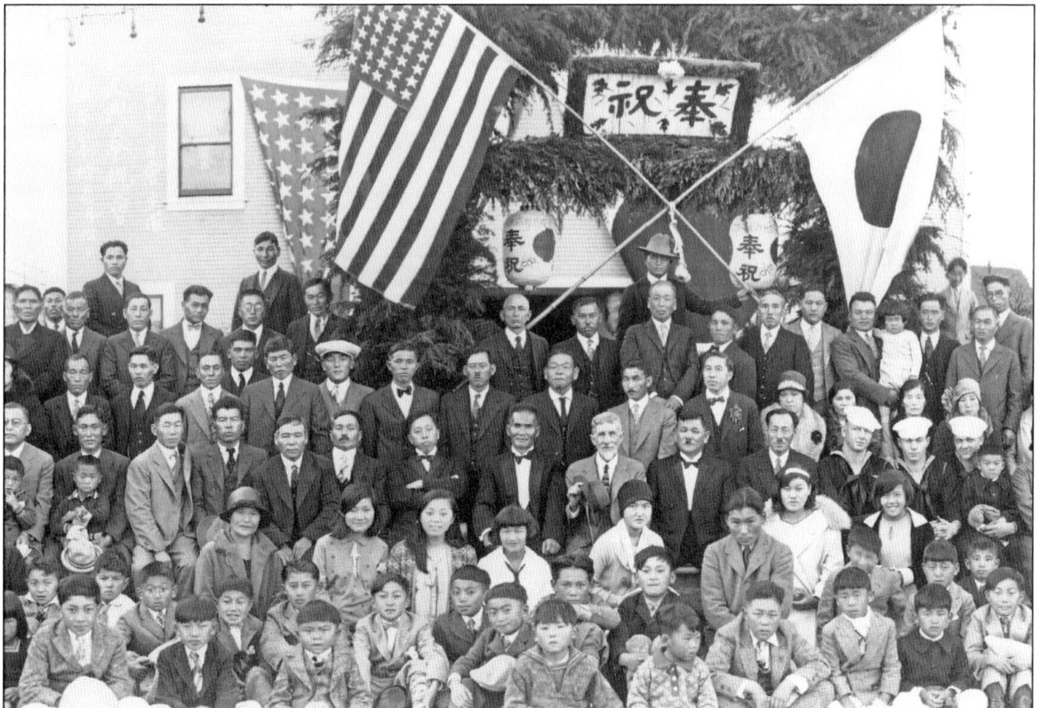

THE JAPANESE ASSOCIATION OF MONTEREY. This building was erected in 1927 for the Japanese Association and for the purpose of creating a community center. It was a meeting place where events, classes, and even Kabuki theater performance, called *shibai*, were held. The association was first developed in 1908 when it donated $100 towards the celebration of the visiting Great White Fleet to Monterey. This photograph was taken in 1928. The whole Monterey Japanese community turned out to honor the emperor's third anniversary. (Monterey JACL collection.)

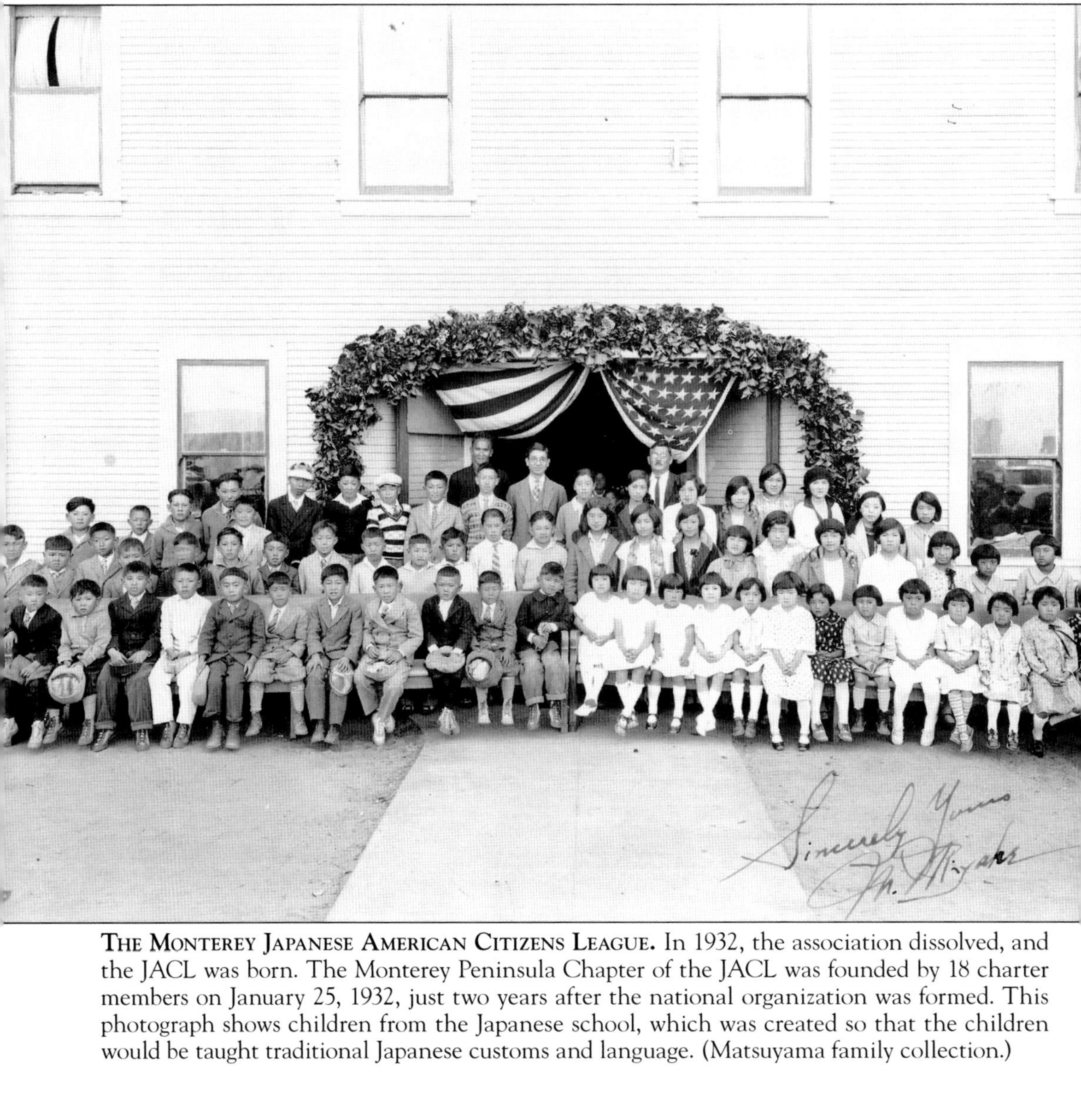

THE MONTEREY JAPANESE AMERICAN CITIZENS LEAGUE. In 1932, the association dissolved, and the JACL was born. The Monterey Peninsula Chapter of the JACL was founded by 18 charter members on January 25, 1932, just two years after the national organization was formed. This photograph shows children from the Japanese school, which was created so that the children would be taught traditional Japanese customs and language. (Matsuyama family collection.)

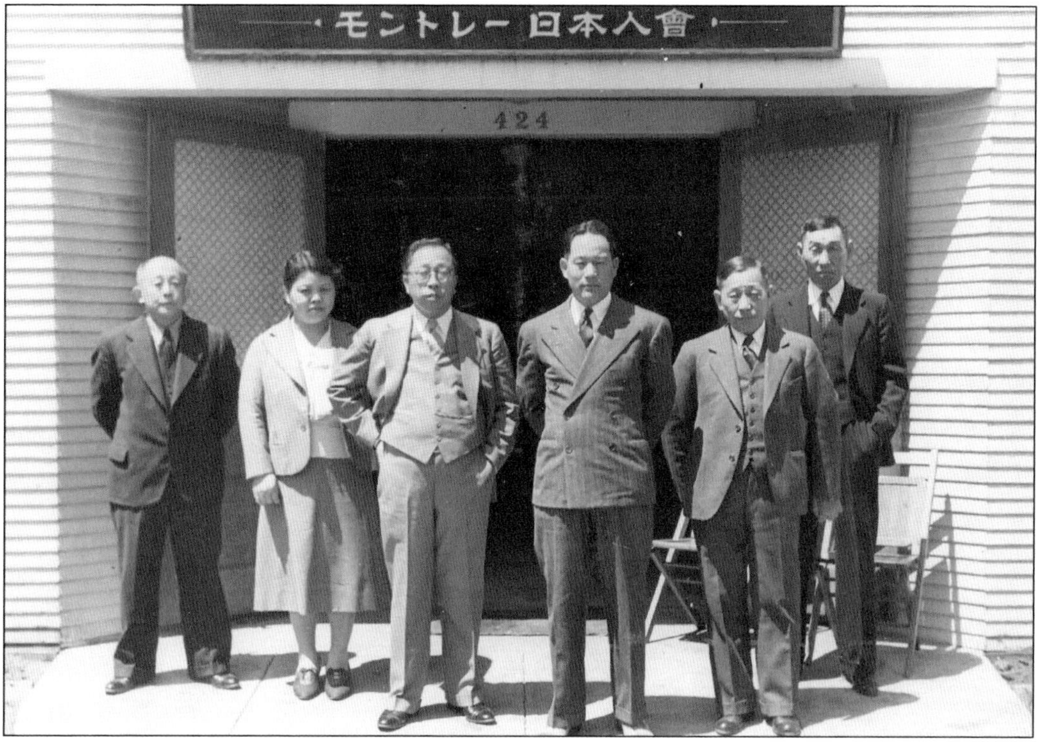

GROUP OF BUSINESSMEN FROM THE JAPANESE ASSOCIATION, 1929. The Japanese Association Building (now the JACL Hall) was a popular place to meet and hold meetings for the Monterey Japanese community. (Kodama family collection.)

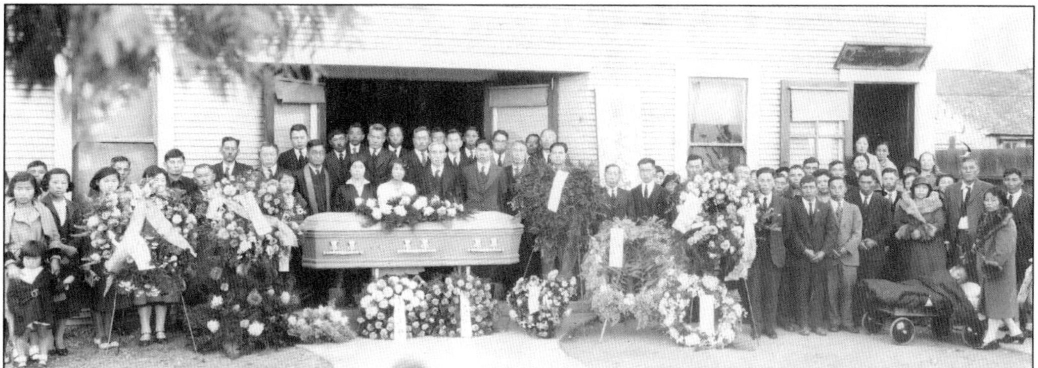

FUNERAL SERVICE, C. 1925. Many families would hold funeral services in the Japanese association's hall and have a group photograph taken in front. (Monterey Library Collection.)

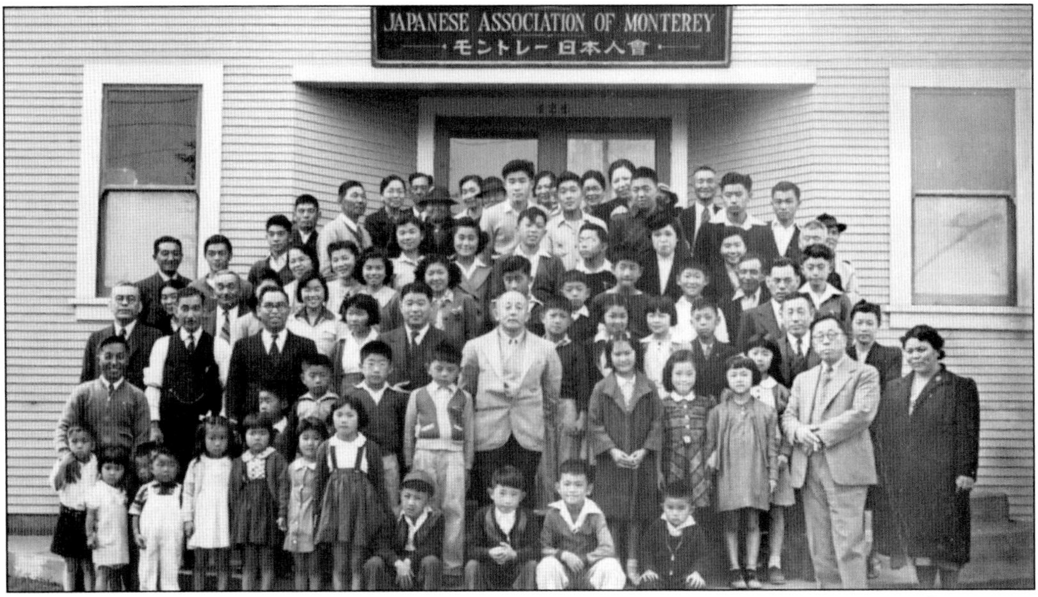

The JACL and Issei, c. 1932. The JACL was formed for the same purposes as the parent organization: to fight against discriminatory legislation and racial prejudice. The group also helps issei with navigating through the American bureaucracy in such legal matters as alien registration and property contracts. Today, the chapter continues to fight for tolerance and diversity, looks after its members to preserve their cultural heritage, and assists new immigrants in assimilating into American society. (Kodama family collection.)

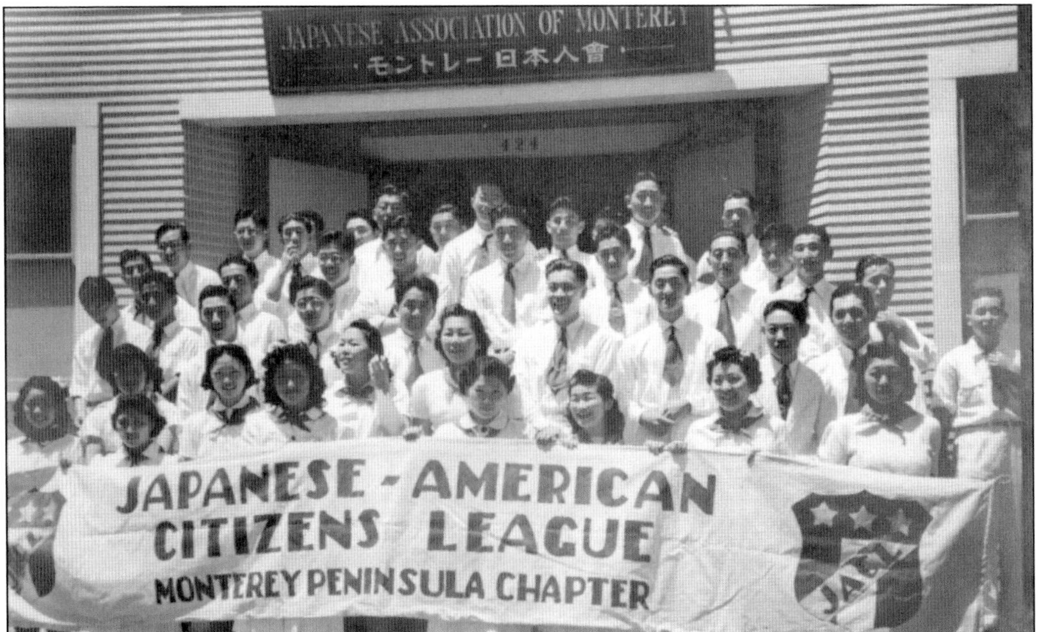

The Local JACL Women's Auxiliary. Throughout the 1930s, the JACL Women's Auxiliary was involved in the larger community. For the 1937 Independence Day parade, it decided to make a giant American flag to carry in parades and at other civic events. (George Esaki photograph, Jean Esaki and Monterey Public Library, California History Room.)

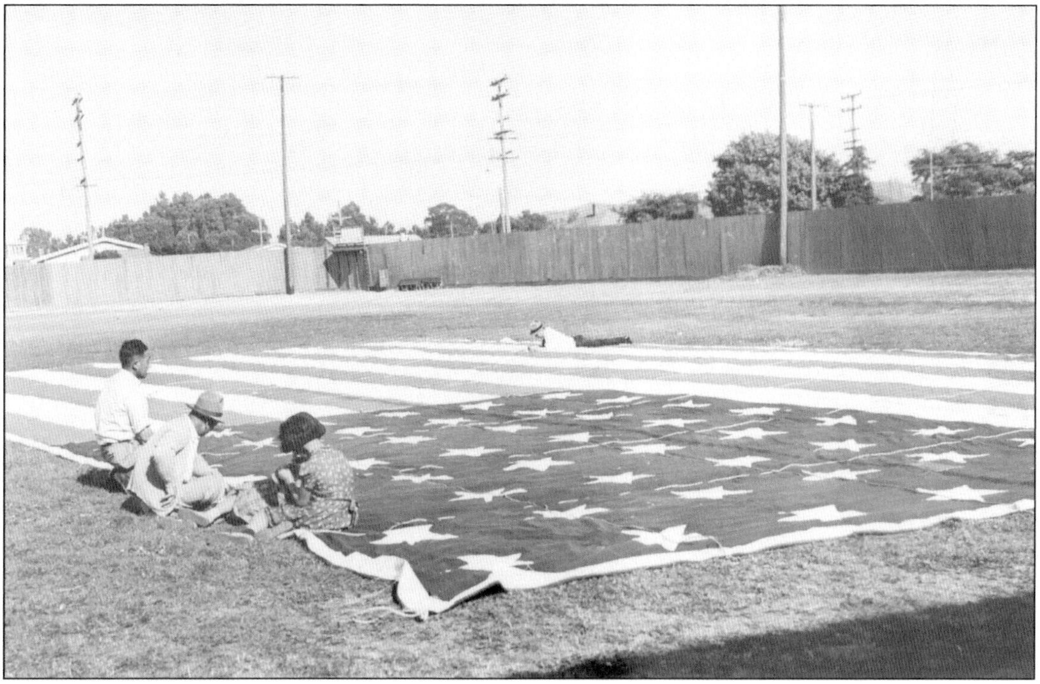

THE AMERICAN FLAG. Here, volunteers work on the flag on the baseball diamond at Jacks Park in 1937. (George Esaki photograph, Jean Esaki and Monterey Public Library, California History Room.)

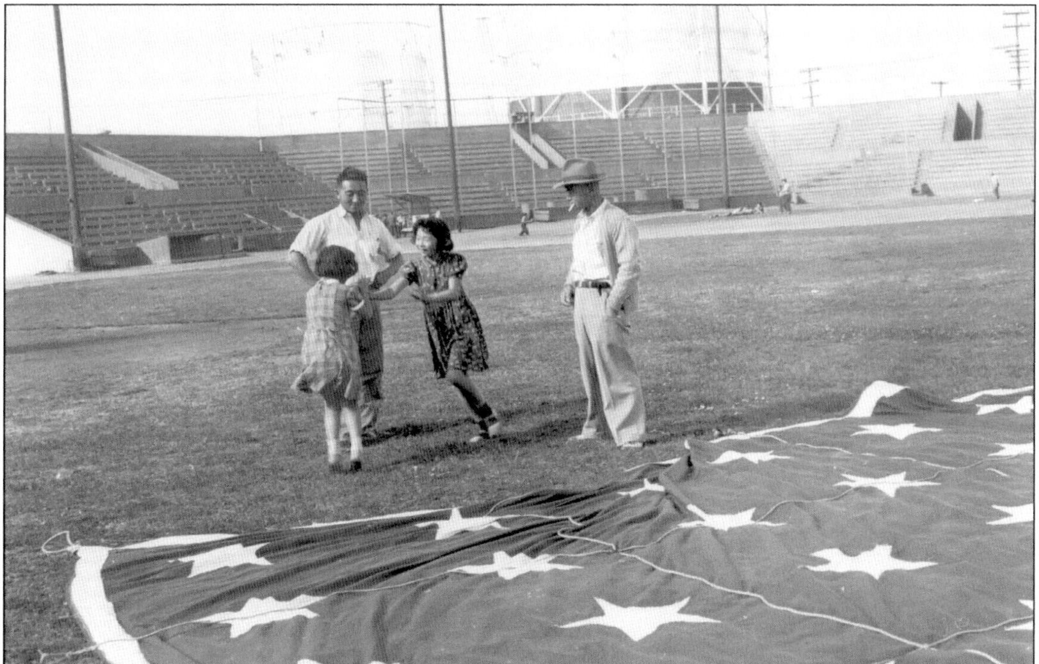

YOU'RE A GRAND OLD FLAG. The flag was measured as 40 feet by 70 feet. The rationale for the size was that only a few people could ride on a float, but it would take 60 people to carry this flag. (George Esaki photograph, Jean Esaki and Monterey Public Library, California History Room.)

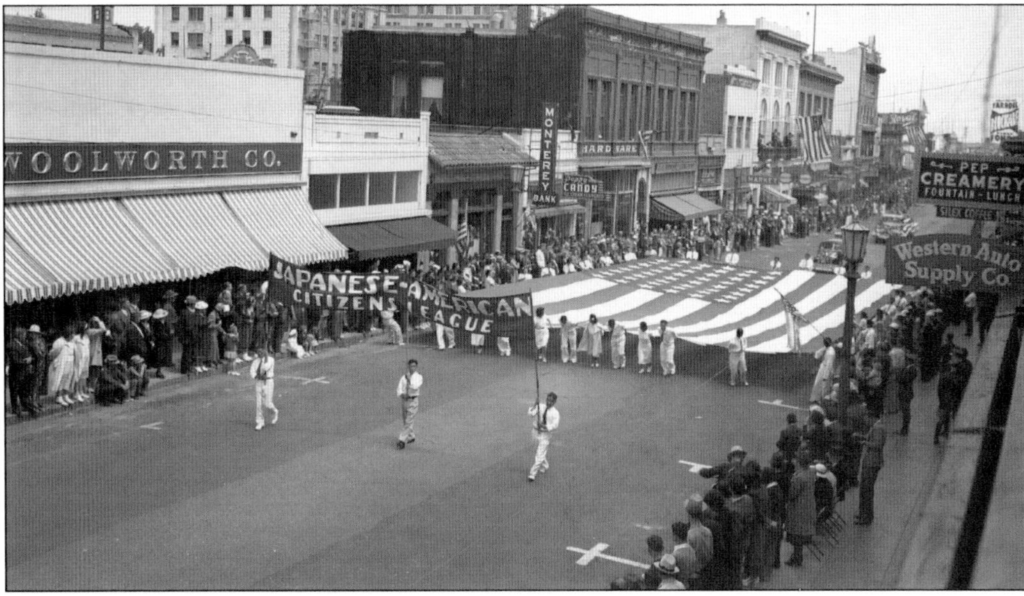

Independence Day Parade. Here is the flag proudly being carried down Alvarado Street in 1938 during the Fourth of July parade. (William L. Morgan photograph, Morgan Collection, Monterey Public Library, California History Room.)

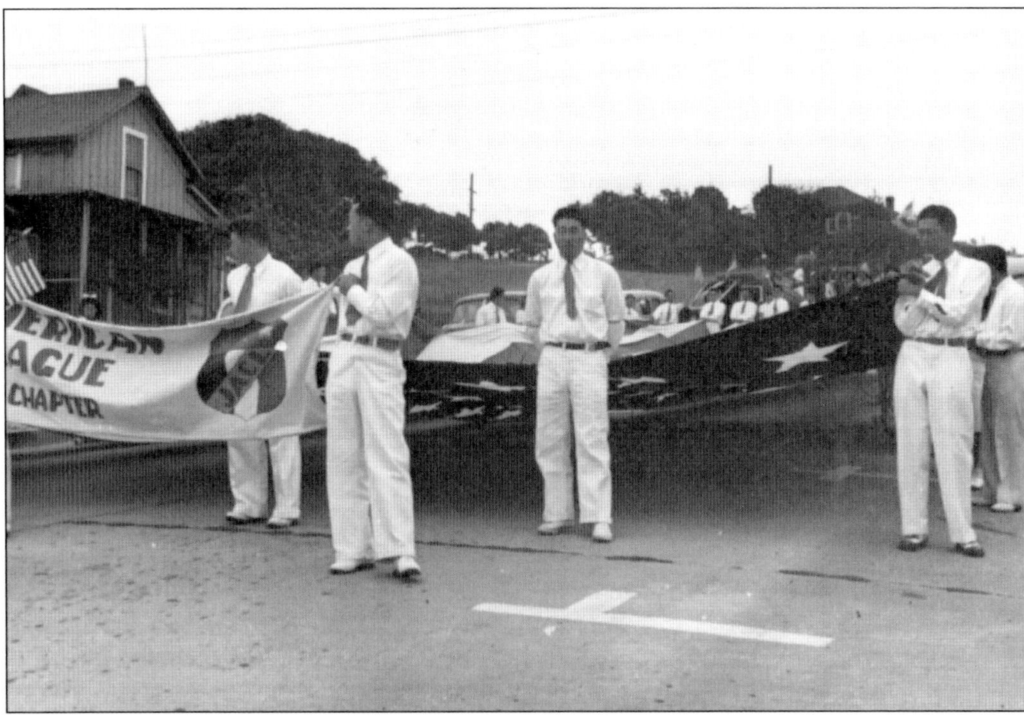

An Important Symbol. Everyone was involved in carrying the flag, which was (and continues to be) an important symbol to the Monterey Japanese community (George Esaki photograph, Jean Esaki and Monterey Public Library, California History Room.)

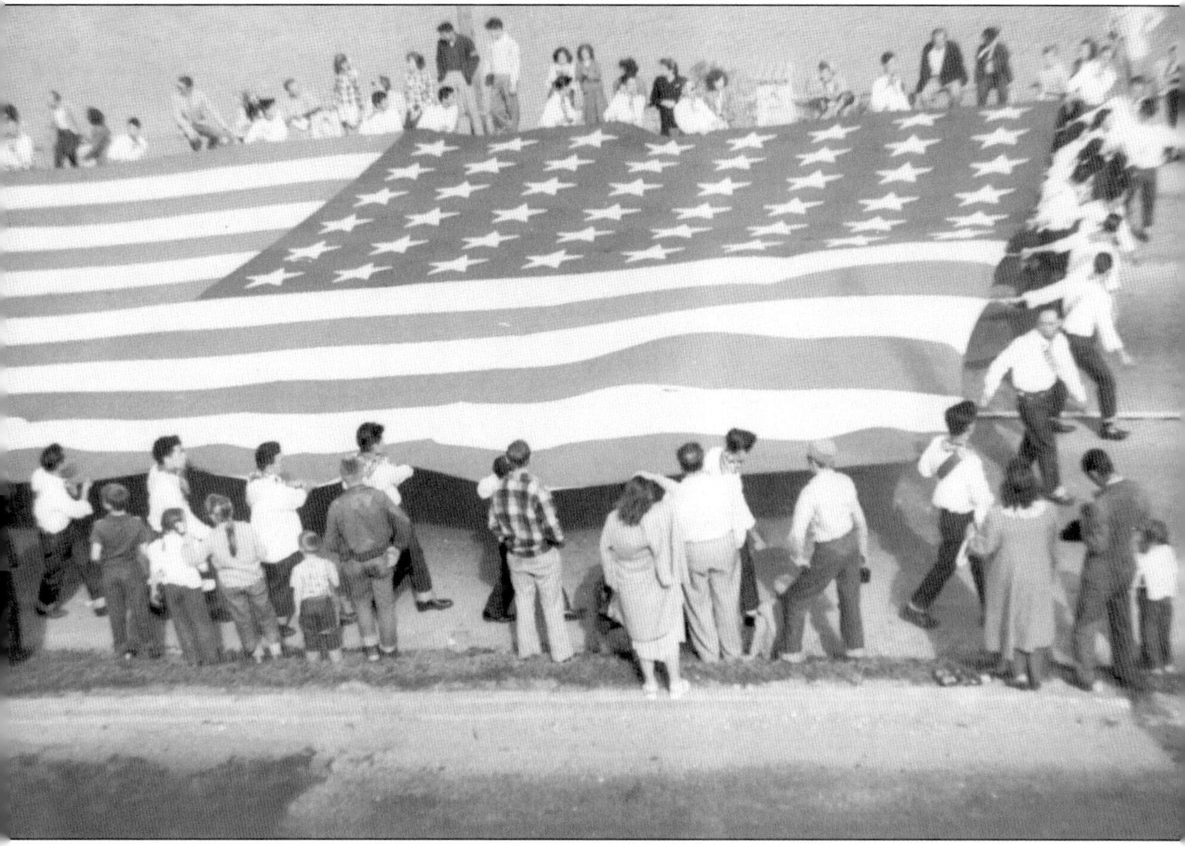

THE AMERICAN FLAG AND THE JAPANESE AMERICAN COMMUNITY. In the early photographs of the first Japanese immigrants and their families, the American flag is usually front and foremost when they participate in some kind of community event or family portrait. This image shows as many as 50 members of Monterey's Japanese community carrying a large Stars and Stripes. (George Esaki photograph, Jean Esaki and Monterey Public Library, California History Room.)

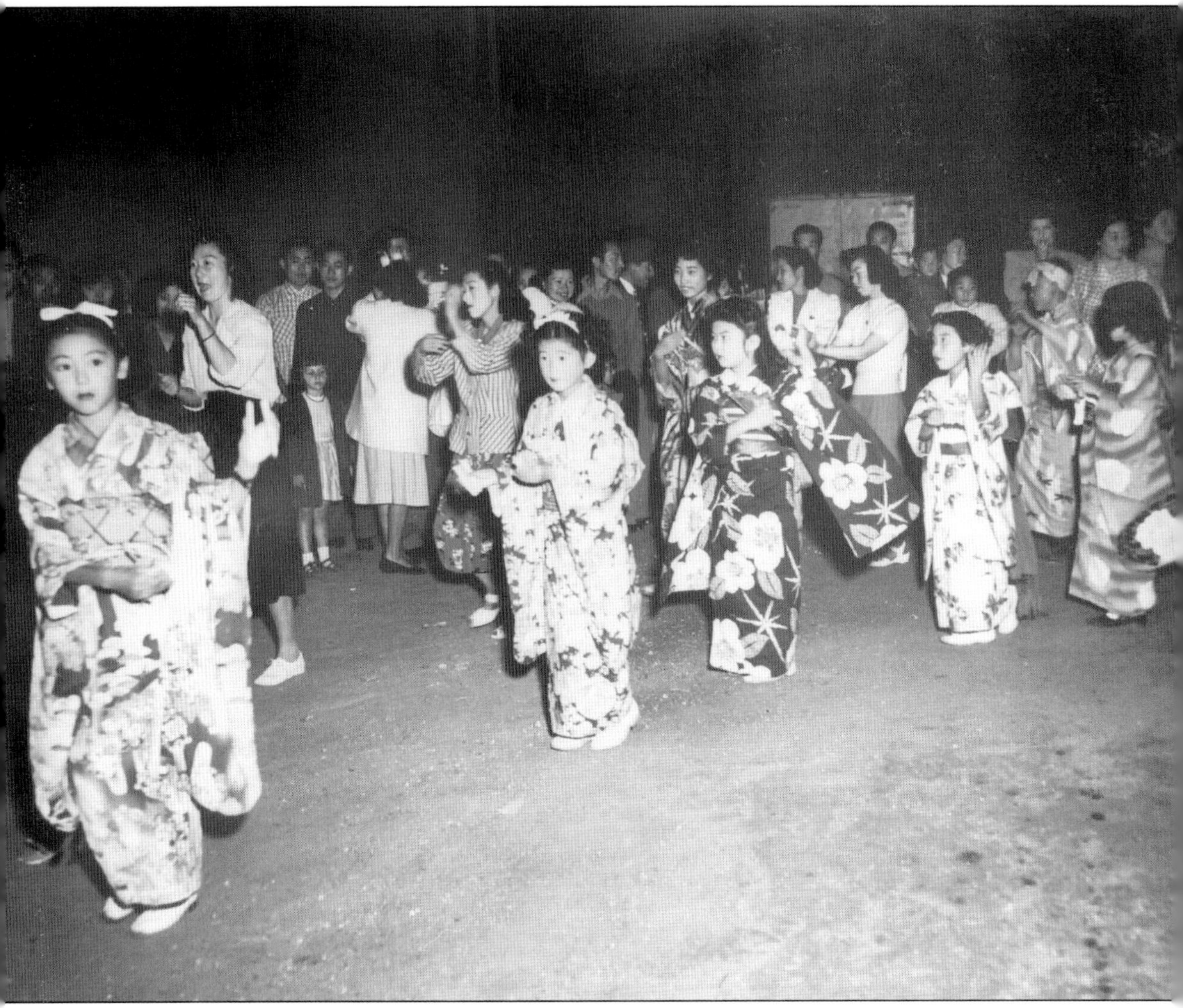

Beautiful Kimonos, c. 1935. JACL Women's Auxiliary members are dressed in traditional Japanese kimonos for what appears to be an early *obon* dance, a Japanese Buddhist tradition, on Adams Street near the JACL Hall. (Monterey Library Collection.)

Eight

Let's Go Fishing—Again!

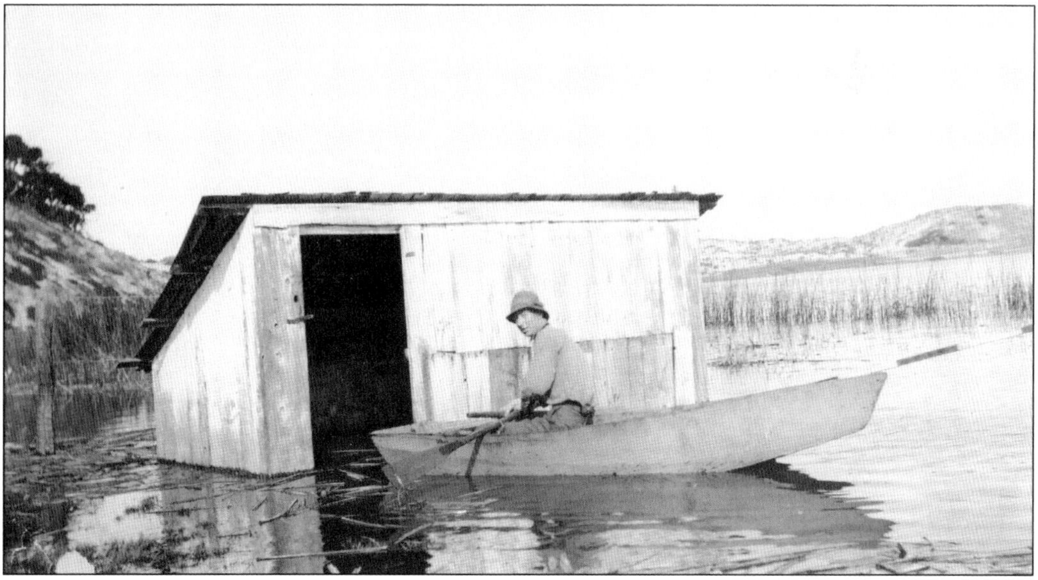

Unidentified Japanese Man Fishing in Roberts Lake, Seaside, c. 1925. When this photograph was taken, Roberts Lake was open to the sea and, like the sea, had both high and low tides. This was a good place to fish in a small boat. (Monterey Library Collection.)

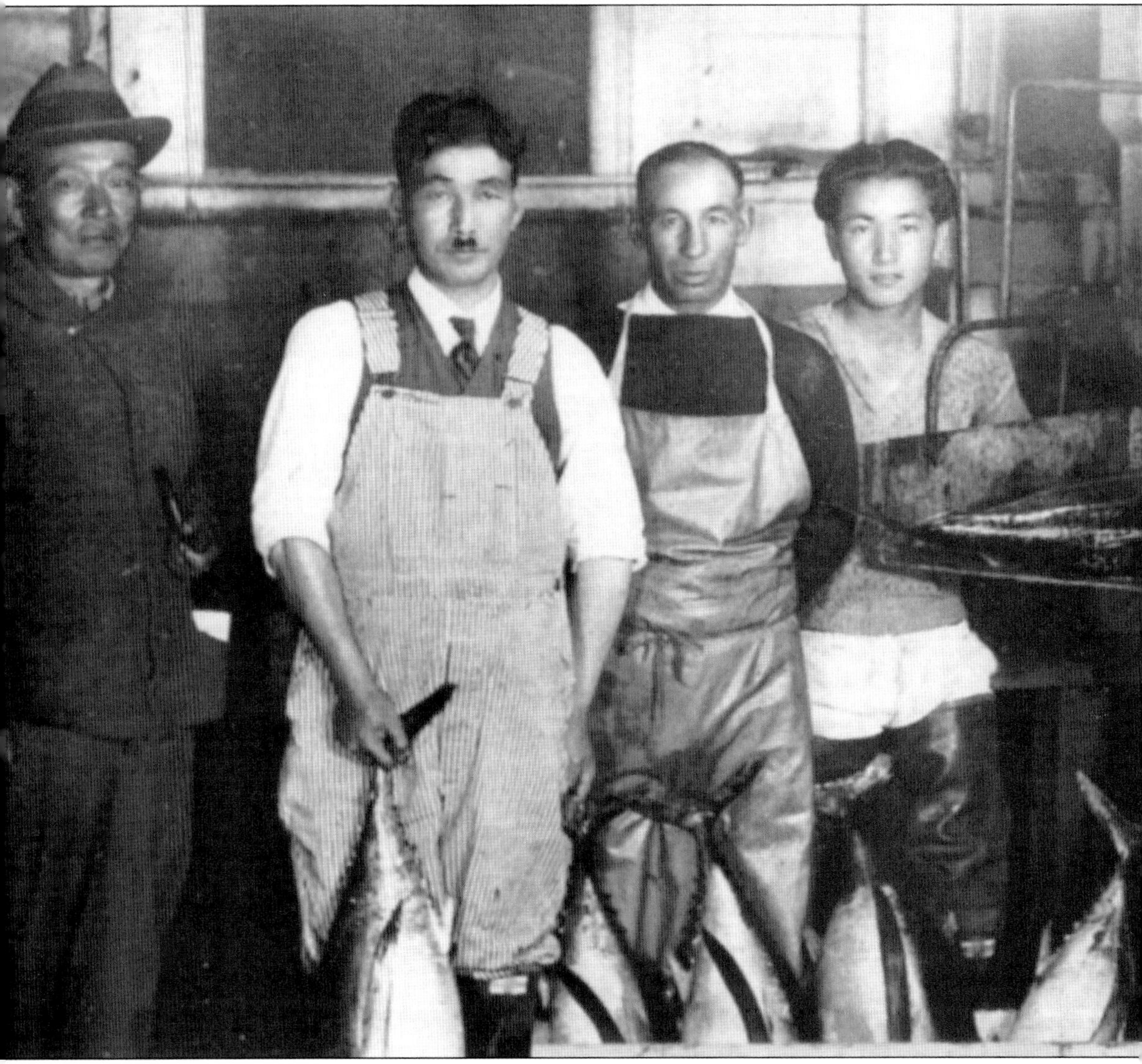

HIGASHI'S FISH COMPANY. Unosuke Higashi, on the left in the overalls, first came to Monterey in 1906 from the Wakayama Prefecture and went into partnership with two other Japanese immigrants, Ikutaro Takigawa and Junichi Oda. He started the Pacific Mutual Fish Company.

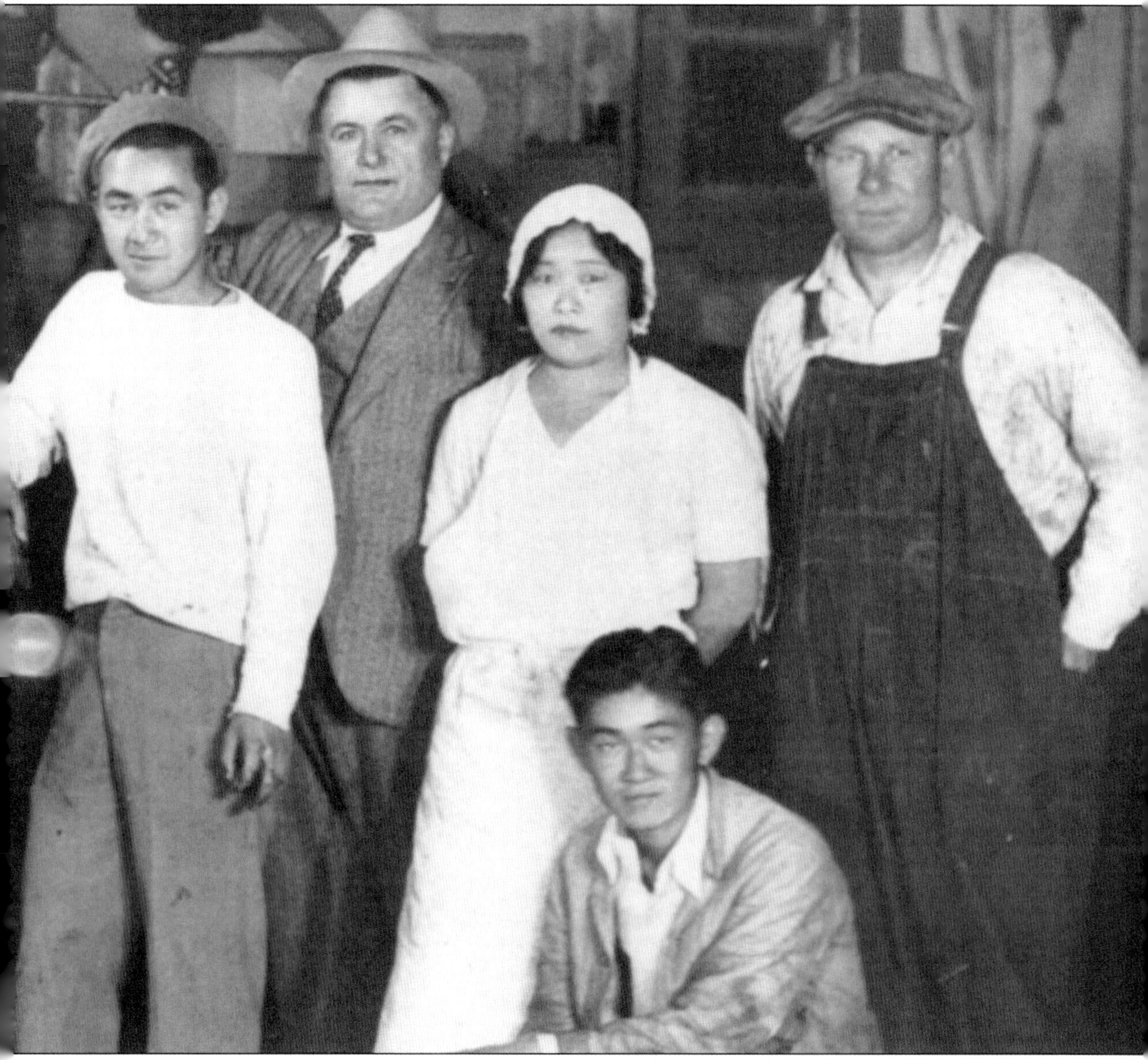

In the early 1930s, he purchased a building on the Monterey Wharf and opened his own market, the Higashi's Fish Company. (Higashi family collection.)

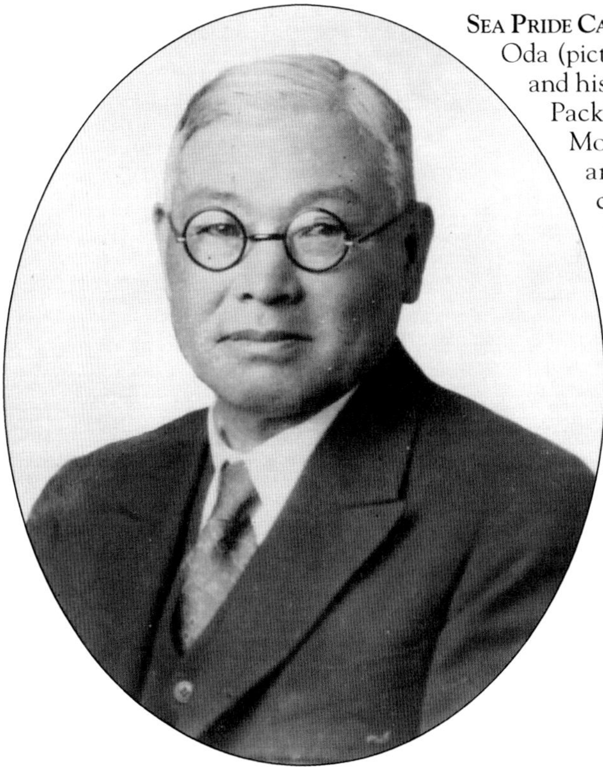

Sea Pride Cannery. On December 17, 1925, Tsunetaro Oda (pictured), from the Wakayama Prefecture, and his partner K. Niino opened the Sea Pride Packing Corp., which is now part of the Monterey Bay Aquarium. It was the first and only completely Japanese-owned cannery on Cannery Row. (Larry Oda family collection.)

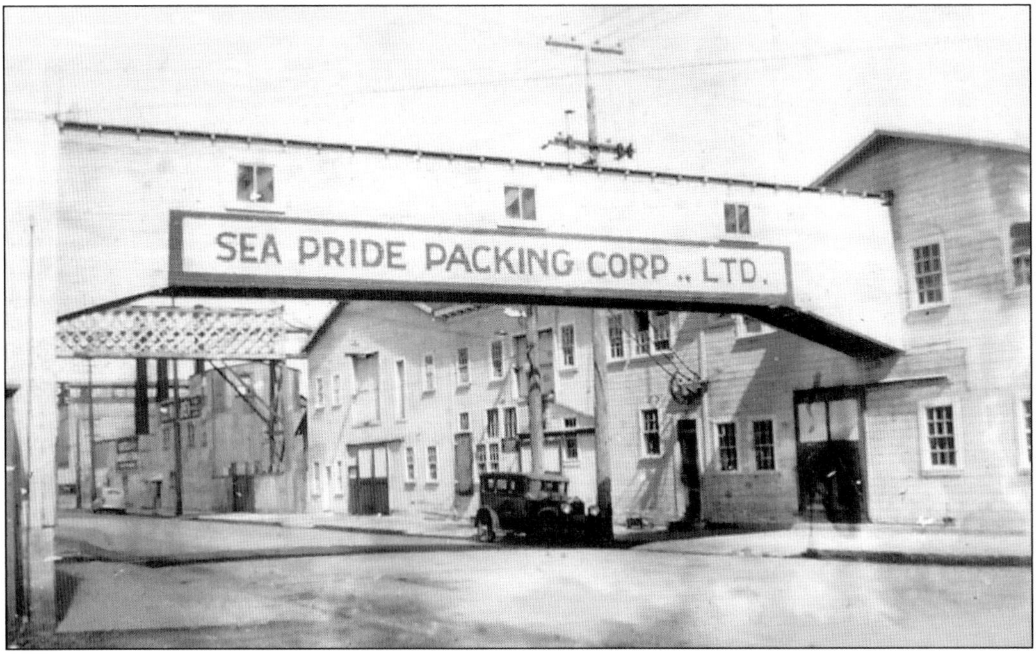

Canning Sardines, Salmon, and Abalone. Sea Pride, like all the other local canneries, packaged sardines, but it also canned salmon and abalone. The business also specialized in reduction products. Reduction is a process where the heads, tails, and offal are grounded up, baked into a powder, and used for fertilizers and animal feeds. (Larry Oda family collection.)

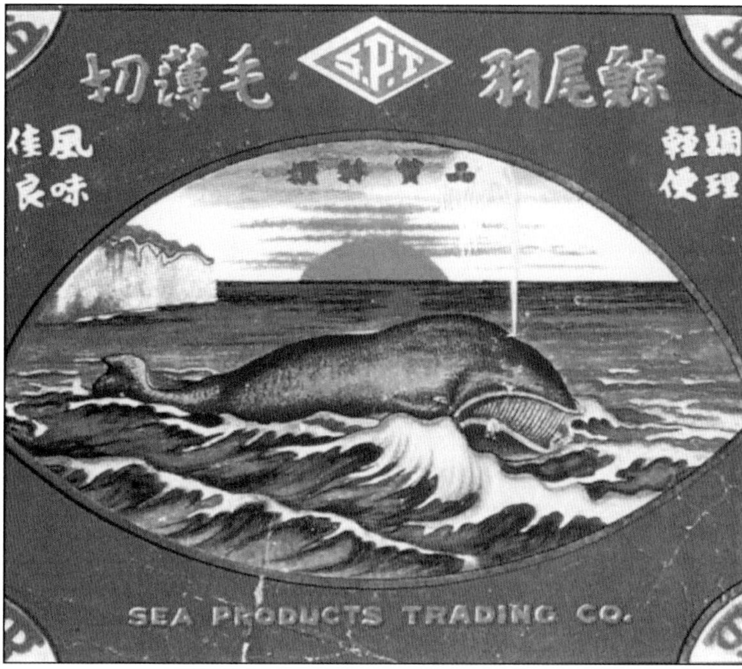

CANNING WHALE MEAT. Working with the California Sea Products whaling company, across the Monterey Bay in Moss Landing, Sea Pride Cannery was also canning whale meat. They had a ready market not only selling to the large Japanese community along the Pacific Coast, from Southern California to Washington State, but they also shipped it to Japan. This lasted for only one year when the whaling company went out of business in 1926. (Pat Sands collection.)

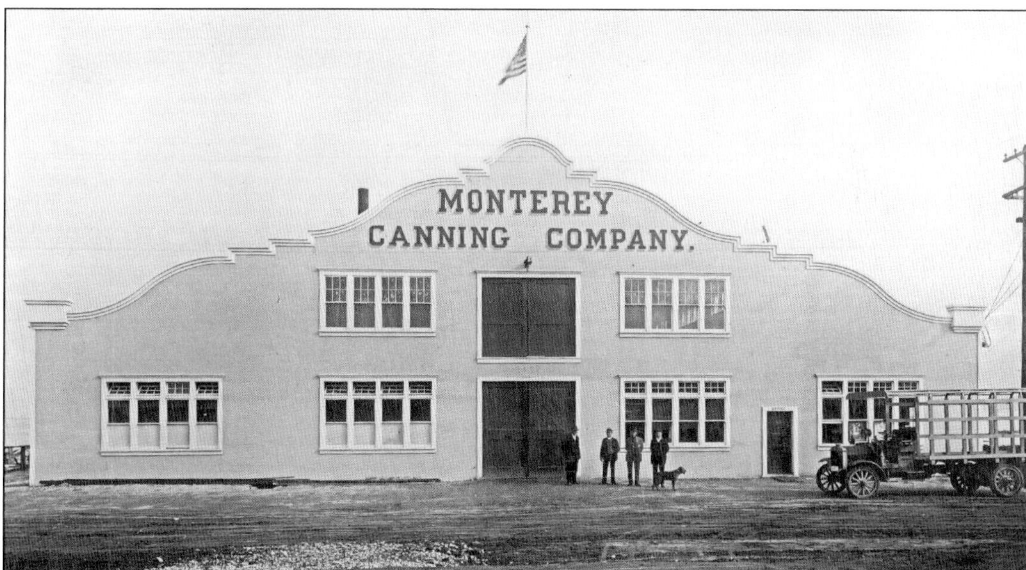

MONTEREY CANNING COMPANY. Built in 1918 to capitalize on the newly developed sardine fishery, Monterey Canning Company was owned by A.M. Allan, of the Point Lobos Abalone Cannery. Before the canneries modernized in the 1920s, all the work was done by hand. It took skilled labor to remove the heads, tails, and offal by hand, and it was mostly Japanese fish-cutters who did that. Allan hired many Japanese workers. (Photograph 1918, California History Room, Monterey Public Library.)

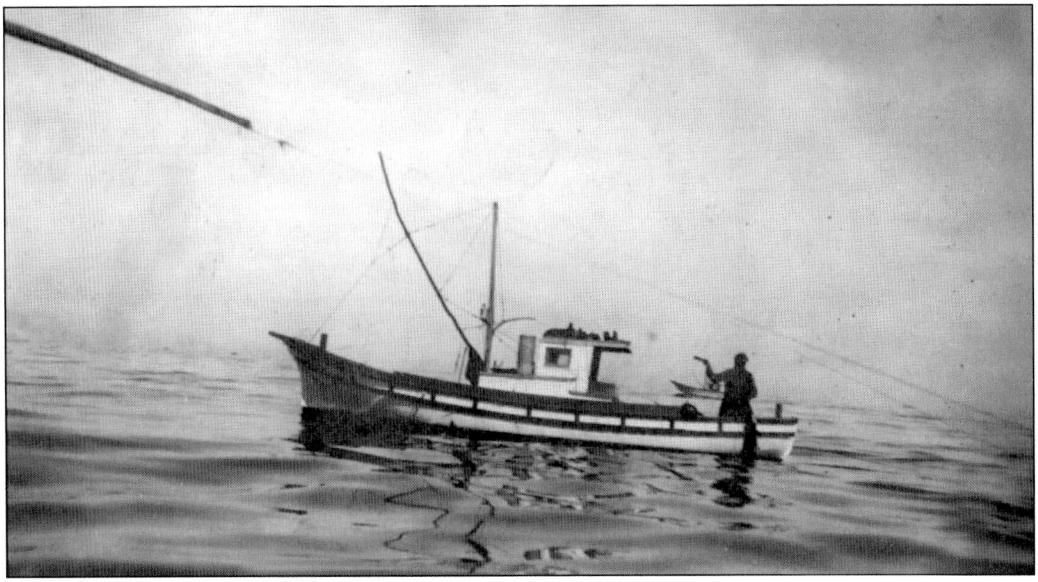

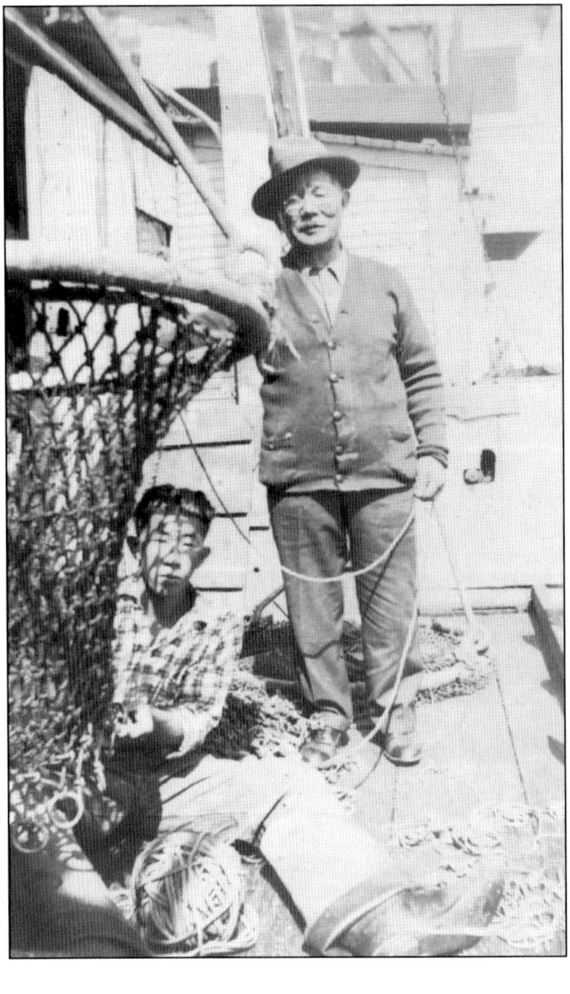

The *Ohio II*. The salmon boat *Ohio II* was owned by the Manaka family in 1918. The Manakas came from the Wakayama Prefecture in 1905 and initially settled in San Francisco, where Tomekichi "Shorty" Manaka first got a job working as a bartender and part-time cook. In 1916, the family moved to Monterey to work in the fishing business with Tomekichi's older brother Yasumatsu "Big" Manaka, who had come to America in 1913. (Manaka family collection.)

Japanese Fish Cutters Strike. During the 1921 Japanese Fish Cutters Strike, cannery owners went to Japanese fishermen and told them that they would not buy any fish from them until the strike was over. The fishermen went to the fish-cutters and asked them to end it, and they did. The end result was no Japanese cannery workers were hired for the entire 1920–1921 sardine season. This photograph shows fisherman Ikuataro Takigawa, owner of Pacific Mutual Wholesale Fishing Co., with his grandson Kiyoshi in 1934. (William Takigawa and Monterey Public Library, California History Room.)

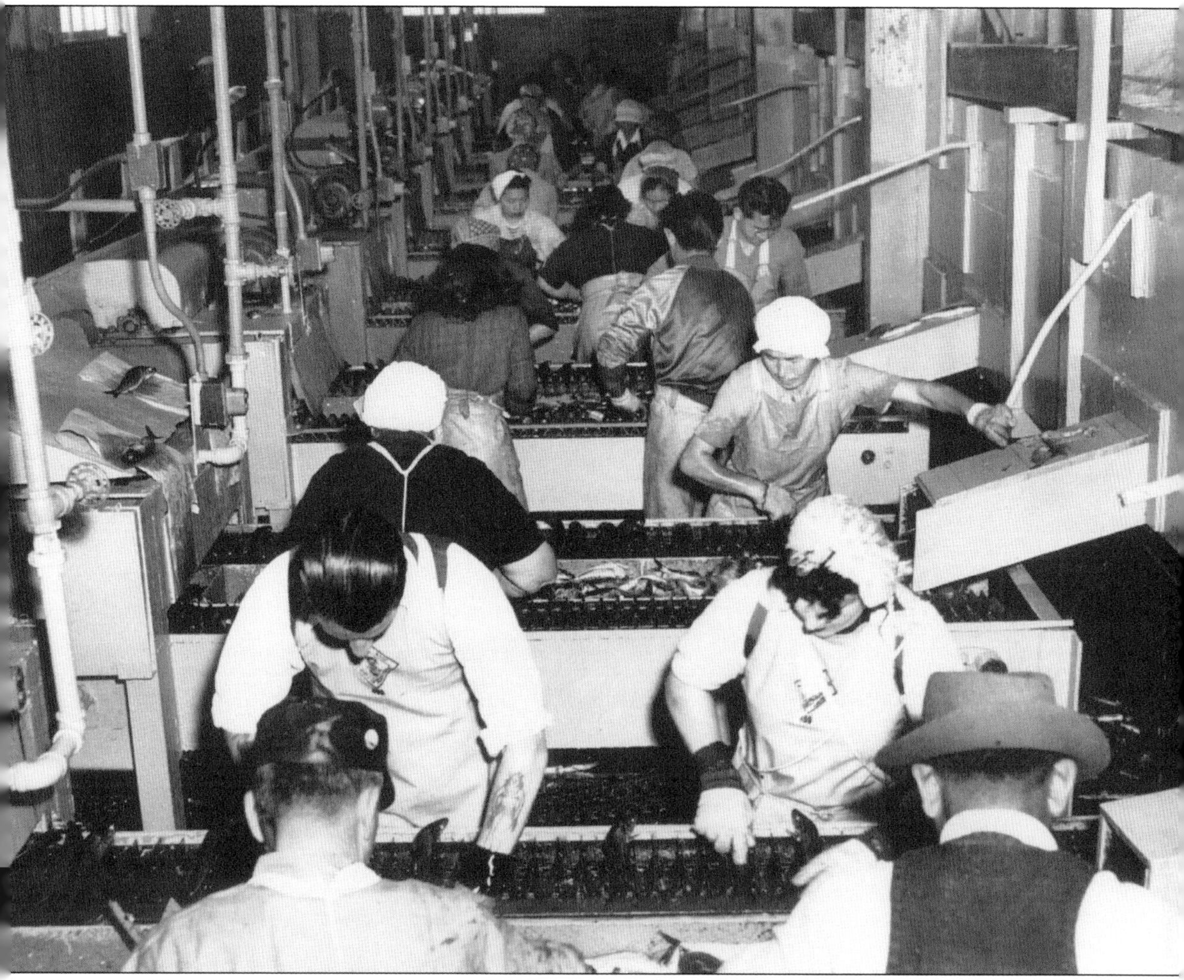

Japanese Fish Cutters, 1930. There were no unions in the Monterey canneries to protect workers until 1938. Conditions and pay varied from cannery to cannery. In 1920, the fish-cutters went on strike. They wanted better working conditions and pay consistency. This became known as the Japanese Fish Cutters Strike of 1920. After a week of work stoppage, cannery owners wanted it to end. They tried to hire housewives, proclaiming that "it's easy work, anyone can do it." (Tom Fordham collection.)

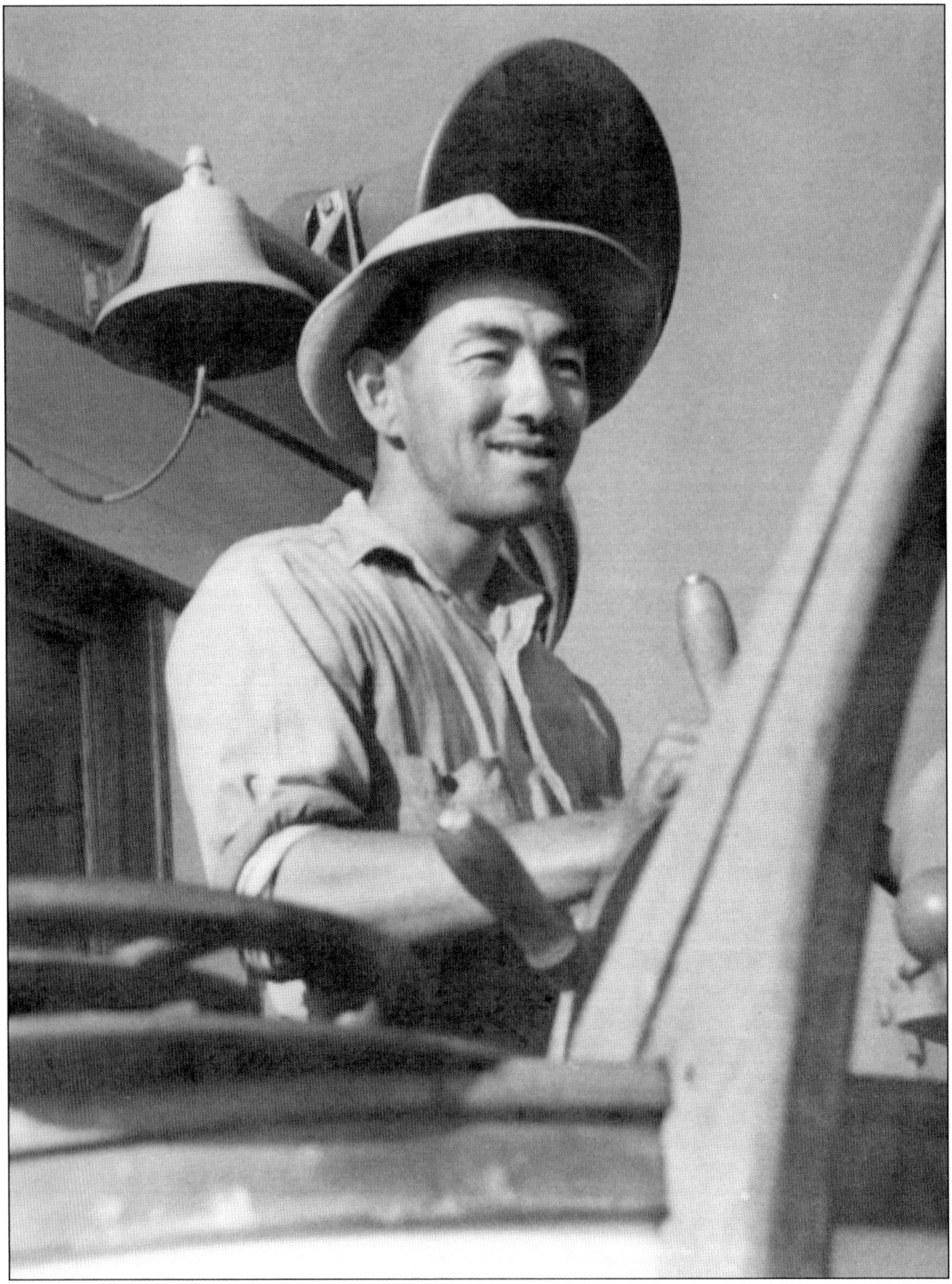

Frank Manaka. Manaka was born in San Francisco in 1908 and moved to Monterey with his family in 1916. The eldest of seven children, Frank went to Monterey schools and dreamed of becoming a baseball player. His father had other ideas and Frank became a fisherman, owning his first boat, *The Ohio III*, when he was just 18 years old. (Manaka family collection.)

Frank's Crew Piles the Net for a Night of Fishing. Frank Manaka was the first nisei, second-generation Japanese resident, to be own a purse seiner, which is a type of sardine boat. In 1928, he struck a deal with the Enterprise Engine Company, agreeing to use one of the company's new diesel engines if it agreed to carry the note on his boat. A new purse seiner in 1928 could cost close to $30,000. (Manaka family collection.)

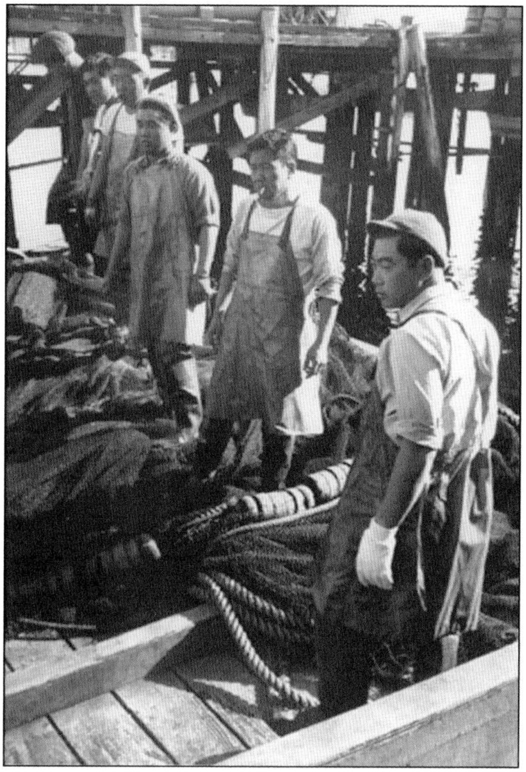

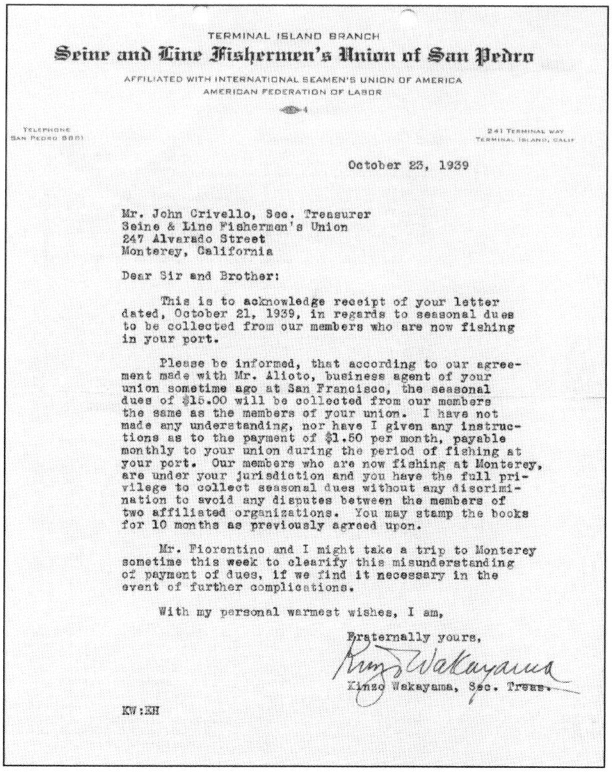

TERMINAL ISLAND BRANCH

Seine and Line Fishermen's Union of San Pedro

AFFILIATED WITH INTERNATIONAL SEAMEN'S UNION OF AMERICA
AMERICAN FEDERATION OF LABOR

TELEPHONE
SAN PEDRO 8881

241 TERMINAL WAY
TERMINAL ISLAND, CALIF

October 23, 1939

Mr. John Crivello, Sec. Treasurer
Seine & Line Fishermen's Union
247 Alvarado Street
Monterey, California

Dear Sir and Brother:

This is to acknowledge receipt of your letter dated, October 21, 1939, in regards to seasonal dues to be collected from our members who are now fishing in your port.

Please be informed, that according to our agreement made with Mr. Alioto, business agent of your union sometime ago at San Francisco, the seasonal dues of $15.00 will be collected from our members the same as the members of your union. I have not made any understanding, nor have I given any instructions as to the payment of $1.50 per month, payable monthly to your union during the period of fishing at your port. Our members who are now fishing at Monterey, are under your jurisdiction and you have the full privilege to collect seasonal dues without any discrimination to avoid any disputes between the members of two affiliated organizations. You may stamp the books for 10 months as previously agreed upon.

Mr. Fiorentino and I might take a trip to Monterey sometime this week to clearify this misunderstanding of payment of dues, if we find it necessary in the event of further complications.

With my personal warmest wishes, I am,

Fraternally yours,

Kinzo Wakayama

Kinzo Wakayama, Sec. Treas.

KW:EH

A Letter for Sardine Hauling. Although the Monterey sardine fishery was a Sicilian fishery, as many as 20 to 25 percent of the fishermen hauling in sardines in any given season could be Japanese, many of them coming up from Southern California. This is a letter from the Japanese Seine and Line Fishermen's Union of San Pedro, California, seeking permission for a group of Japanese fishermen from San Pedro to fish in Monterey. (Tom Fordham collection.)

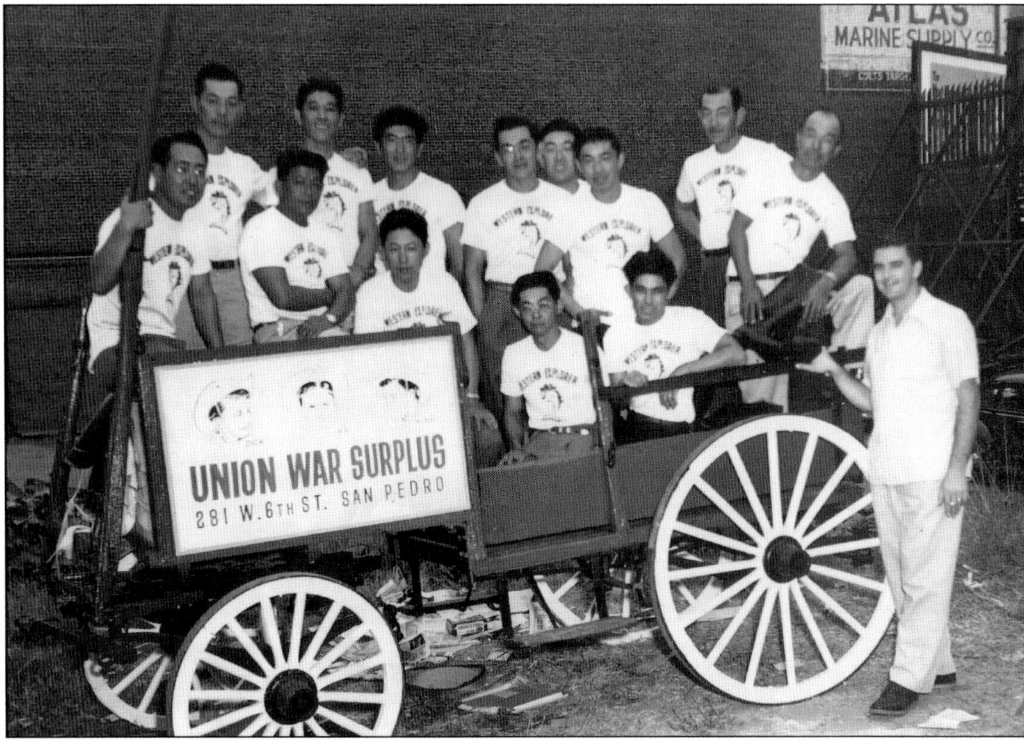

FRANK'S SOUTHERN CALIFORNIAN CREW. After Frank Manaka moved to San Pedro, he hired a crew of local Japanese fishermen. These men came from the same area in Japan as Frank. When the sardine fishery collapsed in Monterey, many of the Monterey Sicilian fishermen moved to San Pedro to fish tuna but had no experience. Frank became their teacher. (Manaka family collection.)

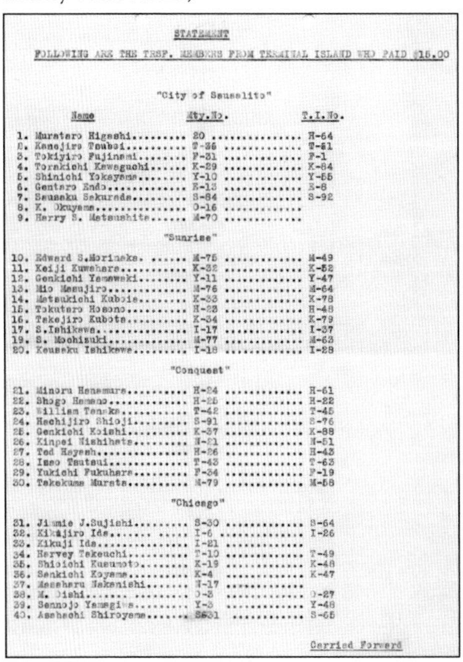

STATEMENT

FOLLOWING ARE THE TRSF. MEMBERS FROM TERMINAL ISLAND WHO PAID $15.00

"City of Sausalito"

	Name	Mty.No.	T.I.No.
1.	Murataro Higashi	20	H-64
2.	Kanejiro Tsuboi	T-36	T-61
3.	Tokiyiro Fujinami	F-31	F-1
4.	Torakichi Kawaguchi	K-29	K-84
5.	Shinichi Yokayama	Y-10	Y-55
6.	Gentaro Endo	E-13	E-8
7.	Sausaku Sakurada	S-84	S-92
8.	K. Okuyama	O-16	
9.	Harry S. Matsushita	M-70	

"Sunrise"

	Name	Mty.No.	T.I.No.
10.	Edward S.Morinaka.	M-75	M-49
11.	Keiji Kuwahara	K-32	K-52
12.	Genkichi Yamawaki	Y-11	Y-47
13.	Mio Masujiro	M-76	M-64
14.	Matsukichi Kuboia	K-33	K-78
15.	Tokutaro Hosono	H-23	H-48
16.	Takejiro Kubota	K-34	K-79
17.	S.Ishikawa.	I-17	I-37
19.	S. Mochizuki	M-77	M-63
20.	Kausaku Ishikawa	I-18	I-28

"Conquest"

	Name	Mty.No.	T.I.No.
21.	Minoru Hanamura	H-24	H-61
22.	Shogo Hamano	H-25	H-22
23.	William Tanaka	T-42	T-45
24.	Hachijiro Shioji	S-91	S-76
25.	Genkichi Koishi	K-37	K-88
26.	Kinpei Nishihata	N-21	N-51
27.	Ted Hayash	H-26	H-43
28.	Isao Tsutsui	T-43	T-63
29.	Yukichi Fukuhara	F-34	F-19
30.	Takakuma Murata	M-79	M-58

"Chicago"

	Name	Mty.No.	T.I.No.
31.	Jimmie J.Sujishi	S-30	S-64
32.	Kikajiro Ida	I-6	I-26
33.	Kikuji Ida	I-21	
34.	Harvey Takeuchi	T-10	T-49
35.	Shioichi Kusumoto	K-19	K-48
36.	Senkichi Koyama	K-4	K-47
37.	Masaharu Nakanishi	N-17	
38.	M. Oishi	O-3	O-27
39.	Sennojo Yamagiwa	Y-3	Y-48
40.	Asahachi Shiroyama	S631	S-65

Carried Forward

SAN PEDRO UNION LIST. This is a partial list sent from the San Pedro Union with the names of the fishermen who would fish in Monterey for the 1939 season. Because the Monterey Sicilian and Japanese boys all grew up and played together, Monterey is the only place in California where there was just one union. In San Pedro or San Francisco, there were separate organizations. (Tom Fordham collection.)

The Net is Being Piled. Frank Manaka employed fishermen whom he grew up with and went to school with. A sardine boat like this one required 12 men to run it. The net is the most important tool on the boat and can cost up to $15,000. It was made of cotton and needed constant care and repair. (Manaka family collection.)

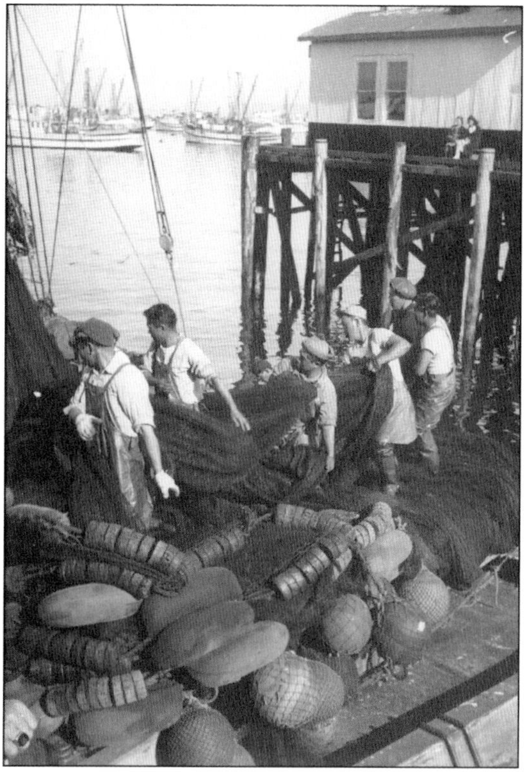

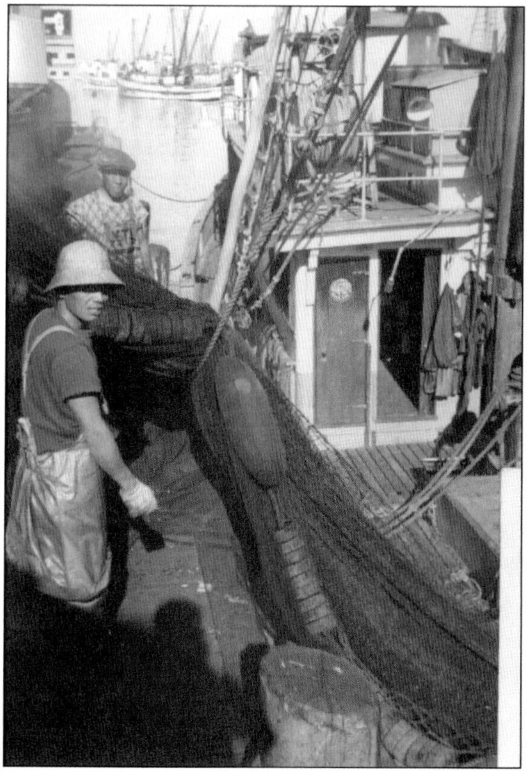

Working the Net. In Monterey, there were a few Japanese-owned fishing supply stores that catered to the Japanese fishermen, such as R. Ono & Co., Menda Ship Chandlery & Grocery, and Owashi Ship Chandlery & Grocery. It was not uncommon for fishing supply stores to have a grocery. The crew needed to be fed. (Manaka family collection.)

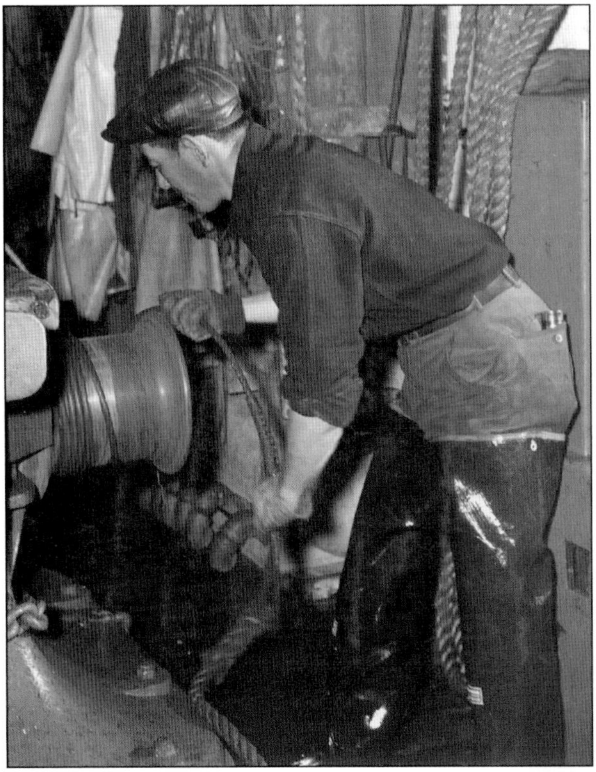

Frank Works the Power Winch, Bringing in the Net, c. 1938. The net was 1,800 feet in circumference and was dropped to a depth of 200 feet. When filled with fish, it weighed up to 100 tons. (Manaka family collection.)

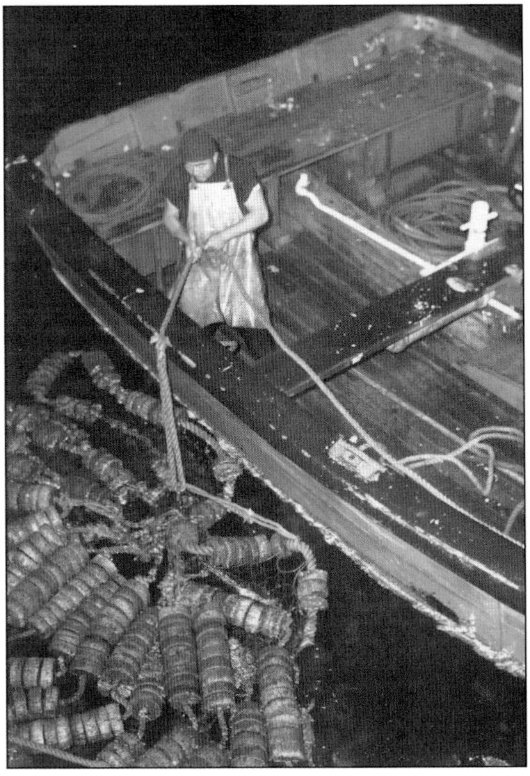

The Cords are Bunched by the Skiff Man, c. 1938. The net is weighed down with lead weights with corks on the top to make it float. When laying out the net, the skiff will take the front end of the net and go clockwise, while the big boat goes counterclockwise until they circle the school of sardines, capturing them in a large hempen fence. (Manaka family collection)

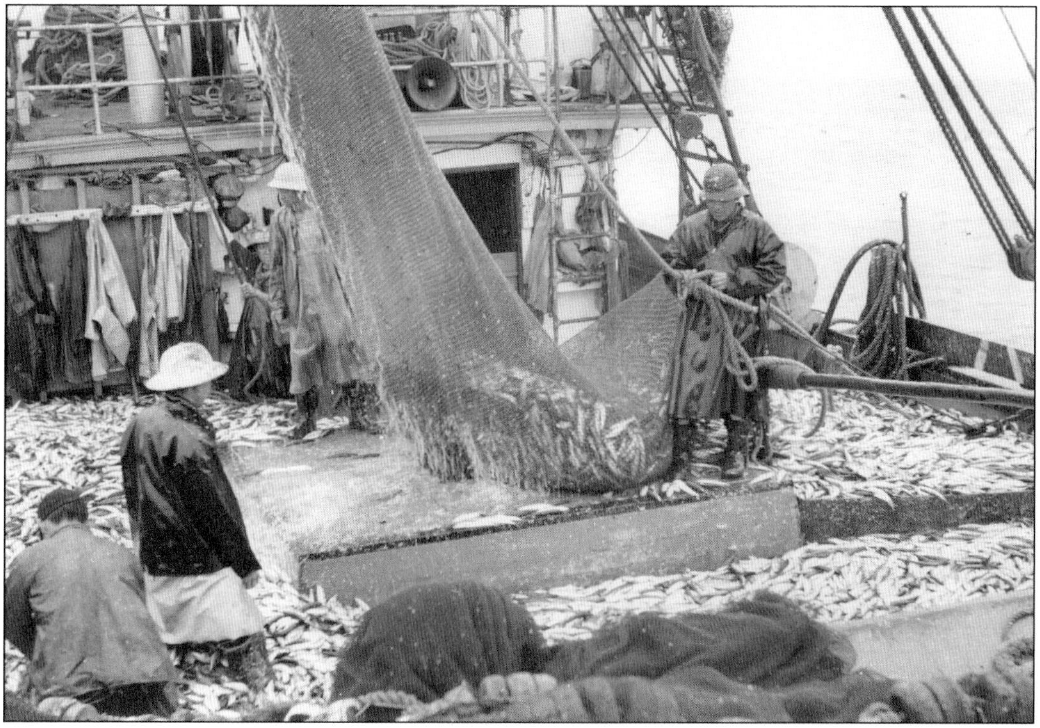

A DECK LOAD, C. 1938. Using the winch, Frank Manaka would close the net at the bottom like a purse. He had so many sardines in this load that he had to put the rest on the deck. There are probably 150 tons of sardines onboard. (Manaka family collection.)

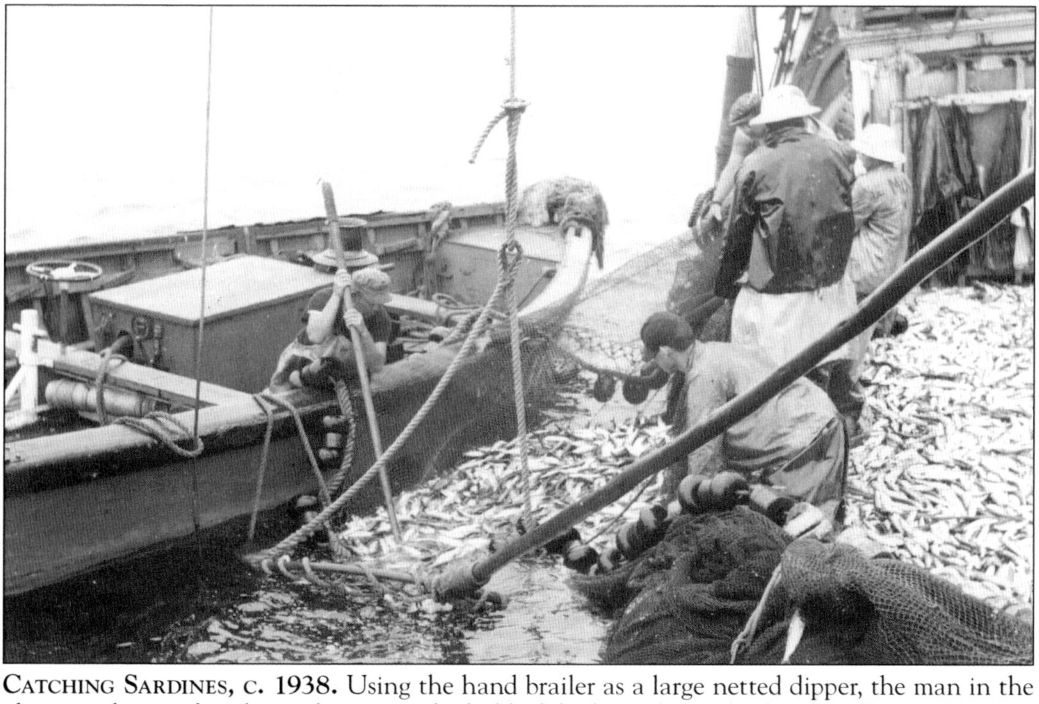

CATCHING SARDINES, C. 1938. Using the hand brailer as a large netted dipper, the man in the photograph transfers the sardines into the hold of the boat. (Manaka family collection.)

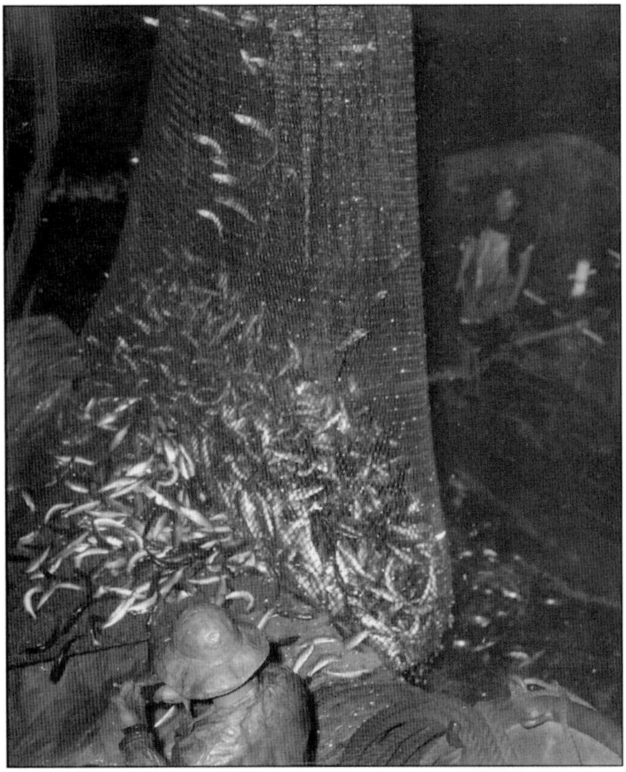

BUTTERFLY NET, C. 1938. The mechanical brailer looks similar to a huge butterfly net. (Manaka family collection.)

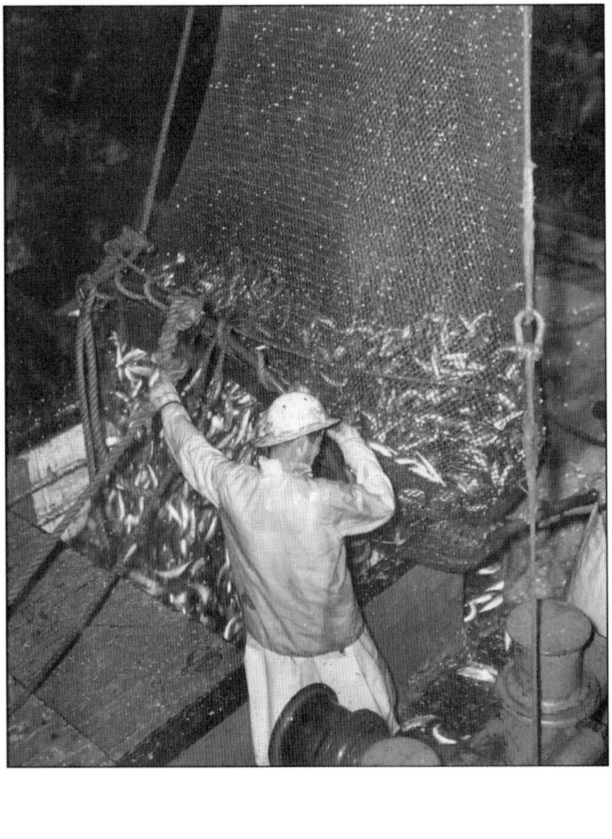

TRANSFERRING SARDINES, C. 1938. Sardines are transferred into the hold of the boat. (Manaka family collection.)

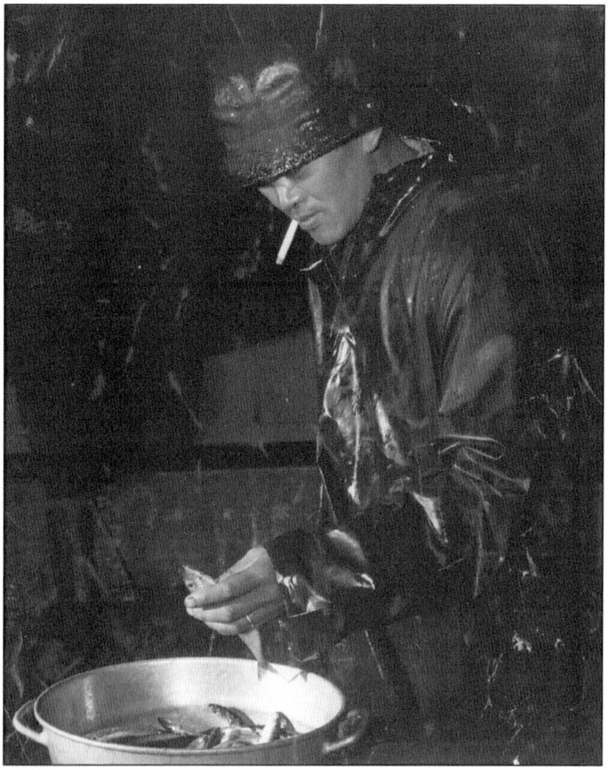

Frank's Younger Brother Harry, c. 1938. Pictured here is Frank Manaka's younger brother Harry who is checking the size of the sardines. Although there was no limit to how many sardines they could catch, there was a limit to the size. They sardine had to be at least 7 inches long before it could be taken. If after measuring a sample and they were too small, even if they were 63/4, they would have to dump the entire catch. (Manaka family collection.)

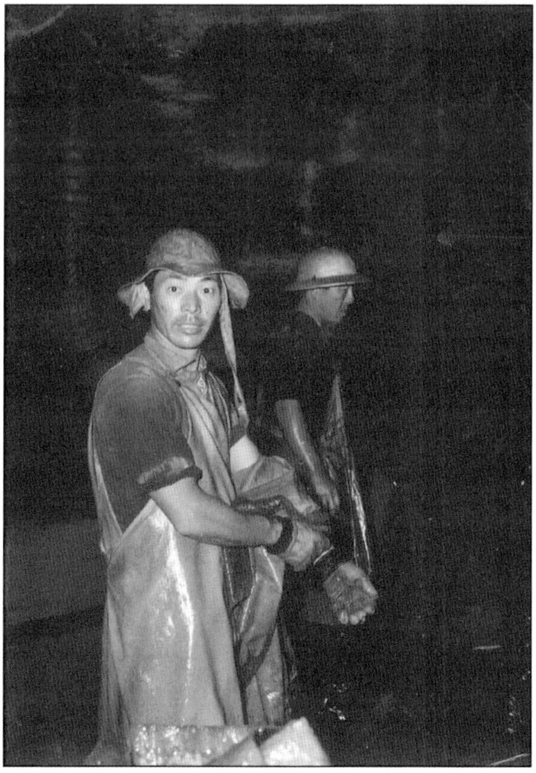

The Dark of the Moon, c. 1938. Sardine fishing was done at night at the "dark of the moon." Sardines are nocturnal and feed on a small phosphorescent animal. So the fishermen would look for the milky glow and the "fire in the water" that could be an acre in size. (Manaka family collection.)

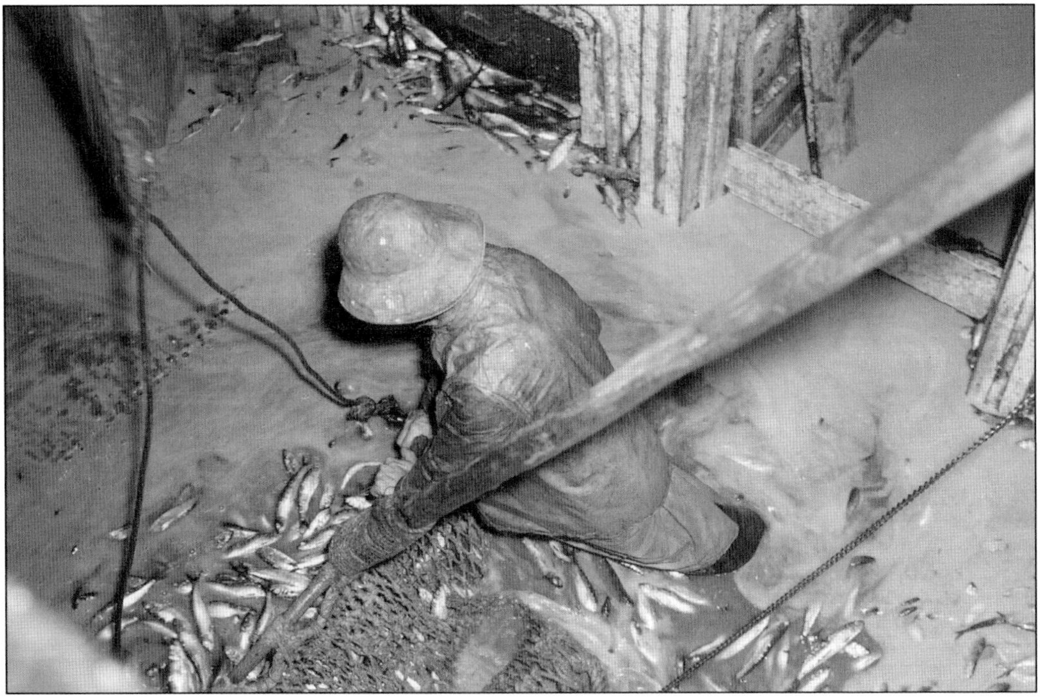

Working Hard, c. 1938. Working in the hold of the boat was a hard, cold, and wet job. (Manaka family collection.)

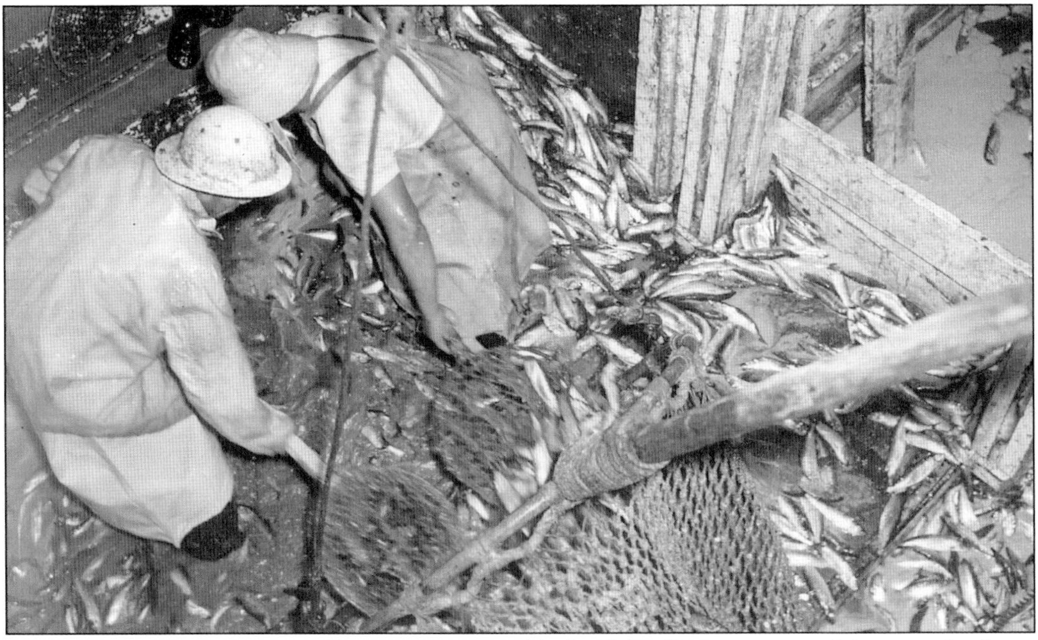

Brailing the Fish into the Hopper, c. 1938. Each of the 19 canneries in Monterey had one or two floating hoppers for the fishermen to unload their catches. The hopper was anchored with two flotation devices about 500 feet from shore. A marine pump sent the fish in the hopper directly through steel pipes to the canneries. These hoppers could take 70 tons an hour. (Manaka family collection.)

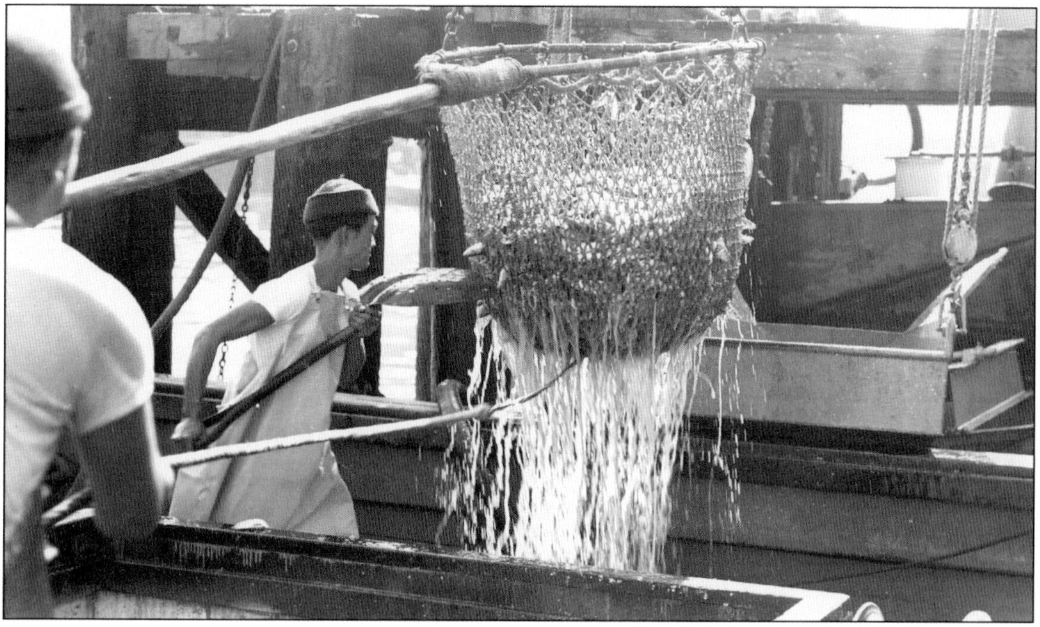

Monterey Sardine Fishermen, c. 1938. At the beginning of every season, the Monterey sardine fishermen would negotiate with the canneries for the price of sardines per ton. From that figure, Frank Manaka would determine the pay for his crew. Wages depended on many factors, such as the job, seniority on the boat, and how many shares a crewman would get. (Manaka family collection.)

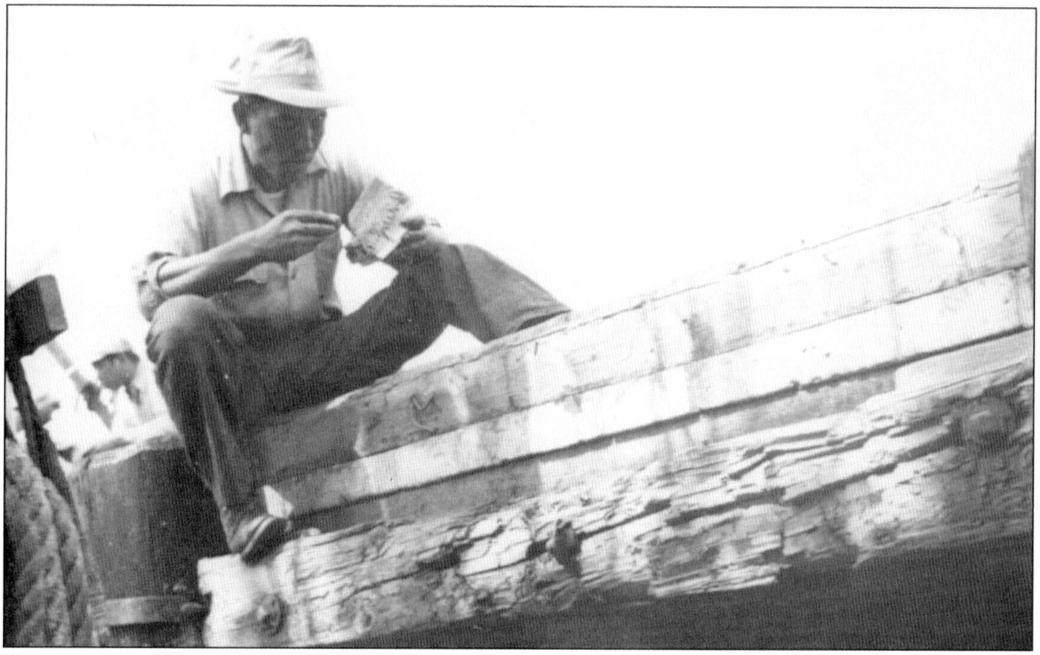

The Monterey Sardine Season, c. 1950. The sardine season in Monterey was from August 1 to February 15, and the fishermen fished Sunday through Friday, except the two days before a full moon and the two days after it, when the moon was too bright. During that time, fishermen worked on the boat, repaired the net, and spent time with family. (Manaka family collection.)

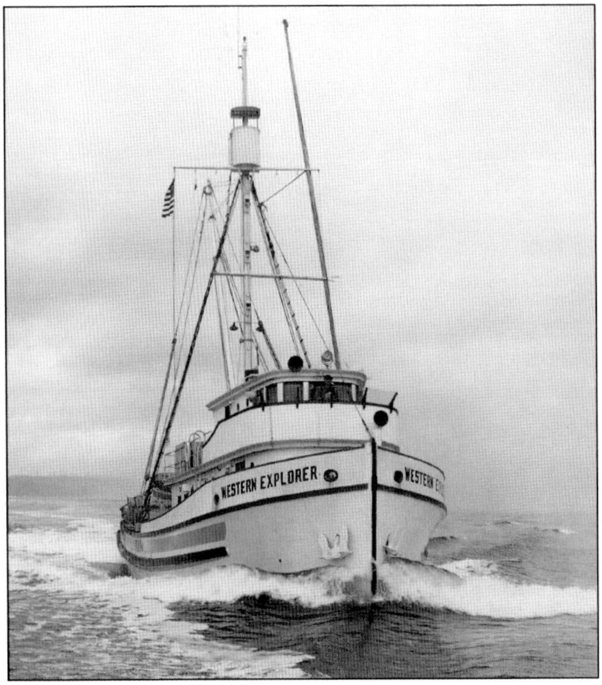

THE *WESTERN EXPLORER*, C. 1948. During the Great Depression, Frank Manaka had a hard time paying the note on his boat *Ohio III*. He went to the Enterprise Engine Company and met with the owner Frank Gilmore to try to work something out. Because Gilmore and Frank were both great baseball fans, they ended up talking more about baseball than financing. And Gilmore agreed to renegotiate the terms on Franks boat. (Manaka family collection.)

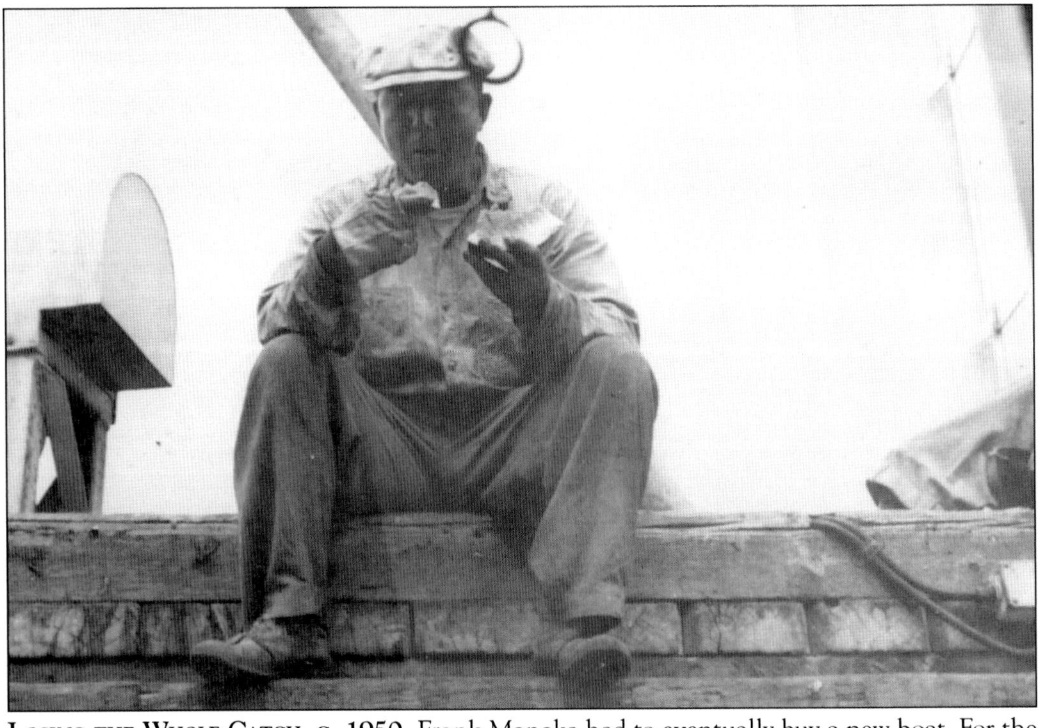

LOSING THE WHOLE CATCH, C. 1950. Frank Manaka had to eventually buy a new boat. For the 1939 sardine season, he leased a boat from San Pedro. He brought it up and fished that first night. When Frank attempted to unload, he was stopped by the Monterey fishermen's union because he had an "outside boat." He had to dump his whole catch. Frank had to lease a local boat for the 1939 season. (Manaka family collection.)

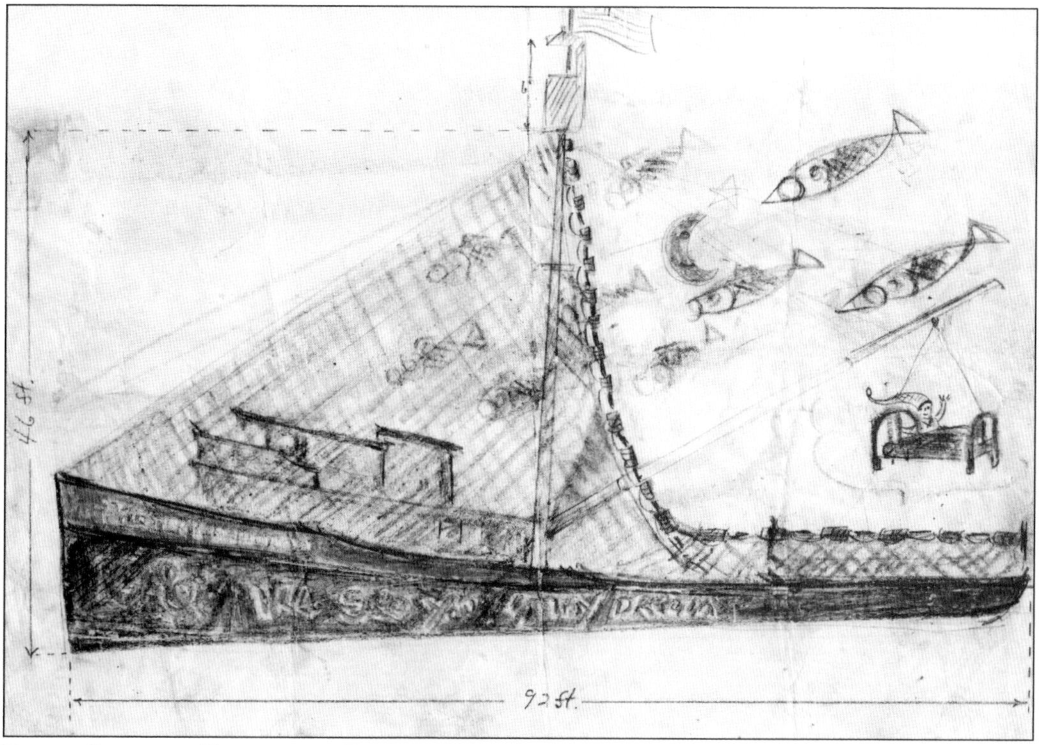

Frank Sued the Union and Bought a New Boat, c. 1950. It took a few years, but Frank Manaka eventually won against the union, giving him enough money to buy a new boat named the *Western Explorer.* He became one of a handful of California Japanese fisherman to own his own boat. After the sardine fishery crashed in Monterey, Frank moved to San Pedro to fish tuna, and he developed the annual Fishermen's Fiesta. This drawing was how Frank decorated his vessel for the 1951 parade of boats. The theme was "In Your Dreams." (Manaka family collection.)

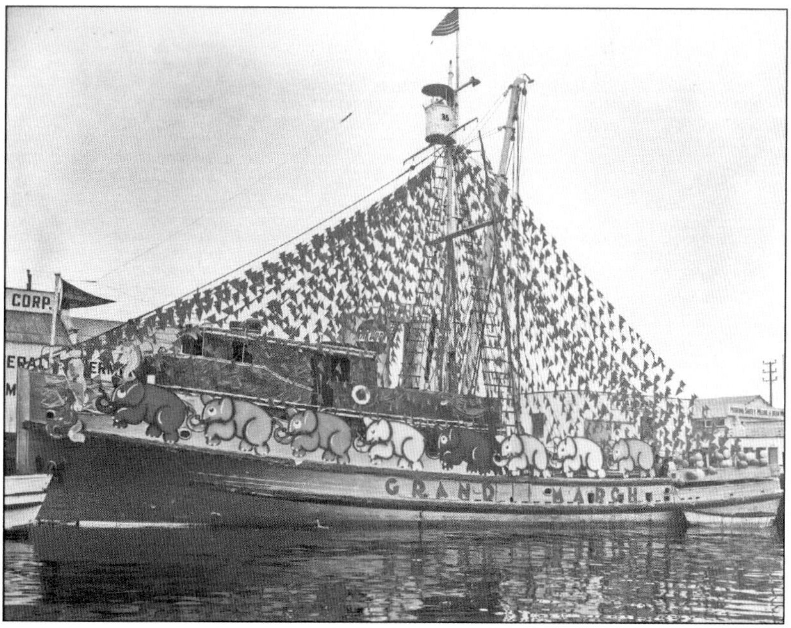

Circus Boat. Here is the *Western Explorer* decorated for a 1952 parade with a circus theme. (Manaka family collection.)

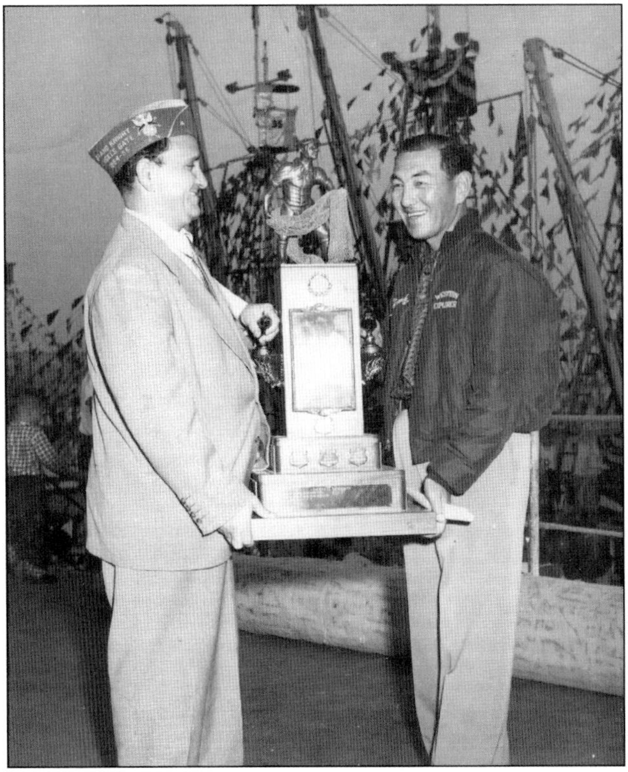

Top Tuna Fisherman. Frank Manaka became one of the best tuna fishermen in all of California. Many of the Sicilian fishermen from Monterey, the same men who made Frank dump his catch in 1939 because he had an outside boat, came to him and asked if he would be their teacher. They wanted Frank to instruct them how to fish tuna, and he did. He won Top Tuna Fisherman for the 1952 season. (Manaka family collection.)

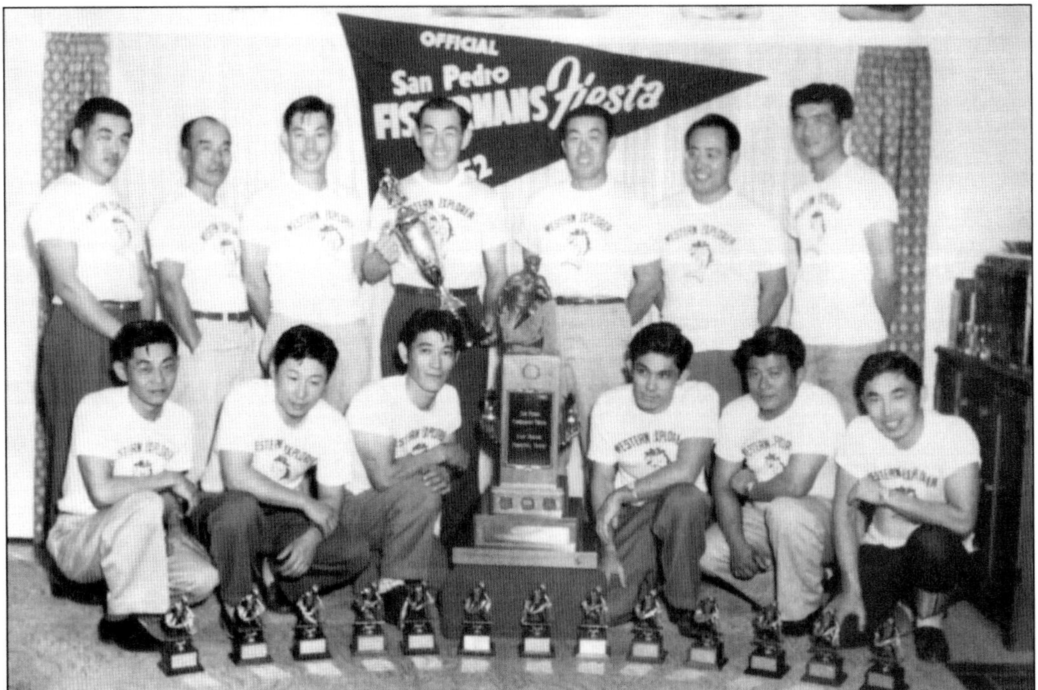

The Top Boat Prize. Here are Frank Manaka (second row, fourth from left) and his crew with their trophies after winning the Top Boat prize in the 1952 season. (Manaka family collection.)

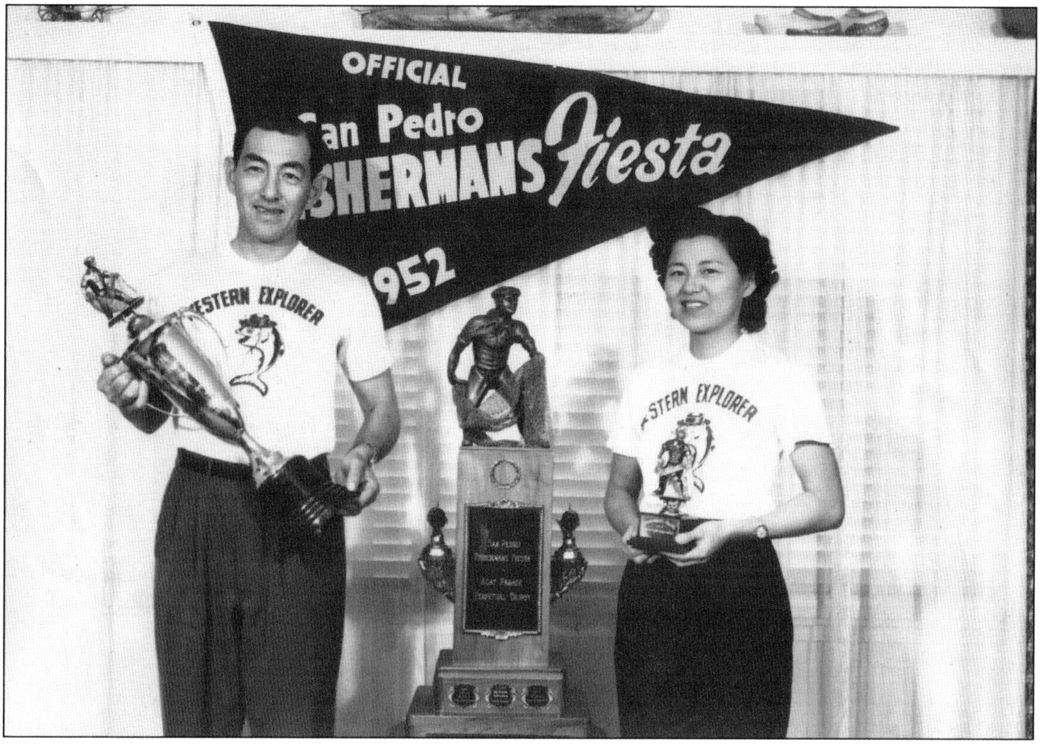

Frank and his wife, Mitsie, in 1952. Frank went on to become one of the best tuna fishermen in all of California. This image shows Frank and his wife holding the championship trophies for top boat and best in show at the 1952 Fisherman's Fiesta. (Manaka family collection.)

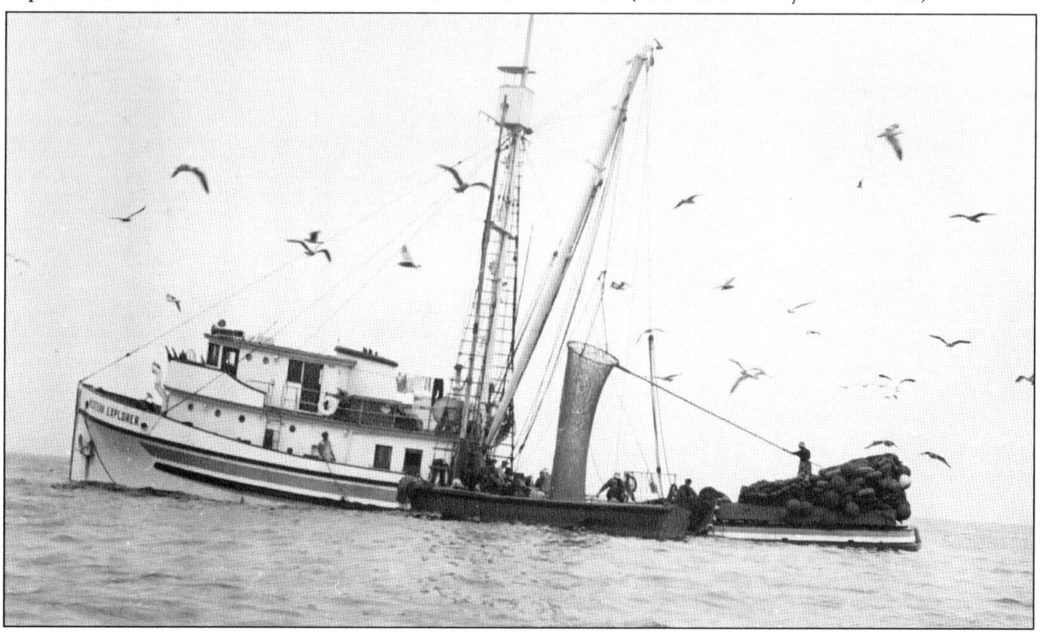

The *Western Explorer* Coming in with a Full Load, c. 1948. The boat is sitting very low in the water. Frank Manaka fished into the early 1970s and was a lifelong baseball fan. He died on his 100th birthday. (Manaka family collection.)

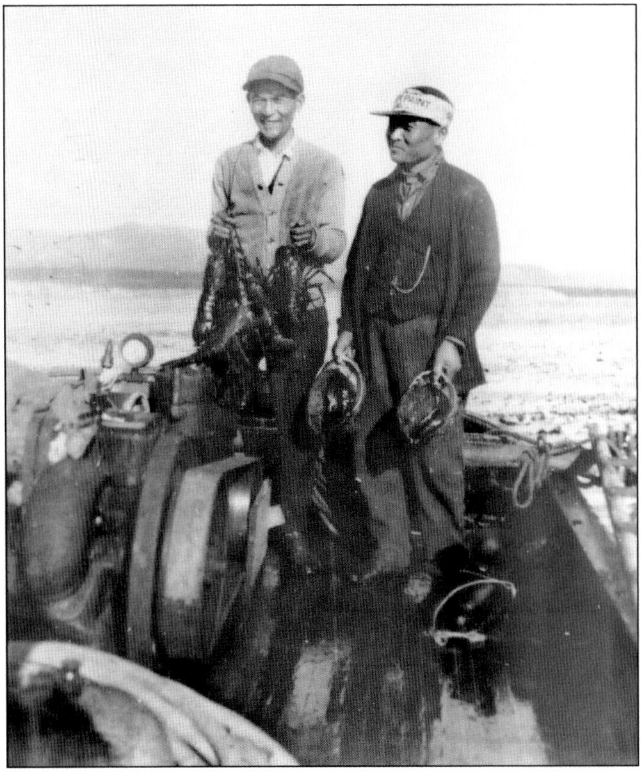

Japanese Abalone Companies. It was abalone that first brought the Japanese to Monterey. By 1920, Pop Ernest's abalone recipe resulted in nine different Japanese abalone companies that worked off the Monterey Wharf. Pictured here are two Monterey abalone fishermen, Toichiro Takigawa (left) and Tanosuke Esaki, in Takigawa's abalone boat in 1925. (William Takigawa and Monterey Public Library, California History Room.)

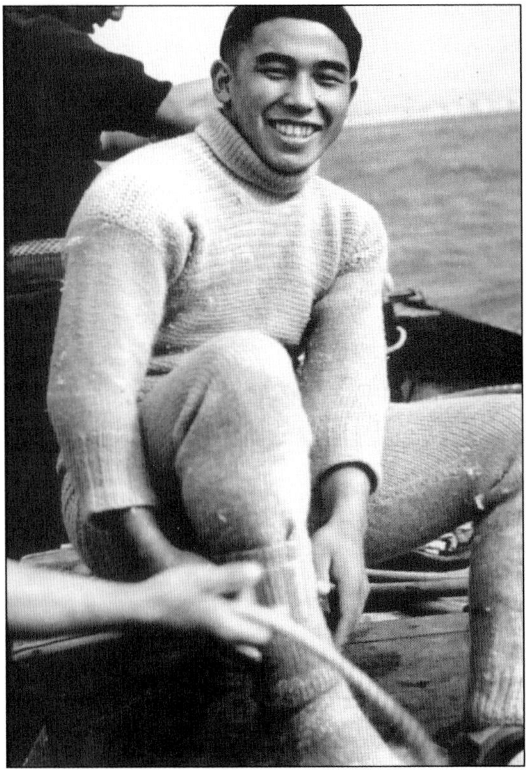

Roy Hattori in His Wool Diving Underwear, c. 1938. Roy was the only nisei diver in Monterey. All the other divers came from Japan and, with few exceptions, most returned to Japan. But Roy was born in Monterey in 1919. His father wanted to start a cloisonné business but could not find the proper clay. With no fishing experience whatsoever, he came to Monterey because he heard the fishing was good. (Hattori family collection.)

Dive Boat, c. 1938. Roy Hattori (diver) was 17 years old when he learned to dive. His father borrowed some equipment and took him out into the harbor, dressed him in the gear, bolted on the helmet, and tossed him off the boat. He told him to "start running down there." Luckily for Roy, a few of the old-timers showed him what to do. Roy's brother James is on the ladder, and their cousin stands in back. (Hattori family collection.)

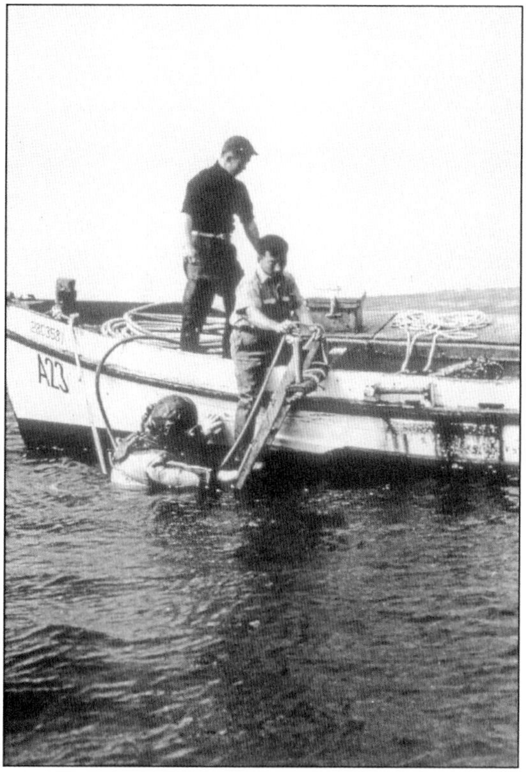

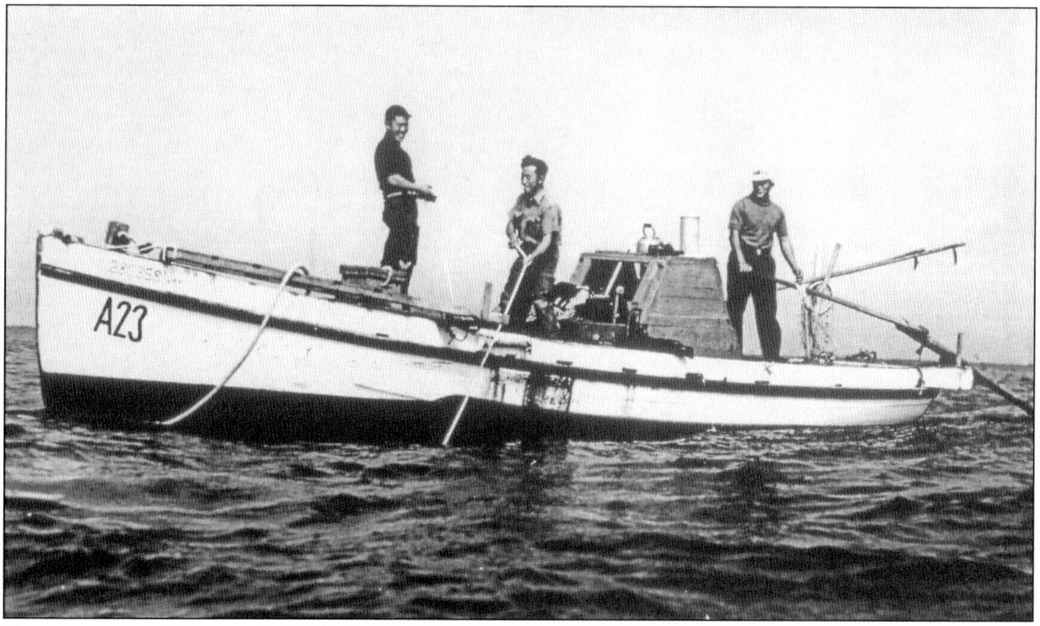

Divers in the Water, c. 1938. Sometimes the currents can be very strong, throw a diver against a cliff, and cause many problems. Roy was thrown once and cracked the glass in his helmet. With little time to think, he reached into his abalone basket, pulled out a large abalone, and stuck it on his mask, which sealed up the crack and saved his life. Note the shoes and teakettle. (Hattori family collection.)

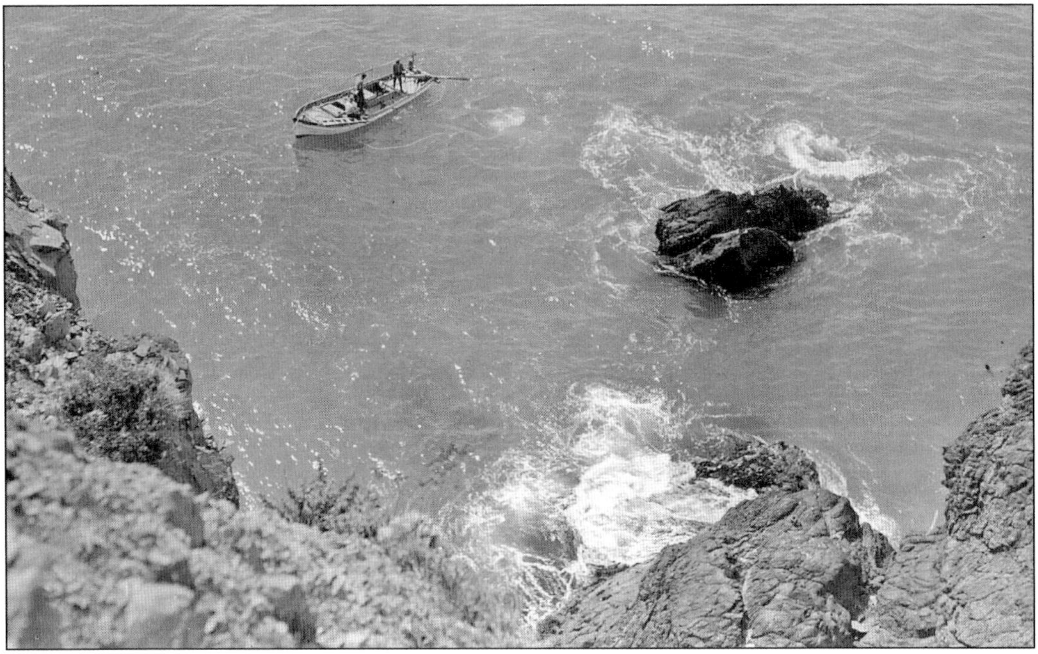

A Typical Abalone-Fishing Day. Taken in 1938, this is the only known photograph of a working abalone boat in Monterey Bay. A typical day for a diver in 1930 would start at 9:00 a.m. with the first dive, which lasted three hours. After returning to the surface for lunch, the diver would continue with the second dive at 1:00 p.m., and the men stayed down until 4:00 p.m.

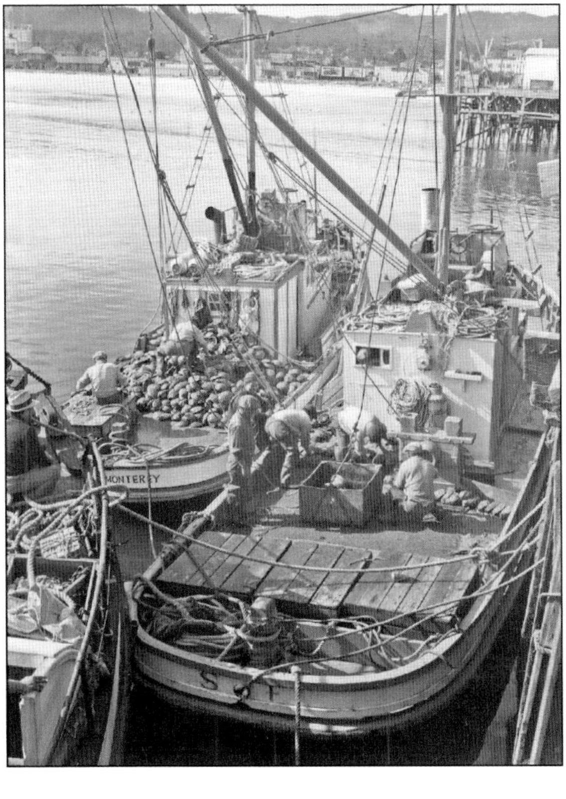

The Mother Boat, c. 1938. Besides pulling the smaller dive boat, the diver and crew lived on this boat during the three-to-five-day abalone trips. A typical diving trip would yield 150–200 dozen abalones. The fishermen received about $1.50 a dozen. (Tom Fordham collection.)

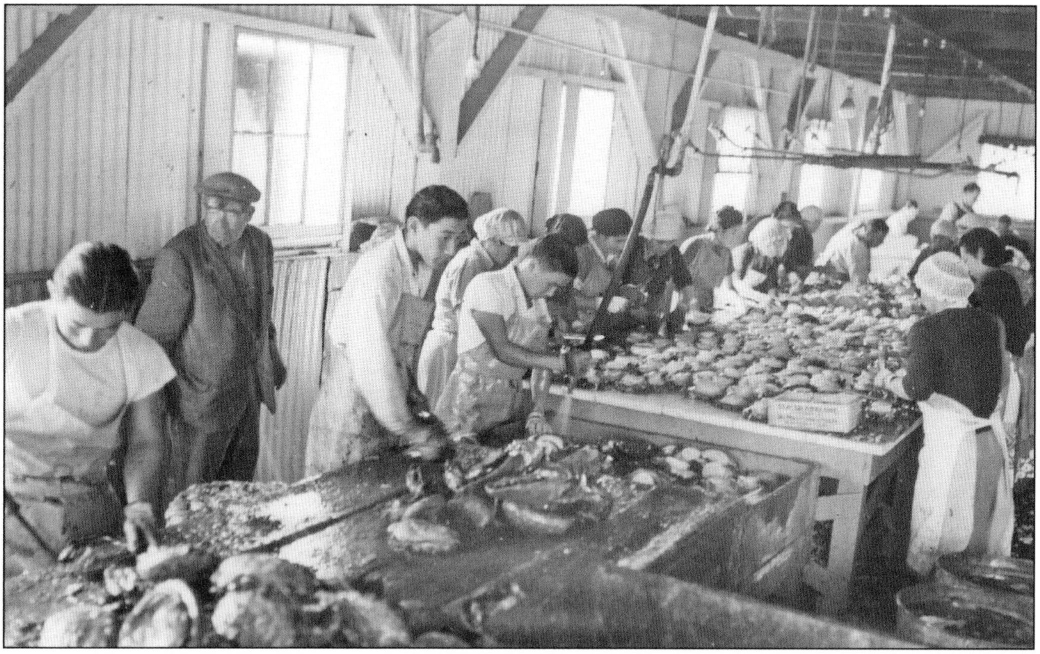

In the Abalone Cannery, c. 1938. The abalone canneries operating on the Monterey Wharf were almost all Japanese-owned and, with few exceptions, used mostly Japanese labor. These workers are removing the abalone from the shell in preparation for processing. (Monterey Library Collection.)

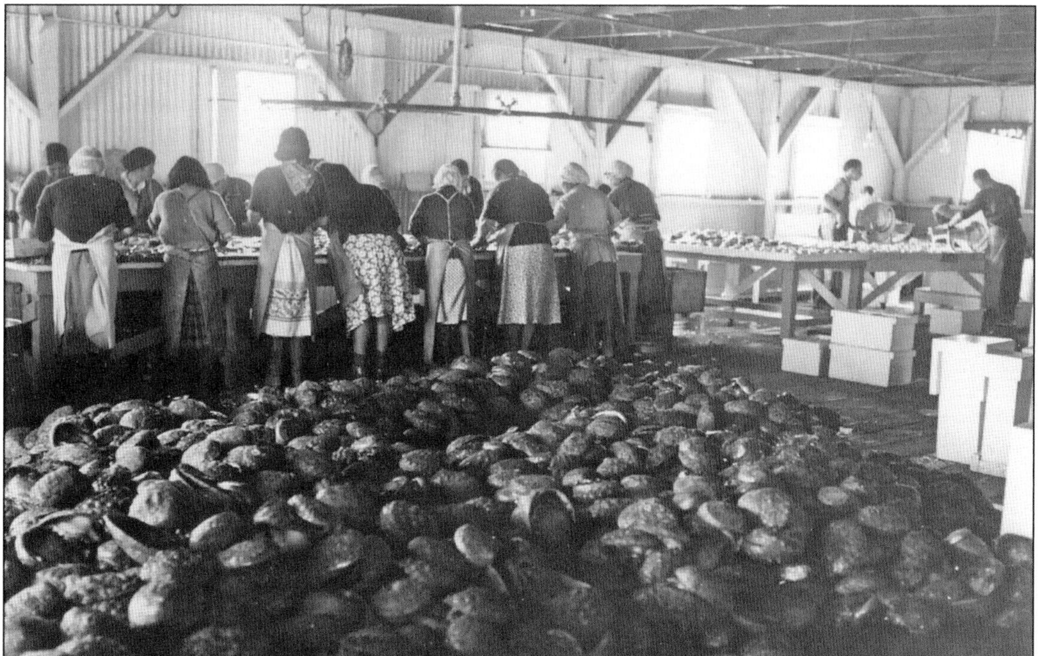

Processing the Abalone, c. 1938. These ladies are trimming the abalone and getting it ready to be sliced. Special large abalone steaks would be cut just for Pop Ernest's restaurant. (Monterey Library Collection.)

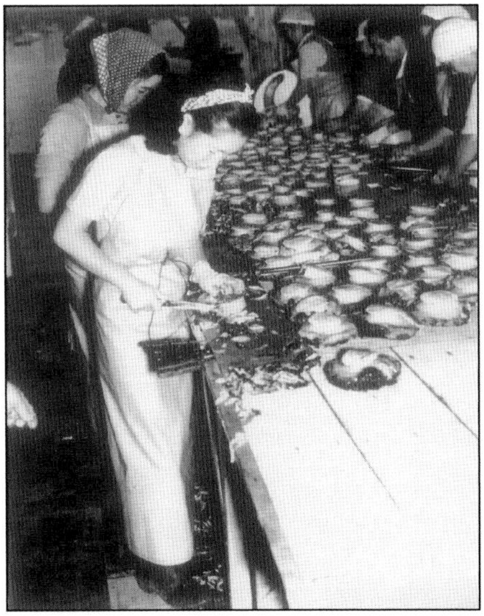

Abalone Worker, c. 1938. Hiroko Fumoto is trimming the edge of the abalone. Like in the sardine canneries, most of the workers in the abalone cannery were female. Since abalone was mostly processed in the spring, most of these ladies worked in the sardine canneries as well. (Monterey Library Collection.)

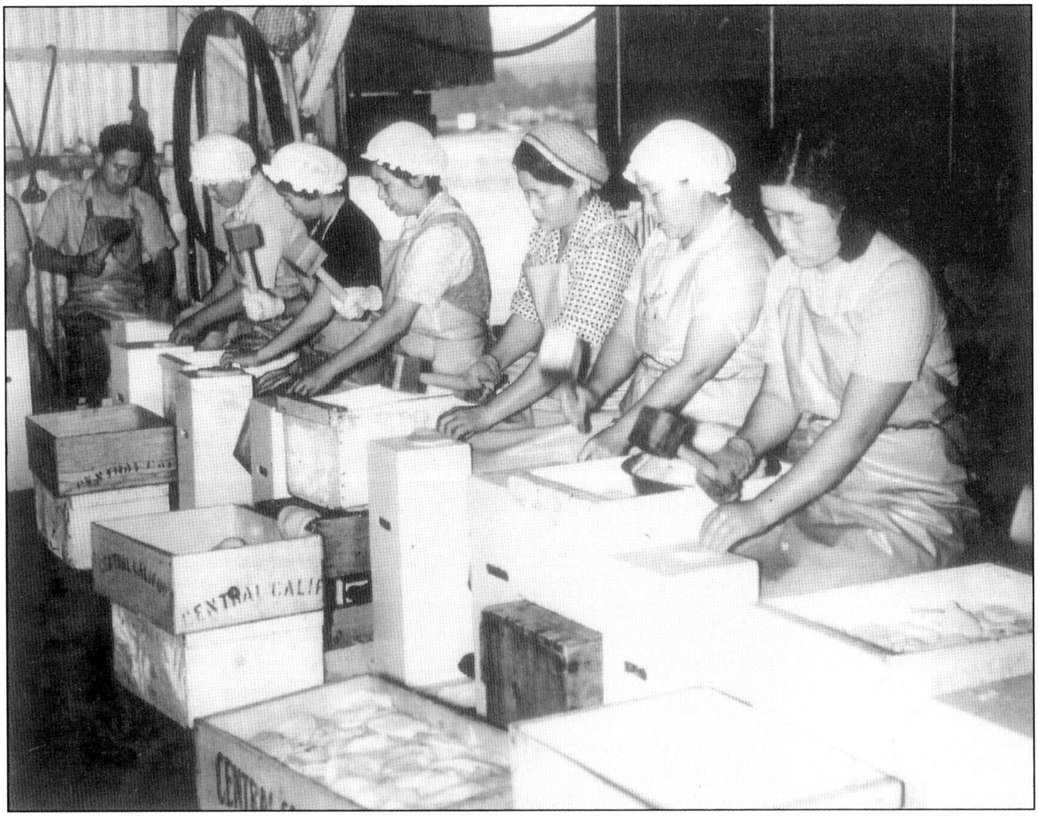

Pounding the Abalone, c. 1938. It was Pop Ernest who came up with the famous abalone recipe known today. He learned that the abalone had to pounded to make it nice and soft. He would put it in an egg wash and add his secret ingredient (juice from the abalone) and cracker crumbs, cooking quickly in olive oil. Among those in this photograph are Sao Nishiguchi (third from right), Mrs. Yokogawa (second from right), and Saze Nishiguchi (right). (Monterey Library Collection.)

Nine

In the Army during World War II

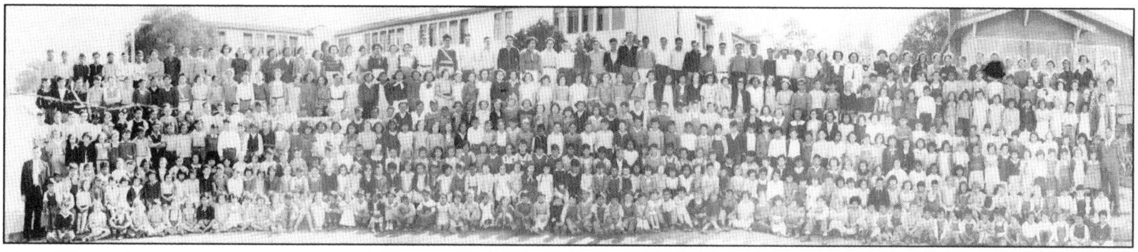

Bay View School, c. 1939. Many of the students in this class are Japanese American citizens. When Japan bombed Pearl Harbor, the world changed for the Japanese in Monterey. In February 1942, the FBI rounded up 15 issei who were leaders of the Monterey Japanese community. They were sent to special security camps in Bismarck, North Dakota; Santa Fe, New Mexico; Alexander, Louisiana; or Crystal City, Texas. These issei were considered to be high-risk. (Monterey Library Collection.)

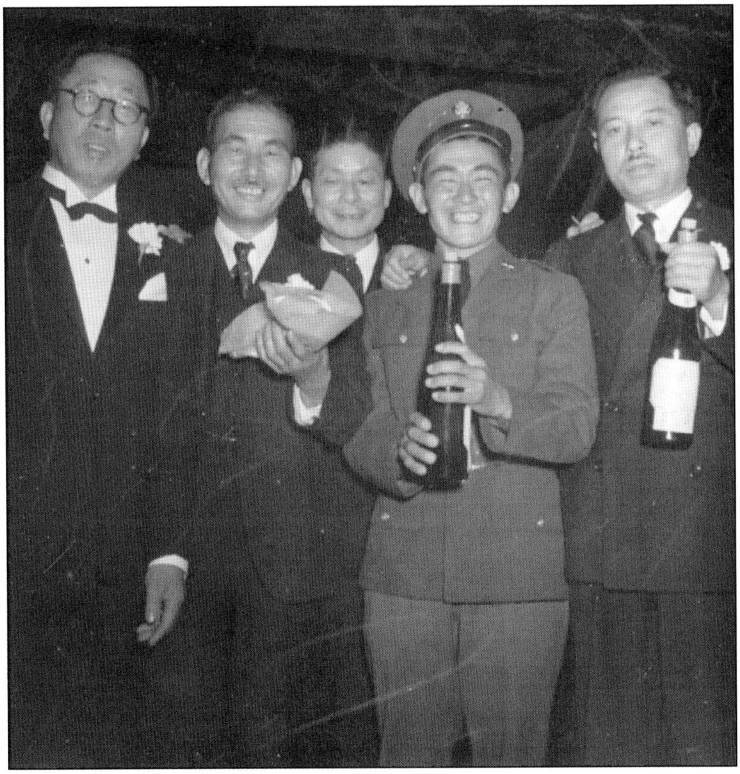

Executive Order 9066. When Executive Order 9066 was put in place on the Monterey Peninsula on April 30, 1942, the Monterey Japanese community had little time to prepare. Its members were sent initially to the Rodeo Grounds in Salinas and put into hastily built barracks and horse stalls. Eventually, families were sent to various internment camps. In contrast, Yoshikaza Higashi (second from right) is pictured here on the night before he left for overseas deployment as a soldier for the United States. (Miyamoto family collection.)

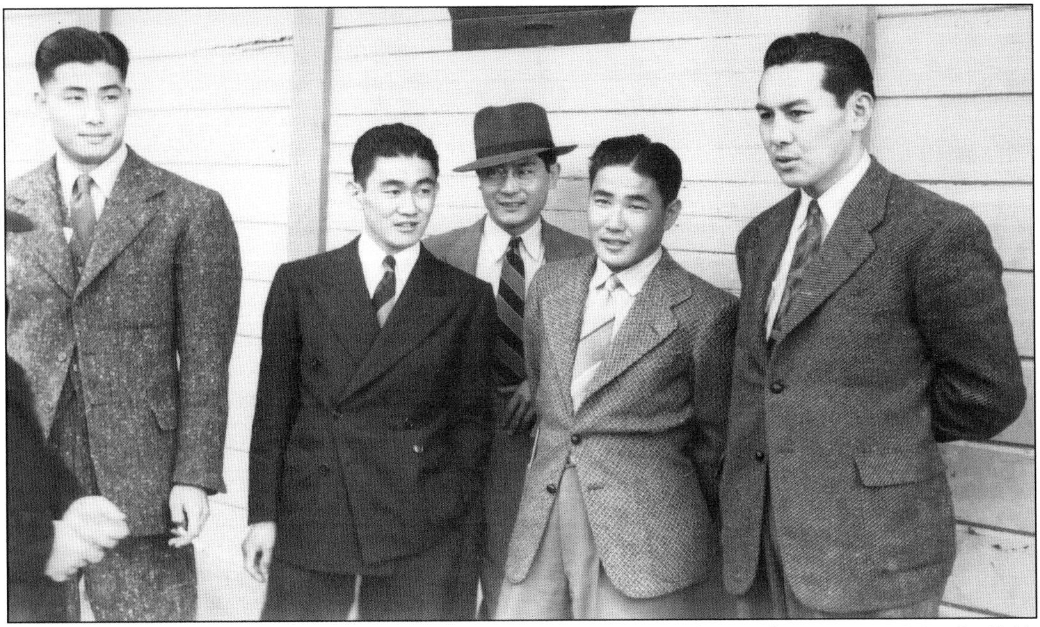

Nisei in the Army. Six nisei men from Monterey were inducted into the Army in March 1941, including Yosh Higashi (second from left), Mas Higashi (third from left), Ky Miyamoto (right), Royal Manaka, and George Kodama. A party was held in their honor at the JACL Hall the night before they left for boot camp, and many came to the train station to say goodbye to them the next day. (Kodama family collection.)

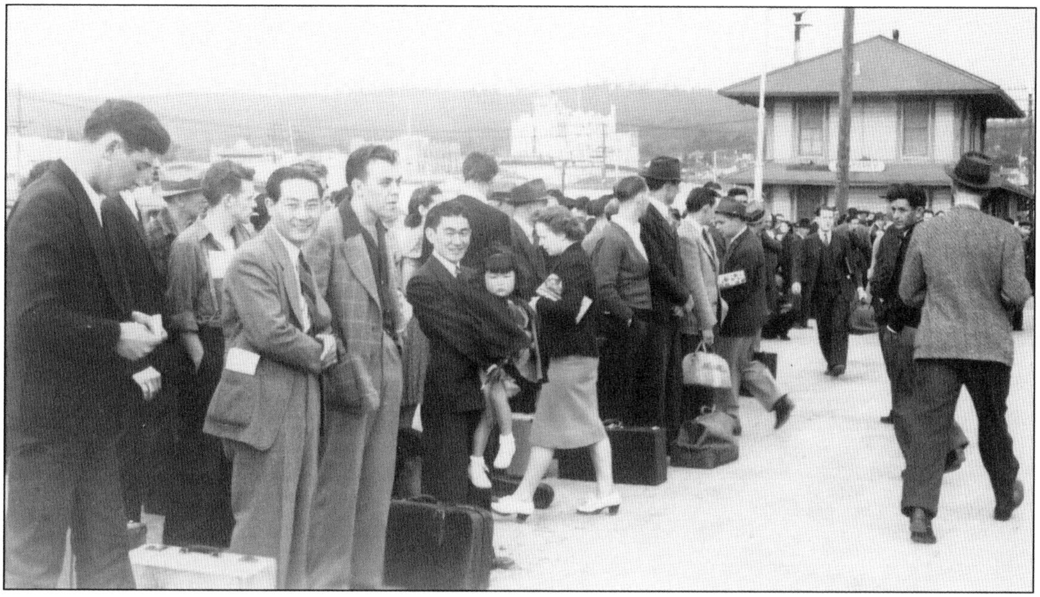

READY FOR DEPARTURE. Here, men are at the train station ready for departure. It seems that the whole Monterey Japanese community came to see them off. That day, Royal Manaka's father, Tomekichi Manaka, said to him, "Whatever you in do, Louie, don't bring shame to the Japanese community. Do whatever you can." Royal went on to be a member of the 442nd Regimental Combat Team (RCT), an all-Japanese American unit and the most decorated in US history. (Miyamoto family collection.)

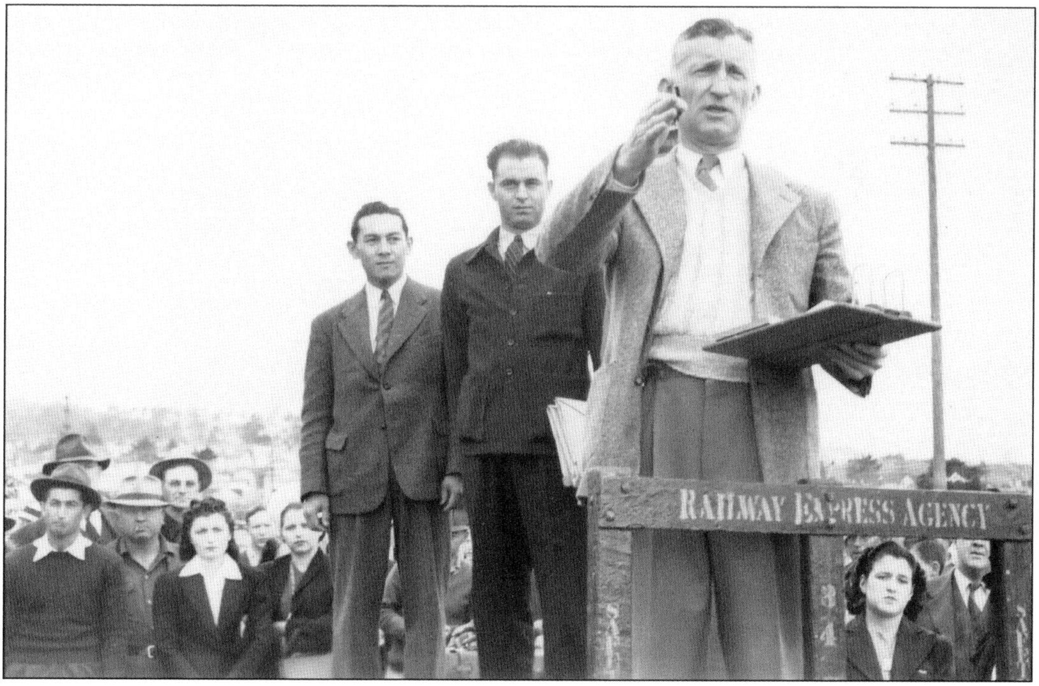

COACH'S SPEECH. Star baseball player Ky Miyamoto and his friend Charlie Frost listen as coach Roy Hughes from Monterey High School says a few words of encouragement. (Miyamoto family collection.)

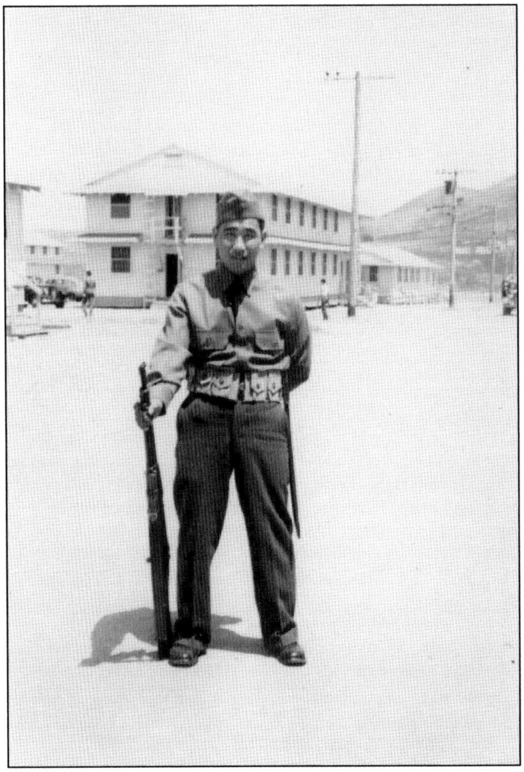

MAS HIGASHI AT CAMP SAN LUIS OBISPO, 1941. When Unosoke Higashi was unjustly sent away to a concentration camp in Bismarck, North Dakota, before he was led away, he turned to his son Mas and said, "Masamai, you go fight for America." (Miyamoto family collection.)

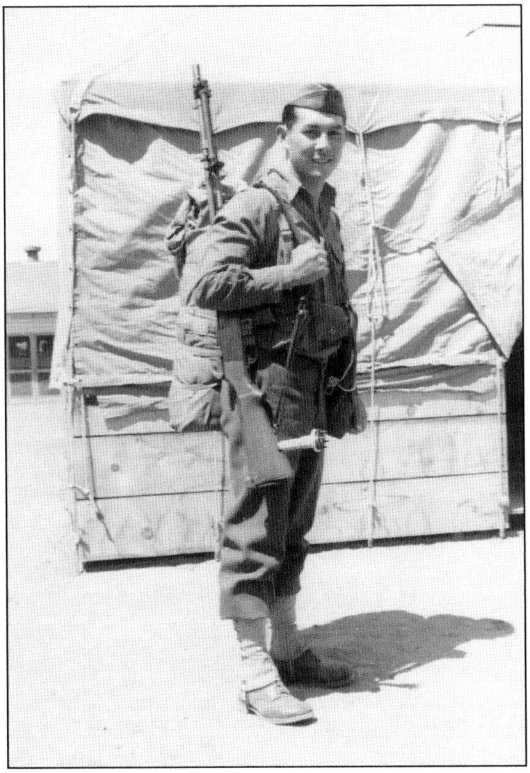

KY MIYAMOTO AT CAMP SAN LUIS OBISPO, 1941. Besides being a great baseball player, Ky Miyamoto also served his country as part of the 442nd RCT "Go for Broke" unit, the most highly decorated unit in World War II. Some other Monterey men who served in the 442nd include Royal Manaka, Haruo Esaki, Tom Kakimoto, Harry Otani, Isamu Sakai, Kaz Sugano, Noboru Kato, Dick Kawamoto, Eugine Kodani, Bill Omoto, Harumi Owashi, Yukio Sumida, Tak Sasaki, Yoshio Yokomizo , Miyoshi Saito, Mitch Sumida, and Tim Mizokamai, who died in action. (Miyamoto family collection.)

Carmel Highlands Fire Department, c. 1950. Seizo Kodani, son of Gennosuke Kodani, joined the Carmel Highlands Fire Department. While in camp at Poston, Seizo volunteered for induction into the 442nd RCT, but he could not pass the physical. The chief of the CHFD sent a letter to the commandant of the camp at Poston, writing in part that the CHFD has examined Kodani's fire truck and equipment. The chief concluded, "We find no evidence that there has been any attempt at sabotage." (Kodani family collection.)

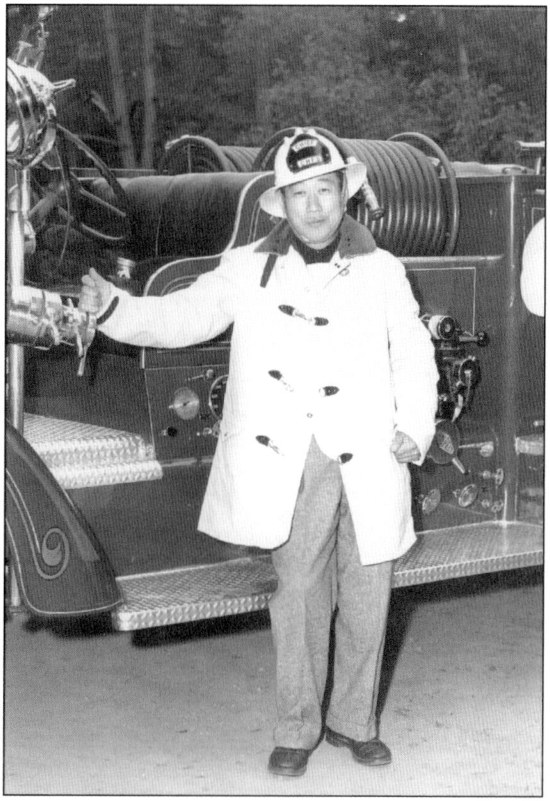

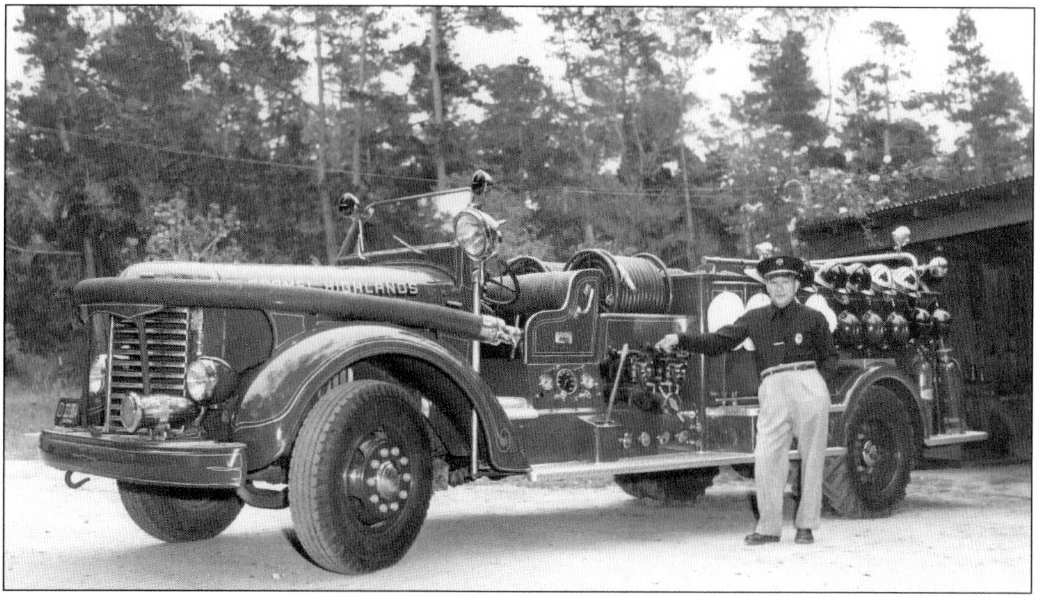

Seizo with His Fire truck and Equipment, c. 1950. Seizo could not join the 442nd, but he was an American citizen. When Seizo was a very young man, still in his early teens, Tajuro Watanabe, who was issei, asked Seizo's father, Gennosuke, if Seizo could "buy" a home for him and his family. The 1913 and 1920 California alien land laws prohibited issei from owning property; for many years, that house in Monterey was registered in Seizo's name. (Kodani family collection.)

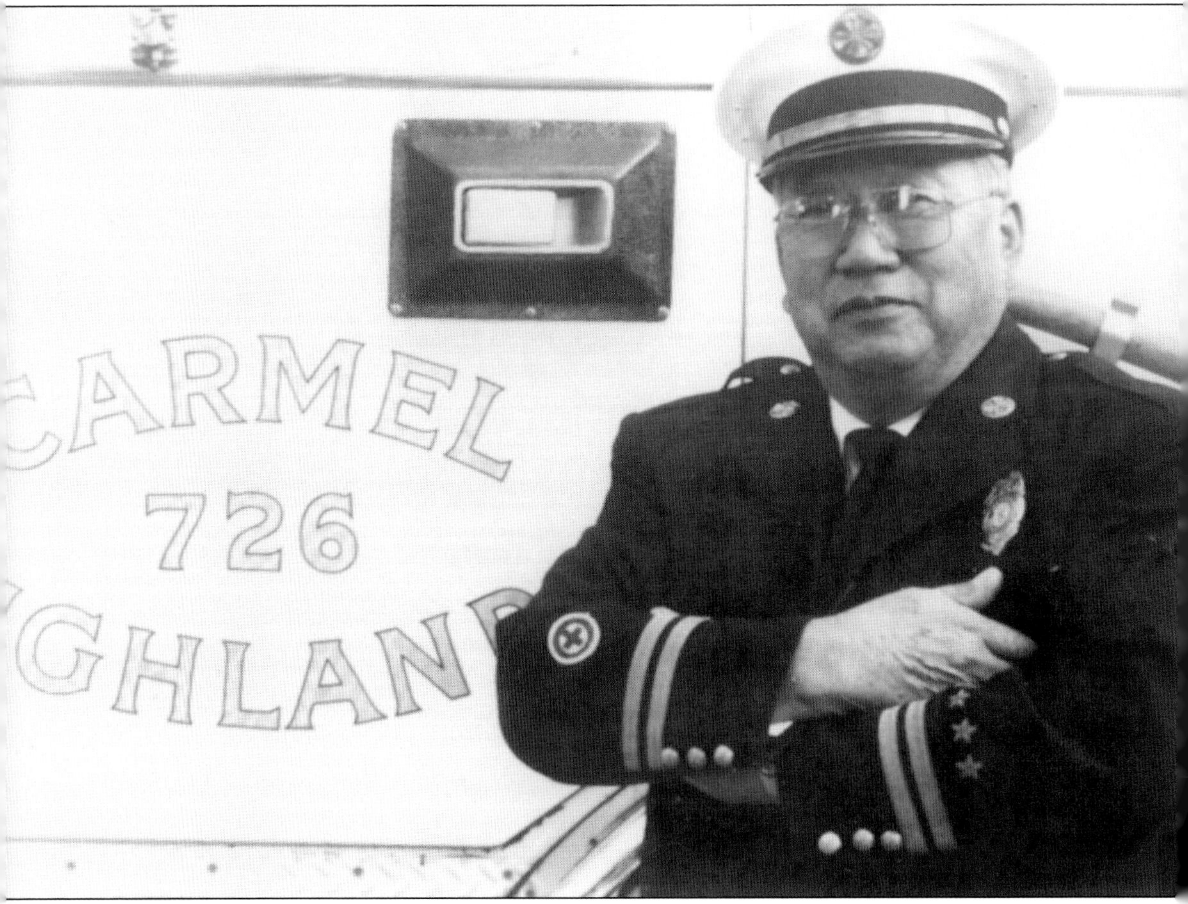

After the War. When the war was over, Seizo returned to the Carmel Highlands Fire Department and had a stellar career. He went on to become the chief of the department. His family still lives near Point Lobos today. (Kodani family collection.)

Ten

The Ama Return

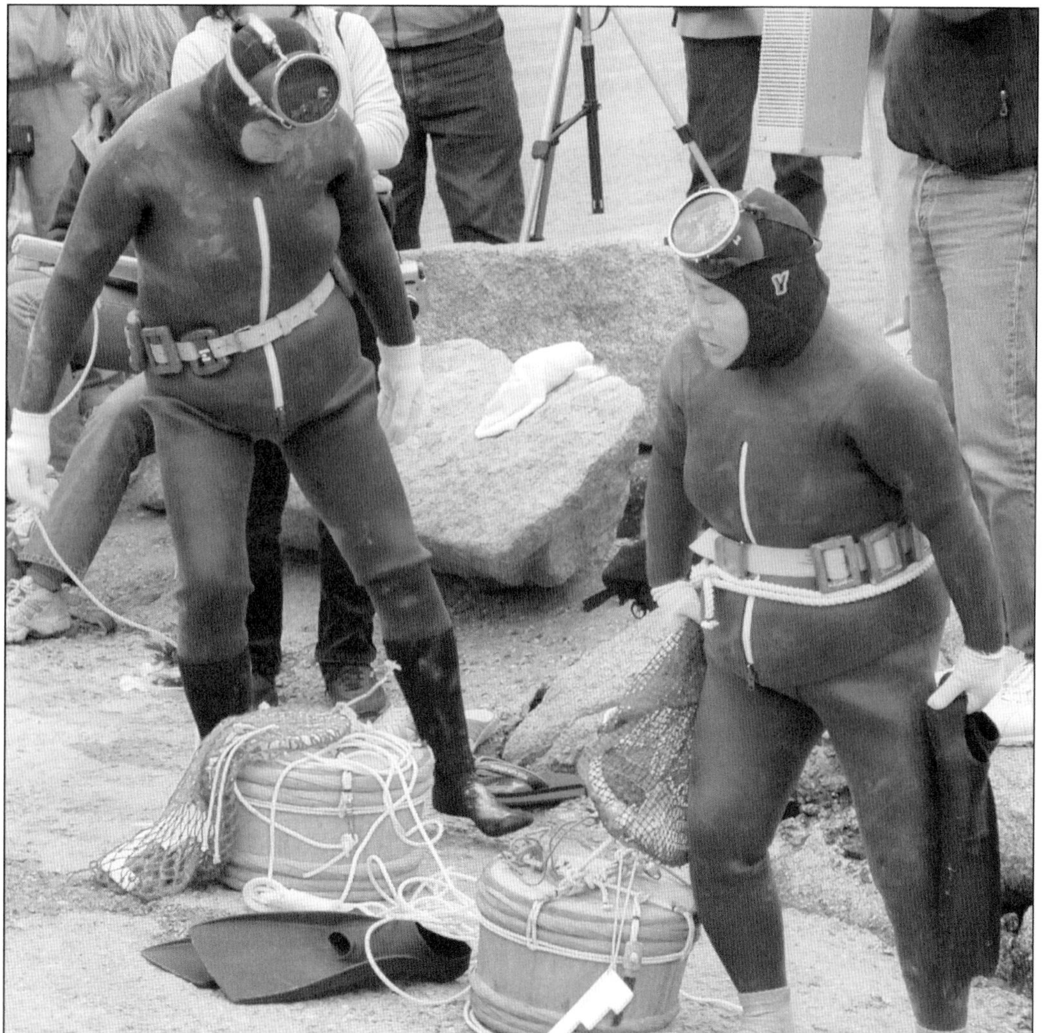

Returning to Point Lobos. In 2006, the ama returned to Point Lobos as part of a program celebrating over 100 years of connection between Monterey and Japan—a connection that still exists today. Just like those first ama so long ago, sisters Reiko Miyamoto (left), age 68, and Emiko Yoshida, age 72, are getting ready for their first dive in Whalers Cove. (Point Lobos Association.)

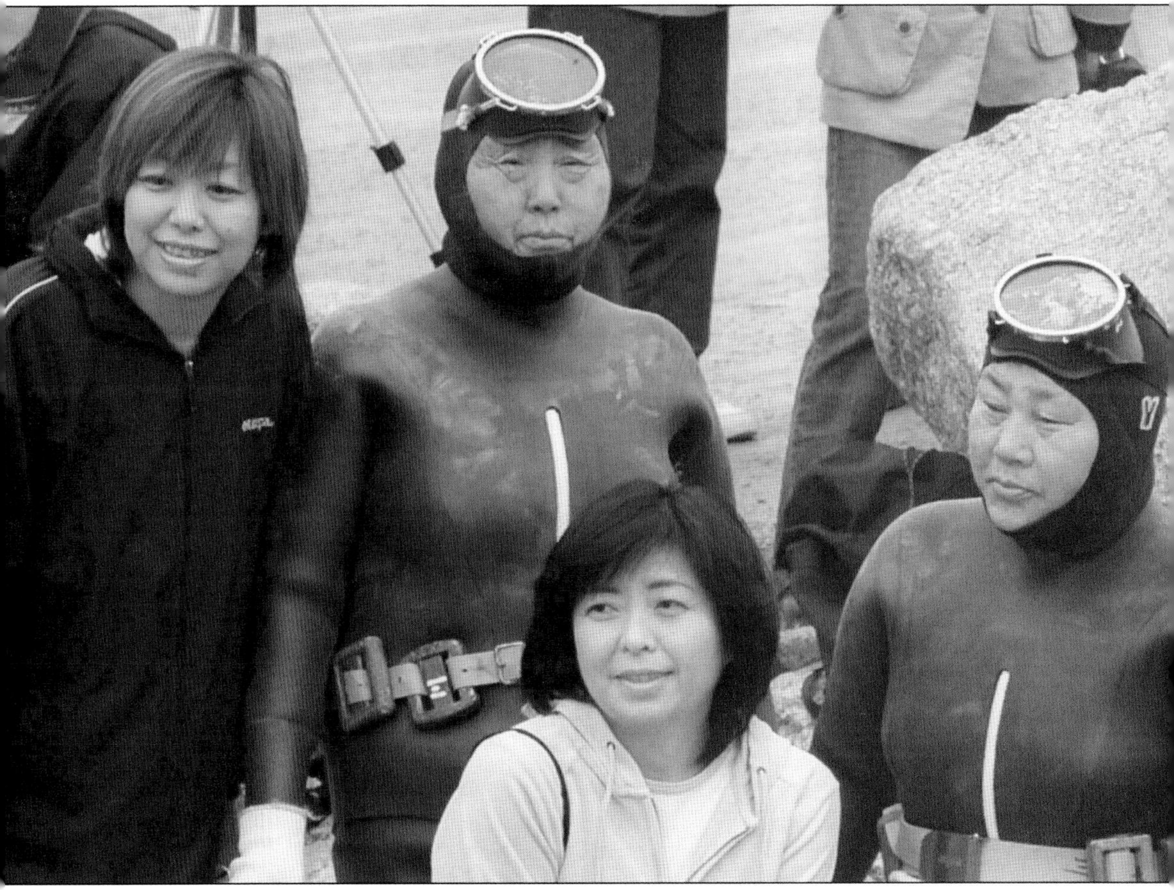

THE AMA ABOUT TO ENTER THE WATER. Sitting between sisters Reiko Miyamoto (left) and Emiko Yoshida, Yoshie Mitsuhashi (center) was their translator. Today in Japan, only women dive for abalone, and it is a dying art. The young girls do not want to become ama. They would rather move to Tokyo. Reiko and Miyamoto were given modern wet suits for their Point Lobos dive. Back home in Japan, they still wear the traditional white, cotton outfits. (Point Lobos Association.)

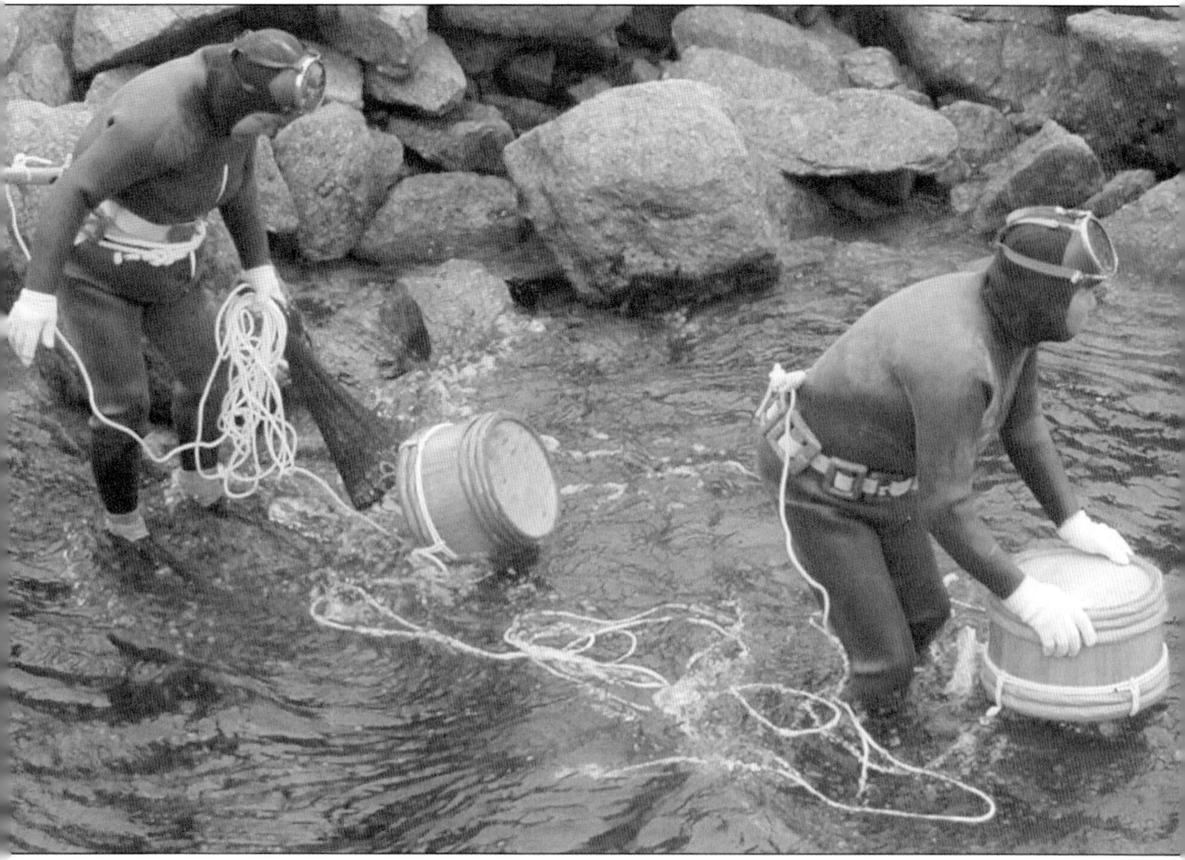

Remembering the Beginning. It was abalone that first brought the Japanese to the Monterey Peninsula in 1897. In almost the exact same spot and 107 years later, the first divers to enter the water are Reiko Miyamoto and Emiko Yoshida, remembering those who came before. (Point Lobos Association.)